Ladies of The Street

Liz Hodgkinson

Revel Barker
Publishing

First published in Great Britain by
Revel Barker Publishing
66 Florence Road
Brighton BN1 6DJ

ISBN: 978-0-9558238-5-5

DEDICATION:

To my dear friend Sandy Chubb,
who as Sandy Brereton shared
many hilarious moments
on the *Sunday People* in the good old days.

Other books by Liz Hodgkinson include:

Property:
The 'Complete' *Guides*: Letting Property, Investing in Property, Renovating and Improving Your Property, Buying Abroad.
Safe As Houses
How to Buy a Flat

Health:
The Alexander Technique
The Zinc Solution (with Professor Derek Bryce-Smith)
The Drinking Water Cure
Smile Therapy
Alzheimer's Disease: Your Questions Answered
How to Banish Cellulite for Ever

Lifestyle and psychology:
Codependency
Drug Abuse: Your Questions Answered
Alcoholism: Your Questions Answered
Addictions
Counselling
Bodyshock: Sex change explained.
Unholy Matrimony: The case for abolishing marriage

New Age:
Reincarnation: The Evidence
Spiritual Healing
Peace and Purity: The Story of the Brahma Kumaris
Psychic Counselling
How to Attract Luck

Biography:
Michael, nee Laura: the story of the first female to male transsexual
Bhagwan: The God That Failed.

Autobiography:
Sex is not Compulsory
Obsessive Love

Career:
The Working Woman's Guide

Cookery
The Anti-Cellulite Recipe Book

More information is available on her website: www.lizhodgkinson.com

Acknowledgements

Huge thanks to everybody who shared their stories, recollections, reminiscences and Fleet Street gossip with the author.

In particular they are, in alphabetical order: Rosemary Bouchy, Ernie Burrington, Sandy Chubb (Brereton), Robin Corry, Michael Crozier, John Dale, Shan Davies (Lloyd), Anthea Disney, John Dodd, Clare Dover, Colin Dunne, Jan Fairfax, Chris Greenwood, Barbara Griggs, Katharine Hadley, Maggie Hall, Colin Henderson, Wendy Henry, Judy Hobson, Derek Jameson, Julia Langdon, Philippa Kennedy OBE, Hilary Kingsley, Jean Morgan, June Penn, Jane Reed CBE, Lee Rodwell, Jo Sandilands, Dr Mike Smith, Doreen Spooner, Charlie Wilson, Lee Wilson and Dan Wooding, plus the current staff of the *Sunday People* and *Sunday Mirror* who kindly showed me round and explained the present set-up at Canary Wharf.

Revel Barker deserves special thanks for commissioning this book in the first place, for generously sharing his deep knowledge of Fleet Street, and for his expert editing; a rare treat for an author. I am also profoundly grateful for the existence of the wonderful *gentlemenranters.com* website, which has become a major Friday pleasure for all hacks, male or female, old or new.

Liz Hodgkinson
Brighton, October 2008

CONTENTS

One

First lady

The way that Jean Rook always told it, was like this. She was lying in bed when her husband Geoff Nash brought in the morning papers and started to read aloud from one of them.

'She's formidable, she's fearless, she's every other adjective you can think of beginning with an F.

She is, in fact, the First Lady of Fleet Street.'

Obviously riled, Rook interrupted him to say: 'And she's obviously a bit of a f...'

But Geoff, himself a skilled reporter but a necessarily anonymous foot-soldier working for the Press Association, who had always been immensely proud and encouraging of his wife's glittering success, silenced her by saying fondly: 'It's you that they're talking about, you chump.'

Rook had been up and writing from five o'clock the previous morning and had delivered the copy for her weekly column in the *Daily Express*. She had checked the proofs but hadn't waited to see the completed page. After she'd left the office an assistant editor – one, apparently, with a limited vocabulary – had dreamt up the wording for the top of the page.

'It wasn't my idea,' Rook insisted. 'I had never called myself the First Lady of Fleet Street. But if I'd thought of it, I would – believe me, I would.'

And the title would stay with her for ever. Jean Rook was to become, in her lifetime, possibly the most high-profile female journalist ever known.

Although a handful of women journalists had enjoyed their own columns from about the 1930s, the years from the late 1960s to the end of the 1990s are remembered as the time of the highly-feted, highly-paid and highly-publicised personal columnists whose weekly or occasionally even fortnightly pages gave a hard-hitting and, they hoped, often amusing take on the week's news and current events and on their struggles with school sports days, children's illnesses, husbands' funny little ways or the agonies of employing a cleaner.

The most successful personalised columns were always easy to read and for that reason may have seemed easy to write: so easy that it could look as though anybody could produce them. In fact it takes a particular kind of mind to be able to turn any trivial occurrence into copy that thousands or millions of people are eager to read, and also to have instant opinions on any and every event that crops up in the news.

Although Jean Rook may have been known by the title First Lady of Fleet Street she was not the only female journalist to be given a huge picture byline and enormous space and prominence in her newspaper. At the same time as Rook was holding sway at the *Daily Express*, Lynda Lee-Potter, Katharine Whitehorn and Jilly Cooper were also effectively being promoted as 'first ladies' in their own papers.

Their guaranteed presence week after week helped to give women journalists a new prominence and influence in the world as well as providing shining examples of what could now be achieved by women writers.

Each of these columnists was long lasting, incredibly tenacious and hung on to her position for years, even decades in most cases. The era of the First Lady is now over, and there are no such big-name columnists any more. But it was fun while it lasted – especially for the first ladies themselves who secured huge salaries and enormous prominence in their papers, thus giving other aspirants something to aim for.

The First Ladies have been collectively derided over the years as Glenda Slagg in *Private Eye* and are often considered to be not 'real' journalists, at least not worthy to stand alongside those who undertake dangerous undercover work or campaign to correct major injustices or financial scandals. The 'Glendas' have been seen as essentially lightweight and self-indulgent, but the best of them had a unique quality impossible to copy. There has never been another Jean Rook, another Katharine Whitehorn, or another Jilly Cooper, although there have been plenty of pale imitations. These writers demonstrated a quirky, witty take on life that, at the time they wrote, resonated exactly with their readers.

As such, they performed a valuable service. Their abiding talent was to spot subjects and issues that they believed would be of interest to their readers but which the readers themselves had not yet clocked. Thus they had to be just a little ahead of the time with their incisive and (they hoped) perceptive comments. In other words, they knew what their readers were thinking, or were about to think. They were there to take the words out of the reader's mouth but only after they had installed it there in a wittier and more entertaining way than the average reader could manage.

Jean Rook reigned supreme at the *Daily Express* from 1972 until the Grim Reaper carried her off in 1991.

She was born in November 1931 in Hull, the only child of consultant engineer Horace Rook and his wife. She had a comfortable middle-class upbringing and although she was upset not to get into Oxford or Cambridge, she was accepted at Bedford College, London University, where she got a 2:1 in English and later wrote an MA thesis on the plays of T S Eliot. This academic background was not, perhaps, an ideal start for a rabble-rousing tabloid journalist and Rook says in her 1989 autobiography, *The Cowardly Lioness*:

'I didn't aim, from pramhood, to grow up into Britain's bitchiest, best-known and loved woman journalist.'

Her father hoped she would be a barrister and she herself initially longed to be an actress. But she considered that as a big, raw-boned girl of 5ft 8 and certainly no raving beauty, she would never make it as a leading lady on the stage.

However, she wanted to be famous one way or another: 'Fame was not just my spur. My consuming ambition slashed me to ribbons even as a fat kid in plaits. Whatever I was going to be, it had to be big. I always saw my name in lights. If the actual light bulbs failed me, I've at least seen it in the biggest, boldest type ever used on a Fleet Street byline... I am the highest paid woman in Fleet Street... I've always said what I think, forcefully, and, I hope, amusingly, at the given moment. Hundreds who feel as I do write back.'

In answer to the often-asked question as to whether her column came naturally to her, Rook responded: 'The sentiment, in a flash. Expressing it in readable form can take mere heady minutes when your mind is up and running or tedious, sweating hours when it's not and every word has to be dragged out with pliers.'

Rook was 25 years old before she decided to try to become a journalist. After finishing her MA on Eliot she felt she was not cut out for the plodding, academic life and she applied for, and landed, a job on the graduate trainee scheme of the *Sheffield Telegraph*. From then on 'I knew I would make Fleet Street if I had to crawl from the Strand to St Paul's in gutters running with my own blood.' In the event, Rook's first editor, Ernest Taylor, told her there was no opening for women columnists at the top and she had better stick to reporting, on which she reflected later: 'I've often hoped Ernest has looked down to see the massive openings I've dug for a whole new genre of women columnists.'

She met her future husband, fellow journalist Geoff Nash, at the Sheffield paper where he advised her to forget about news and concentrate on becoming a great feature writer. Times were changing for women, he told her, presciently, adding: grab the chance.

Rook next went to the *Yorkshire Post* where she was sent to Paris and 'it was here that I first saw Fleet Street's mighty, throned in their red plush chairs on the front row. Iris Ashley of the *Mail*, Jill Butterfield of the *Express*, Felicity Green of the *Mirror*... the terrifying old American tiger, *Sunday Times'* Ernestine Carter.'

For all her ambition, Rook could not find an immediate opening in Fleet Street and so became fashion editor of a (now long-defunct) magazine, *Flair*, which she hated. She wrote: 'either you have a monthly magazine mind or you haven't and I was strictly a racy, pacy daily newspaper journalist. *Flair*'s snail pace was killing me.'

The Welsh-born newspaper giant Hugh Cudlipp was one of the most influential personalities in the history of newspapers in the twentieth century; according to Jean Rook: 'He was the sexiest man I have ever known, who ever made a woman draw heavy breath. He had a voice like a Welsh harp and looked like a cross between Richard Burton and Owen Glendower.' She found him even more appealing when he asked whether she would like to be fashion editor of the new newspaper he was planning, to be called the *Sun,* and she replied: more than my life.

This was not the current Murdoch *Sun* but the paper that succeeded the trade-unions' *Daily Herald,* and it was an unmitigated disaster. Carrying the astonishingly clumsy banner, *A newspaper born of the age we live in,* the new *Sun* was launched in September 1964 in the biggest blaze of advertising publicity ever known for a national newspaper, in spite of which it sank like a stone. Cudlipp later wished he had never heard of it and it was rescued by Rupert Murdoch, who already owned the *News of the World.*

Rook's boss on the old *Sun* was Amy Landreth: 'hell in high heels'. She was Rook's first female newspaper boss and, Rook swore, would be absolutely her last. Rook's stint as fashion editor did not really suit her and soon Howard French, then editor of the fast-failing *Daily Sketch,* offered her a job at twice what the *Sun* was paying. Rook jumped at the chance and soon met David English, who had been brought onto the *Sketch* to oversee its merger with the *Daily Mail* and was 'the most demanding and inspiring editor I have ever worked for'.

The *Sketch* folded on 'the night of the long envelopes' in 1971, and Rook landed her own column on the quickly-rising *Daily Mail.* After 18 months at the *Mail* she had a call from John Junor, then editor of the *Sunday Express.* Rook went to lunch with Junor but did not go to the

Sunday paper. Instead, she was offered the top columnist's slot at the *Daily Express*, a job she decided to take as she was finding the *Daily Mail* a fairly unhappy ship with two people for every job.

As her mentor, David English was predictably furious and made Rook an offer he thought she could not refuse – loads more money, a seat on the board, a trust fund for the baby and other riches beyond the dreams of avarice but in the event Rook jumped ship and joined the *Daily Express,* where she was to make her name. She admitted in her autobiography that this largesse being offered was not so much because she was particularly valuable personally, but because of the bitter rivalry at the time between the *Express* and the *Mail*.

There was always a certain amount of ego in the salary game – which newspaper could pay the most, or offer the most glittering golden handcuffs.

Rook's apparently vast, although undisclosed, salary at the *Express* prompted some of the sub-editors on the back bench there to ask themselves why the *Express* couldn't have paid even more money and to have also hired the re-write man – always assumed to be David English – who could make sense of her copy, while they were about it.

The baby in the deal over which the newspapers haggled was Gresby, Jean Rook's only child, and 18 months old when she crossed the Street. She and Geoff Nash had married when Rook was 31 but in agreeing to the marriage she gave him an absolute ultimatum: no children, ever. This was an agreement that lasted nine years, until their much-loved and – in truth – much-wanted only son, who would become the actor Gresby Nash, was born by Caesarean section when Rook was 40. She had said initially that 'no screaming bilious little bundle was going to come between me and the top job in Fleet Street' – words she risked having to eat when Gresby arrived although, it has to be said, he never did come between her and that 'top job'. Nor, in spite of his own and his fond parents' ambition for him, did he ever enjoy the star billing with which his mother was favoured.

It may have been the fabled Yorkshire grit that got Rook to Fleet Street, and perhaps a tempering of Sheffield steel that kept her there. But she would not have lasted, nor have been given such accolades, unless she had been something special once she had arrived. Many women are called to the Street of Adventure, but few are chosen for the top jobs. Jean Rook had two outstanding journalistic qualities: an ability for clever and often biting wordplay and an instinctive understanding of politics, something few female columnists have apparently been able to match.

Jean Rook had declared that she would never work for a female boss again after her experience under Amy Landreth, but when Albert (Larry) Lamb became editor of the *Daily Express* after being sacked from *The Sun*, she found him even worse than any female boss could have been.

They'd met before. Lamb had tried to tempt her to the Murdoch *Sun* from the *Daily Mail* and had been insulted by her refusal – even when Rook had told him she was earning more money than he was offering. Lamb wanted big-name writers on his paper but, Rook deduced, he was against the system of creating star names. The only star in any newspaper's firmament (according to Lamb) should be the editor.

She called him 'the fiend of Fleet Street' and says he slapped yellow stickers – indicating he wanted the content changing – on everything she wrote. He and Rook hated each other and Lamb did his best to get rid of her.

He might have succeeded but instead he was ousted himself when he fell out with Lord Matthews, then the proprietor of Express Newspapers, and Derek Jameson took his place as editor. According to Rook, Jameson was 'a brilliant intuitive editor, farcically conceited. He was inspirational and ran the paper like a knees-up.' She says she survived herds of editors, and certainly in her last days at the *Express* there were herds of them to be survived.

In common with many journalists, Rook had a dab of greasepaint along with the printing ink in her veins; although the actual acting could be handled vicariously by Gresby, Rook would never disguise her desire to perform – posing in such stunts as taming a lion in a circus, driving a chariot with Charlton Heston as 'Ben Her' and posing at the drop of a flashbulb with politicians and celebrities, ostensibly always as big a star as they were.

By the mid-1980s, Rook had achieved everything she wanted: a huge, five-bedroom house in Kent, a 4.2 Jaguar car, a trendy Wapping flat and a son at Eton. It was all, she wrote, 'the sweet fruit of 31 hard years in journalism.' She added: 'I fervently believe if you're well paid, well advertised and well-plastered across the country's billboards, you've a duty to deliver the goods.' She would start writing her column before sunrise when two alarm clocks knocked her out of sleep, and usually finish around 4pm, when she was, in her own words, wrung dry.

But Rook's life, so sweet, successful and blessed in an upward-only direction, was to end in terrible tragedy. At the age of 56, she was diagnosed with breast cancer and underwent the first of several agonising operations. While she was severely jet-lagged from a trip to America in 1985, the family home in Kent was invaded by armed robbers, who tied both her and Geoff up at gun point before they stole and made off with valuable jewellery and other goods.

She believed the aftermath of the armed robbery killed Geoff, slowly. Not long after the attack, he started showing unmistakeable signs of Alzheimer's and died a pathetic, shambling wreck. Rook's cancer returned and she herself died in 1991, at the age of 59. She had written, bravely (and always entertainingly) just before her death: 'If the op goes wrong... I wonder if they'll hold my memorial in the journalists' Fleet Street church, St Brides. Or in St Paul's? After all I was... still am... the First Lady of Fleet Street.'

Milk is regularly spilt and often spewed along Fleet Street but there is no time for crying over it. Before Rook's seat at the *Mail* could get cold her instant successor was enthroned in it. While Rook was queening it in a plush room overlooking Fleet Street from the 'black Lubyanka' of the *Express*, a substitute columnist was wheeled into place to continue preening for the *Mail* from a dingy office in Whitefriars Street.

Few readers will have been aware of the switch; hundreds, possibly thousands, of readers who if asked would have described themselves as devoted followers of the column will not even have noticed that the name and the picture at the top of the page had changed overnight.

David English had created – or at least (credit where it's due) had helped, inspired and promoted – Fleet Street's First Lady; now, without pausing for a breath, he had to create a second First Lady, as good as or even better than the first. And he had to do it before the page came out the following Wednesday,

Like Jean Rook, the young Lynda Higginson had harboured ambitions to be a famous actress; opportunities were not exactly plentiful for council house lasses from Leigh in Lancashire but this daughter of a painter and decorator showed early persistence and at least made it from the mining town of her birth as far the Guildhall School of Music and Drama.

There she learnt to lose her 'working class' accent, and it was while she was appearing in *Dry Rot*, a Whitehall farce starring Brian Rix, that she met a young medical student from Guy's Hospital, and they married in 1957.

Her husband served as a medical officer with the RAF in Aden and to pass the time Lynda started writing short stories that she would read on the radio. She also wrote for the *Aden Chronicle*. Her light touch soon became popular and on their return from Aden Lynda, who by now had three children, landed a job on *Woman's Mirror* as a feature writer. This led to a job on the *Daily Mail* in a similar capacity in 1967 and her big opportunity came when she was offered the most glittering prize after Jean Rook suddenly decamped to the *Express.*

She had not been the first choice. David English had initially approached Jilly Cooper, then making huge waves at the *Sunday Times,* and offered her the eye-watering salary of £15,000 a year. Cooper, although tempted, and being offered sums 'beyond the dreams of avarice' as she put it, eventually declined and stayed with the *Sunday Times* at the vastly lower (but still good for the time) salary of £5,000 a year, especially as her column appeared on the *Look!* pages only once a fortnight.

Rejected by Cooper, English decided to promote from within. It was, after all, far cheaper and – even more importantly – much quicker. Sitting in the feature-writers' room, totally unaware of how her life was about to change, was Lynda Higginson, now Mrs Jeremy Lee-Potter. While nervous at first and even though never quite mastering Rook's quick wordplay or fiercely barbed repartee, Lee-Potter soon gained confidence and before long became a major star in the *Mail*'s galaxy, hugely promoted along with diary editor Nigel Dempster. At first guided by David English at every step, Lee-Potter eventually found her own, individual, feet, even if she continued to be seen in some circles as a pale imitation of Jean Rook – particularly by Jean Rook herself.

Although it was Lee-Potter, rather than Rook, who had actually trodden the boards as an actress, albeit briefly, she was content to leave the theatrical performing and daft stunts that Rook loved to her rival. Instead, she became a serious interviewer in addition to writing her weekly column, talking to all the celebrities of the day and also to the victims of serious tragedies, some of whom would be tempted to open their hearts to Lynda Lee-Potter from the *Mail* rather than to any competing columnist by the inducement of a large Associated Newspapers cheque.

Her critics said Lee-Potter showed no great style or perception in her interviews, but she was always dogged enough to come out with masses of quotes from her subject, and was able to fill several pages of the paper at short notice. Her mindset and attitudes appeared to be exactly in accord with those of her readers, although obviously she was much richer and more successful than the average *Mail* reader.

The one word to describe the readership of both the *Mail* and the *Express* in those days was 'aspirational'. Hugh Cudlipp once mockingly remarked that 'the *Express* thinks its readers all have two-point-four children, live in mock Tudor homes in Surrey and have two cars in the garage – but in fact they don't, that's just how they want to live.' The point was not lost on Bob Edwards, who edited the *Daily*

Express twice in the 1960s. When his deputy pointed out one night that they had two stories in the paper about public schools – 'and our readers can't actually afford to send their children to public school' – Edwards replied: 'I know that. But our readers like to think that the editor thinks they can.'

So when Mrs Lee-Potter referred in her column to the grassy area at home as 'the lawns', she probably knew exactly what she was doing, and for whom she was writing. She had also, by this time, started referring to her father as 'a painter' – seeing no necessity to add 'and decorator'.

Sometimes witches, sometimes bitches, the argument raged across Fleet Street about who was the better. Some said that Rook had the edge because she was sharper and wittier; others claimed it was Lee-Potter because she, not to put too fine a point on it, had David English. Some said Rook had a lighter touch (not necessarily a compliment when dealing with bitchiness); others said Lee-Potter was heavy handed (not always a positive factor in dealing with commentary-style journalism).

The important thing, however, was that outside the close environs of London EC4, nobody cared, nor did anybody even give the question a second thought. Fleet Street believed that the universe revolved around its own being; fortunately they didn't believe it sufficiently to let the navel-gazing permeate into the paper. The readers liked what they got. When *Mail* subscribers got Rook, they were content; when they suddenly started getting Lee-Potter instead, there was little evidence that anybody could be bothered to trek to the newsagent to switch allegiance. By the time they went round to pay the newspaper bill (and the majority of newspapers were home-delivered in those days) they had probably forgotten what the fuss was about.

The columnists were, nevertheless, household names. And if you failed to notice that somebody had been attacked in one of their columns, you'd learn all about it soon enough. Just in case you'd missed it, when Lee-Potter homed in on Miriam Stoppard, the good doctor felt obliged to ask everybody who would listen: what has she got against me? The answer was, most probably, nothing at all; it was just that Stoppard was an easy target that week. People wrote about people being written about; it was perpetual motion. It was fame of a kind,

Journalist Michael Leapman, emphatically not a Lee-Potter fan, said of the columnist: 'She recognises that it does not matter what opinions you express, whom you choose to hold up to contempt, whose physical appearance and dress sense you mock, as long as you write with verve and venom, especially venom... So what has nourished the spite, the anger, the sheer nastiness of Lee-Potter's print persona?'

He felt that she invariably picked the soft targets, the ones who could not easily hit back, and subjected them to 'withering scorn and personal criticism, unsupported by anything except her prejudices.'

Lee-Potter, Leapman said, was careful to come across as charming, giggly, sympathetic, in public but was always fulfilling her mission to make life miserable for such celebrities of the day as singer Elaine Paige, TV presenter Anthea Turner, Princess Michael, Prince Andrew and Germaine Greer, who she described as being 'muscly, greying and scrawny with a skin like leather'. She thinks of herself, according to Leapman, as the 'hooded avenger. But – avenging what, exactly?'

Paul Dacre, David English's successor as editor of the *Daily Mail*, decided not to try to replace Lee-Potter immediately after her death in 2004 as he realised she had become a kind of national treasure who had also been much in demand as a public speaker. And for all that Lee-Potter's column had originally been a kind of revenge on Rook, it lasted for 13 years after Rook's death, during which time no new Rook had been found at the *Express*. During the months of Lee-Potter's long, last illness, the words 'Lynda Lee-Potter will return soon' appeared every week underneath what would have been her column, even though everybody knew she never would return.

After a decent interval, her place as a 'Wednesday witch' was taken by Allison Pearson, a worthy successor and wittier and more insightful than her predecessor, it has to be said. There has never been a true successor to Jean Rook at the *Express* which shows just how rare these true tabloid stars really are.

Katharine Whitehorn, who held court at *The Observer* for about 36 years, was not a gritty northerner like Rook or Lee-Potter. Far from it. Her father was classics master at a public school and her mother's father founded the National Marriage Guidance Council. Whitehorn's mother had herself secured a place at Cambridge, although she was considered too delicate to go up, but Katharine went in her stead, after being educated at Roedean. Her brother John went to Trinity College, Cambridge.

There may have been little spare money in the Whitehorn household but there was plenty of gentle culture and the Whitehorns knew a lot of influential people. For example, after university Katharine landed at job at Methuen's publishers when Dr E V Rieu of Penguin Classics and a friend of her father's, happened to mention there was a job going as a

16

junior publisher's reader. The novelist L A G Strong, also a friend of the family, got her some reviewing work on *John O'London's Weekly*.

Whitehorn said that she grew up with career women all around her and admitted that her background definitely gave her an early leg-up. Even so, no family background could have been responsible for her sparkling success as a columnist and media personality, and though her early jobs came from asking around her friends or being in the right place at the right time at a party, her talent soon shone through.

She landed a job on *Picture Post*, and was used as a model for a now-famous picture of a 1950s girl alone in a London bed-sitter. After *Picture Post* folded, Whitehorn worked at *Woman's Own* although claiming later that she never felt she got her head round that essentially working-class publication and in the event resigned after six months.

She first began to be noticed with her *Roundabout* column on *The Spectator*. This column made an instant impact as all previous *Roundabout* columns on the weekly journal had been about cricket or foreign policy or cars and although they were supposed to be funny, they had never been written by a woman before. The editor of *The Spectator* at the time was Brian Inglis, a brusque, monosyllabic man, difficult to talk to, who nevertheless liked women and who later wrote avant-garde books about alternative health and spiritual healing.

Roundabout attracted the eye of the bisexual George Seddon, an executive on *The Observer* who was at the time looking for a woman's editor. Half of London, as well as Whitehorn, applied for this job and the upshot was that she briefly became fashion editor, taking over from Alison Settle, who was about to retire. Whitehorn has said in her memoirs and in several radio and print interviews since, that at the time – the early 1960s – journalism was bridging an 'immemorial gap' between male writing and female writing. George Seddon, she says, invented women's pages that weren't exactly women's pages and which were soon copied the world over.

Considerably gentler than either Rook or Lee-Potter, Whitehorn was tough in her own way and has said she would like to throw down a steep flight of stairs any woman who writes that women would be happier staying at home with their children than having a big career. Parenthood, she asserted, is 'not what you ought to do but what you can stand'.

After a couple of early love affairs, Whitehorn settled down into a comfortable, long-lasting marriage with the thriller writer Gavin Lyall and produced two sons, Bernard and Jake. Her column at *The Observer* lasted until 1996, an astonishing thirty-year stretch, and then it was suddenly stopped by the new deputy editor Jocelyn Targett, a young man who appeared to be going places and who wanted younger writers for the paper. Targett did indeed go places and before long left journalism for the altogether racier world of horse breeding at Newmarket.

Targett had assured Whitehorn she would still be called upon for features, but the final blow came in 1997 when she was asked to do a big piece on nursing. When it didn't go into the paper for several successive Sundays she contacted the woman's editor to ask why, saying that it would be past its sell-by date if it wasn't used soon.

The exasperated answer she got was: 'Really, Katharine, I have 24 freelances telling me why their piece has to go in on Sunday.' This insulting remark made her realise her time was up, that she was no longer a valued contributor and she left to go to *Saga* magazine as an agony aunt.

'Saga was my parachute out of *The Observer*,' she said.

Some may think she was bloody lucky to have lasted so long on one paper, so what was her secret?

In an interview with Stuart Jeffries in *The Guardian* in March 2008 to celebrate her 80th birthday, she was heralded as the 'original confessional columnist' who blazed a trail for women who juggle a career and family life.

'What women of my generation did,' she told Jeffries, after asking him whether he was the window cleaner, 'was to write like women. Before us, women were expected to write like men if they wrote on the serious pages. Now, it's different: women like Polly Toynbee, Carol Sarler and Libby Purves say things that would only occur to a woman. They write just as seriously but have distinctive female voices.'

Whether her voice is distinctively female or not, Whitehorn was one of the original newspaper columnists – Jilly Cooper was another and Hunter Davies (a man) yet another – who looked to incidents in their own lives to provide copy. One of her most famous pieces was about 'sluts', where she asked: 'Have you ever taken anything out of the dirty-clothes basket because it had become, relatively, the cleanest thing?'

This is the quote by which Whitehorn is best remembered and which will probably go down in history in a future book of the wit and wisdom of women journalists. OK, maybe it doesn't sound very startling now but at the time, when everybody pretended they were clean and tidy and perfect in every way, it struck a new note of refreshing honesty.

There was also the famous column about putting an aspirin in a suspender to hold up stockings. But now – who remembers either suspenders or stockings? And even aspirins have changed their shape. The fact that an old-fashioned round aspirin would soon crumble to dust if it was used to secure a stocking to a suspender was somehow never asked. It just sounded amusing and outrageous at the time.

The notion of holding your clothes together with safety pins or, indeed, with an aspirin, seemed even funnier coming from an upper-crust Cambridge graduate – or at least, it did in those days, long before artist Tracey Emin could be paid thousands or millions of pounds for putting an unmade bed surrounded by hideous and unmentionable gunge on public display.

As well as writing her weekly column for 30-odd years, Whitehorn sat on endless committees, was a regular fixture on radio and wrote endearing, very amusing little books about how to survive in the kitchen, or with children, or in hospital and how to cook in a bed-sitter. In fact, she pioneered the art of writing about living in a ditzy, slapdash, booze-filled way which sounded new and daring. It all seemed much more fun, anyway, than the prim, repressed, striving-to-be-perfect way of life to which most women had previously aspired, and which was encouraged by the women's magazines of the time.

Donald Trelford, a former editor of *The Observer*, says of his former star employee: 'Looking back from today, when most newspapers have half a dozen columnists, many of them female, it is hard to convey the bracing sense of fresh air blown in by the pioneering Whitehorn columns... She wrote as she spoke, in that crisp, amused, rather plummy style that used to be called an educated accent.'

In her memoirs, Whitehorn managed to make her long lasting and very public career look like one happy accident. She 'bumped' into somebody at a party who 'gave' her a job; 'happened' to know somebody through the family who could give her a start, landed a job when somebody else left and she was the only girl around to take over, and so on.

In fact, as we who are journalists ourselves all know, there is a kind of eagerness and magnetic vivacity on the part of the ambitious career person that is noticed and the vibes are picked up. At parties, these people shine like stars, and that is how and why they are hired.

But having been given that apparently lucky chance, you then have to prove your mettle by turning copy in on time, every single week, that will make the readers – and the editors – keep coming back to you for more. Most importantly, you have to turn it in on time. Newspaper deadlines are inexorable and will not, can not, wait. As Whitehorn herself admits: 'The average editor's cry is: We don't want it good, we want it Thursday.'

So far as their private lives went, it seems that these lippy female columnists managed to have long-lasting and, reasonably happy marriages. Jean Rook was married to Geoff Nash for 25 years although admitting in her autobiography that for most of that time they had separate bedrooms. There was never any suggestion that either of them had affairs with other people. Rook was probably far too busy and said that she did not socialise. Whether there is a hidden meaning in that word 'socialise' we shall now never know.

Lynda Lee-Potter, who married at 21 also had an enduring marriage to the same man, Dr Jeremy Lee-Potter. Katharine Whitehorn was married to Gavin Lyall for 45 years although there could be stormy moments as both were big boozers and Lyall, who later suffered from alcoholism, was also a chain smoker who frequently appeared to be living on the frayed ends of his nerves. Geoff Nash worked for the Press Association where he was a highly regarded reporter; Dr Jeremy Lee-Potter had a major career as a doctor but was never in the public eye; Leo Cooper, Jilly's husband, published military history books but was probably otherwise unknown beyond that milieu, and Katharine Whitehorn's husband Gavin Lyall wrote thrillers.

These busy writing women probably earned far more than their husbands, who they frequently wrote about in their columns, and they carved out an affluent and interesting lifestyle for themselves and their families, entirely by their own efforts.

Jilly Cooper became a major personality after her *Sunday Times* column brought her to public attention for its apparently intimately revelatory content. In her column, Jilly always made a big thing of being blissfully happily married to 'heavenly' Leo, as his second wife. It was only much later that the world learned of Leo's eight-year affair with another woman.

Primarily a fiction-writer, Cooper had her first outing as a writer on *Petticoat* magazine in the 1960s, where she was noticeably outstanding and her very sexy short stories, highly permissive for the time and later lengthened into novellas with girls' name titles such as *Prudence, Imogen* and *Bella* had the nation's young women gripped from week to week.

Cooper, nee Sallitt, comes, like Katharine Whitehorn, from an upper middle-class background although in her case it was army and landowning rather than academic. Trained as a secretary – her *Who's Who* entry describes her as a 'very temporary typist' – her first job in journalism was as a junior reporter on the *Middlesex Independent*.

She married Leo in 1961, and was soon writing young, exciting and publishable short stories. In 1968, she met the then editor of the *Sunday*

Times colour supplement at a dinner party who was intrigued, and asked her to write a humorous piece about being a young working wife.

The piece duly appeared in the paper and it was obvious that here was a fresh, new and potentially very big talent. Cooper's forte from the start was writing about her home and family in a modern, upbeat way and *Sunday Times* readers loved her as a person they thought of as being much like themselves but vastly funnier and kookier. *Sunday Times* readers were at one with Cooper in all her domestic adventures and mishaps and her persona was, if possible, even more sluttish than Whitehorn's. She wrote, for example, about redecorating her house and just painting round the pictures, not bothering to remove them first.

Again, this apparent bohemianism was a refreshing antidote to the humourless household advice coming from the average woman's magazine at the time and Cooper's life appeared to go from one delightful knockabout calamity to another.

But, as ever with major talents, Cooper's chatty, friendly style and sometimes excruciating puns hid a fierce ambition. Her cleverness was to come over as an impossibly zany but totally lovable housewife, and her columns were such an enjoyable read that one could fail to notice that the pieces were in fact, brilliantly crafted little masterpieces.

Cooper wrote about her infertility, about her experiences at boarding school, about being a bigger earner than her husband, all in a frothy light-hearted way that sometimes concealed the seriousness of the subject. Often, the candour was more apparent than real – she was, of course, not on oath to tell the truth, the whole truth and nothing but the truth but commissioned to amuse readers with her wit and humour.

Cooper often wrote about being hard up and mentioned that she and Leo would have 'starved' unless she had been able to sell her short stories, so it was something of a shock to discover that they lived in a huge house on Putney Common, right next to the Dimblebys. Cooper's Sloaney, upper-class tone earned her the epithet 'Jolly Super' at *Private Eye*, a nickname she turned to her own advantage with her 'Supercooper' and 'Jolly Superlative' collections of columns.

These two Sunday stars, Whitehorn and Cooper, were so big in their day they were satirised in a funny novel, *Sunday Girl*, by Lee Langley, where the madcap columnist runs out of true-life incidents to write about, and so starts inventing them for her Sunday column.

Jilly Cooper delighted the *Sunday Times* readers for 13 years, and then joined the new *Mail on Sunday* in 1982. But although she stayed there for seven years, filling the column started to became a struggle, and the strain was starting to show. Also, the zany life she chronicled was not coming over so irrepressibly amusingly now that she was middle-aged.

In common with most of the 'first ladies' Cooper also did interviews with big-name people of the time for the *Sunday Times*. And again, her byline was as important as the subject of the interview.

Cooper amusingly mythologised herself but her really big career is as a writer of bestselling blockbuster novels, and this is where her reputation will probably rest.

The four 'first ladies' who stormed their way into the male-dominated newspaper world of the 1970s were considered outrageous for their day, and between them they continually pushed back the boundaries of what it was acceptable to say in print. Katharine Whitehorn's famous 'slut' feature mightily offended many of the housewives of her day and another column she wrote on 'smelly grannies' was also considered highly offensive.

Jilly Cooper's revelations about her infertility and details about her intimate operations also seemed a shocking thing to read over breakfast on a Sunday. At the time readers were simply not used to finding themselves confronted by such topics in the serious newspapers, but these columnists paved the way for the even more intimate revelations and disclosures of later women journalists.

(One only has to think of Liz Jones telling all about her marriage to writer Nirpal Dhaliwal; a genuine no-holds-barred account that make Cooper's coy revelations seem like something out of a Victorian novel. And then Dhaliwal, a talented writer himself, 16 years Jones's junior, hits back with his own account of their marriage, writing not just about his own infidelities but how his many partners compare with each other. Dhaliwal is writing – refreshingly – about his own experiences as a highly sexed Indian man desperately trying to go to bed with as many Western women as he can, and this kind of stuff is assumed to be as fascinating to the reader today as Cooper's chronicles of domestic chaos were in the 1970s.)

It was rare that any of the husbands of the four First Ladies ever got a chance to strike back. In any case, the impression given was that they were all blissfully happily and faithfully married, and there was never any hint of the husband's inability to perform in bed.

This is in dramatic contrast to Australian journalist Amanda Platell, who has written columns giving details about her boyfriend's erections, or lack of them, and naming him as well as shaming him.

Julie Burchill, another major and highly revelatory talent, landed her first job in journalism was as a 'hip young gunslinger' on the *New Musical Express*, where it soon became clear she was head and shoulders above all the other writers on the paper, although how exactly one could be either hip or a gunslinger at the International Publishing Corporation's extremely staid offices, has never been revealed.

However Burchill-watchers were not surprised when she was offered a big-byline column in the *Mail on Sunday*, then edited by Stewart Steven. Burchill managed to entertain and infuriate the reading public in equal amounts week after week and, again, has laid every aspect of her private life completely bare for the reader.

Readers who have followed her columns and writings know that she has been married three times, first to Tony Parsons, secondly to Cosmo Landesman and thirdly to Daniel Raven, that she has two sons, neither of whom she brought up, that she lives in Hove, has struggled with weight problems and drug addiction, and has had eight sexual partners. Burchill has also written about the sexual prowess, or lack of it, of her various lovers and husbands, and about her lesbian affair with Daniel Raven's sister Charlotte.

When given the chance, women journalists have almost always proved themselves to be vastly more uninhibited and far less hidebound than their male counterparts.

The 'first ladies' gave female journalists a prominence they had never previously enjoyed, and they each became public figures, at least during the lifetime of their columns. They were famous names, their columns were both prominently and highly promoted, and they were hugely well paid. But the era was not to last. For most later female columnists, such as *The Times'* Libby Purves, their newspaper column is just one aspect of a portfolio career – a necessary precaution in these days where there is no security of tenure in any journalistic job.

In the days of the 'big four' light, frothy, personal columns were rare in newspapers. But nowadays it is difficult for any one columnist to stand out and columns are seen as a cheap way of filling up space – compared with sending reporters out on real stories, and what used to be known as newsgathering.

Former newspaper editor Bernard Shrimsley regards columnists as the 'sauce' in a newspaper and reckons that a 'lip smacking' flavour disappeared from the *Daily Express* when Jean Rook died. Can you invent columnists, Shrimsley asked, and answered: 'Trouble is, true stars make it all look so damned easy'

Shrimsley has also said that one reason for the proliferation of columns nowadays is that they are cheap to run and, from the look of them, very few columnists these days stray far from their ivy-clad manors: 'This is a far cry from the days of the First Lady of Fleet Street (peace be upon her) who wouldn't board a Jumbo without a top cameraman alongside, and one she chose because he could be trusted to help her with the luggage and *not* help her with the interviews.'

Many of today's columnists, such as Deborah Orr and Rebecca Tyrrell of *The Independent*, are reporting mainly from the domestic arena; they rarely go out and get stories as Jean Rook, Lynda Lee-Potter and Jilly Cooper did.

The original – and best – First Ladies were out there, true professionals, not just reporting from the home front but interviewing all the celebrities of the day, establishing a huge range of contacts and earning their vast salaries.

The real sadness is that so many journalists who were big, or even household, names in their day, are soon forgotten when their columns no longer appear. Few, if any, of today's young journalists have even heard of Jean Rook, Katharine Whitehorn or Lynda Lee-Potter, although Jilly Cooper remains well known because of her bestselling novels. But they need to be remembered and honoured because, as Jean Rook said, they created 'massive openings' for today's confident young journalists who are, mostly, completely unaware of the debt they owe to these brave, outspoken and trailblazing first ladies.

Two

Women on The Street

There are two glamorous and exciting professions – apart, that is, from the oldest one – where women have proved themselves pre-eminent, once given the chance.

One of these professions – or, strictly speaking, these *crafts* – is acting and the other is journalism. In each, it is possible to rise to become an international celebrity, and in both, men have tried with every tactic at their disposal to keep these thrilling occupations to themselves.

For a long time, women were excluded by law from performing in the theatre and even when they were reluctantly allowed onto the stage, acting was not considered quite 'respectable'.

With the more recent glamour profession or craft of journalism, women were also for a long time excluded from working in certain areas of the industry. But even where there was not exactly a legal ban on female employees, the powerful men's club atmosphere of Fleet Street was for decades a strong enough disincentive to dissuade all but the most ferociously ambitious and talented females from even attempting to make their way into 'The Street'.

Yet there were pioneer women who somehow managed to blast their way into the newsrooms, feature rooms, editing rooms and pubs of Fleet Street, in the days when it was difficult for women to have any career at all, let alone gain a foothold in the tough, ruthless world of national newspaper journalism. The twentieth century can be seen as the era when women finally came into their own, and nowhere more spectacularly than the somewhat disreputable and frightening but hugely entertaining world of Fleet Street.

The type of women worthy of celebration are those who in previous times would have had no outlet at all for their writing or observational talents. The only power available to most women in the past was to tyrannise over vast families of a dozen or more children or perhaps be the mistress of some rich man. It is true that a few, very few, exceptionally talented and spectacularly single-minded women could occasionally succeed as novelists and some, such as Harriet Beecher Stowe, author of *Uncle Tom's Cabin*, combined being a world-famous author with bringing up a huge family.

Later, the biographer Antonia Fraser managed to combine writing scholarly tomes with rearing six children, as did her mother Elizabeth Longford, the mother of eight. But such women could be counted almost in single numbers. In any case, writing novels, or indeed any kind of book was (is) essentially a solitary occupation, quite unlike the chatty, jostling camaraderie that is newspaper journalism.

But, as national newspapers began to establish themselves and slowly and grudgingly inch open their doors to women, here at last was the opportunity to have fun in a career and give full public rein to the witty, playful, throwaway type of writing previously regarded as an exclusively male talent.

Where, one might ask, were the Jean Rooks, Julie Burchills and Jilly Coopers of past centuries? The answer is: nowhere – because there were simply no public outlets for their wry witticisms and clever literacy. It was widely considered in the past that women had no sense of humour at all, and certainly no sense of fun, a notion that was comprehensively disproved when this supposedly humourless gender started to write for newspapers.

Once women were able to write popular journalism, and given permission to appear in national newspapers, they were at last able to put all their formerly pent-up energy, vigour and writing talents into entertaining literally millions of grateful readers through their sharp, observant and iconoclastic columns and features.

But it was never easy for women to break into the untidy, disorganised, chaotic, hectically busy and essentially amoral world of national newspapers, for a number of reasons. In many instances, the powerful men-only print unions kept them out of course, but even in areas where the unions did not hold sway, the small, highly elite world of Fleet Street was not exactly female-friendly.

The mass-market newspaper industry itself, brought into being by such extraordinary men as Alfred Harmsworth and Lord Beaverbrook, had had its beginnings in the 18th century coffee houses, where the leading male minds of the day would gather to exchange satire, biting wit and scurrilous jokes or compose wicked political pamphlets and cruelly brilliant cartoons.

The only women allowed into those coffee houses were blousy barmaids and serving wenches, and they were there simply to wait on the men and look decorative, not to add their *bons mots* to the sparkle of the conversation. The early boozy and boisterous days of Fleet Street took their cue from this all-male world of clever talk and high-octane wit.

Fleet Street itself, as a centre of literacy and printing, goes back much further, to the 15th century, when printing was invented. There were two monasteries in the Street, the Black Friars and the White Friars. The monks soon understood the importance of printing, as they could then print the Bible and religious tracts, documents that previously had to be laboriously hand written. Printing allowed The Word to be disseminated and when newspapers began to be produced, the area had already established itself as a centre of printing and mass communication.

The first daily newspaper to be produced from Fleet Street was the *Daily Courant*, in 1702. From the first, unlike many other countries, Britain had a relatively free press, and so from the start there was a tradition of being allowed to slag other people off with a degree of impunity.

The passing of a spate of Literacy and Education Acts in the 1870s meant that a lot of previously illiterate people would now be able to read, and they would want something to read that was not intellectual and did not depend on a university education. Thus the mass market was born, ushered in by such newspapers as the *Daily Mail*, *Daily Sketch* and *Sunday People* in the late nineteenth century.

Fleet Street itself was also coincidentally near all the main railway stations and this meant that newspapers could be transported overnight to every part of the kingdom including Wales and Scotland. The new railway system ensured that Britain could have national newspapers, something that did not happen in any other country. Britain was the right size for a national newspaper industry, whereas nearby France, for example, was too big.

Once all these factors came together, Fleet Street rapidly grew in power and influence. The large, confident *Telegraph, Express, Mail* and *Mirror* buildings underlined the enormous power and prestige of the early days of the national press.

But although the masses needed to be entertained and informed, there was also a place for serious newspapers, papers of record that would be read by the leading politicians and opinion formers of their day.

27

Downmarket newspapers also had their serious element – they had to contain at least some news to count as newspapers – and news reporters, initially all men, were required to report from battle fronts, houses of parliament, courts of law and the City on the major stories and scandals of the day. The very early newspapers were not only written entirely by men but were aimed more or less exclusively at a male readership.

Once the uncompromisingly masculine pattern was set and underlined by the acres of grey print and seven-point columns that characterised the early newspapers, Fleet Street remained overwhelmingly male, even down to the continuing existence of all-male bars and clubs, right until the 1980s. Even in the late 1970s, the wine bar El Vino did not allow women to go to the bar and also had its men-only steak bar where women were not allowed.

In 1970, a contingent of leading female journalists, led by Unity Hall of the *News of the World* and Jill Tweedie of *The Guardian*, stormed El Vino and while the exploit attracted a lot of attention, it was still several years before women were allowed into the wine bar on equal terms.

Also, until new technology finally and brutally ousted hot metal, and put an end to Fleet Street itself as a geographical centre, most newsrooms were men-only strongholds consisting of a sea of shirt-sleeved, chain-smoking, wisecracking males bonding over their typewriters, fags, dirty jokes and endless lunch hours. It was rare then for a mere woman to be a news reporter, sub-editor or photographer on a national title, and absolutely unthinkable that a woman might one day be the actual editor of a Fleet Street newspaper.

The Street in its prime, both as a geographical location and as a concept, was characterised by high wages, hard drinking, dozens of pubs and huge amounts of alcohol-fuelled talent. Because many newspapers enjoyed very high circulations, there were also oceans of money to be spent. Former *Mirror* journalist Anne Robinson, now a television celebrity, has said that in her day Mirror Group Newspapers raked in more money than many a small country. Not only were wages sky-high, thanks to the bargaining power of the unions, but expenses were virtually unlimited and even quite modest executives would have chauffeur-driven cars to take them a few yards up the road to the Savoy or on to Claridges, where they would order vintage wines, brandies and ports, often before as well as during and after lunch.

No wonder these men, enjoying a fast-paced life very high on the hog with their wives safely tucked away in the home counties, and often

28

having affairs with secretaries, did not want to admit women on equal terms. Keith Waterhouse writes in his autobiography *Streets Ahead*:

> Wives were never seen in Fleet Street. Newspaper widows lived in Petts Wood. I was something of an absentee husband myself, as were perhaps the great majority of newspapermen with ink in their veins. To go home before the first editions were 'up' was like leaving a party before anybody else had arrived.

However, Waterhouse's second wife was seen in Fleet Street, as she was the journalist Stella Bingham.

So, Fleet Street was never just a job but a way of life, a permanent men's party that nobody ever wanted to leave, and it was, above all, a repository of towering male egos and overweening vanity. The top crime reporters and showbiz correspondents of the day strutted around holding court and many were, in fact, the celebrities and household names of their time.

No woman in those days could visualise herself being a female version of Arthur Helliwell, Donald Zec, Hannen Swaffer, crime reporter Duncan Webb (with his hat set at an eternally rakish angle), Cassandra, Godfrey Winn or even of Keith Waterhouse. These men behaved like kings and were treated like kings, with kings' ransom salaries and expenses showered upon them. Many journalistic leading lights came, in those days, from lowly origins but they rapidly got used to earning lots of money and being feted wherever they went.

The Street itself, starting at Ludgate Circus and going up to The Strand and round into Fetter Lane, acquired a patina of ineffable, bohemian glamour and a kind of stardust clung to those journalists who had managed to make it onto a national newspaper.

The main print unions, which held newspaper proprietors to ransom for decades, had a strict policy of no women and no blacks, and their tactics were slavishly copied by the leading journalists' union, the NUJ, with its closed shops, Fathers of the Chapel and threats to come out on strike if they were not happy with a management decision. The NUJ did not exactly forbid women but acted as a forbidding presence, frightening many women from even embarking on journalism as a career.

In the 1960s, when graduate training schemes were established, less than five per cent of the intake was female. The strange thing is that that percentage seemed perfectly normal in those days, as journalism was still seen as being very much a man's job, with just a few token women allowed in on sufferance.

Before the days of computers and recording machines, journalists badly needed the skills of shorthand and typing, and the ratio of females to males at colleges of commerce and night schools was just the opposite, about 20 to one.

But it was not just the men with their powerful unions, all-pervading egos and closed shop systems who kept women out. In a way, the women kept themselves out. In order to get to Fleet Street at all in the old days, you had to have not only a towering ambition, but also the ability to kick doors down, to fight your way in and also, crucially, be able to take rejection and setbacks. Few men were tough enough for this life, let alone women. Only the supremely self-confident ever had the ghost of a chance and the majority of women, apparently, simply had no self-confidence at all.

Most women did not imagine they could remotely survive the cut-throat world of the national newspaper, and even talented women desperate to write for a living did not believe they could handle the hard-swearing, minute by minute decisions, quick thinking, instant repartee and sheer bullying needed to bring out a daily news sheet. Many were too nervous even to apply for a job as a reporter or feature writer on a newspaper.

There is no time for politeness or consideration of delicate feelings when deadlines are approaching, and women in the early days were terrified of what might be expected of them. Keith Waterhouse – one of the men who did make it, with spectacular success – writes, of 1950s newspaper offices:

> One heard bloodcurdling tales of grown men reduced to tears by the tongue-lashings of sarcastic newsroom executives who themselves were said to live in fear of their own superiors.

And he is talking about men, men who had been in the Army or had faced the horrors of public schools of the day, and were schooled from the start in toughness and bullying. Women of the time could not begin to cope with that kind of behaviour, brought up as they were to be compliant, acquiescent, silent and passive, not loud, bossy, pushy and brassy, as you needed to be – and still do need to be – to succeed as a newspaper journalist. The Street has never been a place for the shrinking violet of either sex.

Female journalists could expect to be balled out in exactly the same way as men. A story is told of Joyce Hopkirk, who had several executive positions on newspapers. When she was in charge of features at the *Daily Mirror*, she had to organise a lunch in the directors' dining room for Spike Milligan, with editor Mike Molloy as host.

The executives were all drinking in the editor's office waiting – and waiting – for their celebrity guest. Eventually, Molloy asked Joyce to ring the dining room to see whether there was any sign of Milligan, only to be told he had been taken straight to the dining room as directed and, finding nobody there, had stormed out. Molloy was furious, turned to Hopkirk and yelled: 'You couldn't organise a piss-up in a brewery.' There was simply no quarter given to a lady's delicate feelings.

Hopkirk was not one to accept such a pronouncement meekly. She decided that she would prove Molloy wrong and so set about organising a genuine piss-up in a brewery. In the event, she managed to fix up the wrong brewery on the wrong day, thus – so it seemed – proving Molloy's point with a catastrophic and achingly funny mix-up that has since gone into newspaper legend.

Then again, those women who did make it into Fleet Street had to endure being patronised at every turn and also putting up with a constant barrage of sexual harassment, which the men often found extremely amusing. Because there were so few women there was no safety in numbers and in any case not a shred of sisterhood.

One simple example will underline the kind of sexual harassment and blackmail that prevailed in the old Fleet Street. At the *Sunday People*, expenses had to be signed by the managing editor. One day, with an unmistakeable leer, he invited a young female reporter to a party. She said she would have to check with her husband, and he intimated that this wasn't the idea at all, and that he wanted to go only with her.

As politely as she could, she turned down the invitation. The next week the managing editor would not sign her expenses and said they would have to be cut considerably before he would pass them. Yet if she had gone to the party – if indeed a party existed – it seems a fair guess that he would have passed any reasonable amount. Several women had similar stories about this particular executive.

Many female journalists have tales about how they were led to believe they would get rapid advancement if they went to bed with their immediate (male) boss.

You needed to be opinionated, courageous and supremely thick-skinned to be able to stand up for yourself in such an environment, and these were not qualities much encouraged in women in the past. In fact, quite the opposite, as women were universally advised to hide their cleverness, not flaunt it, and certainly never to argue or be forceful or forthright. There was also the abiding fear that if you were too strident or opinionated you would never find a husband.

The other aspect was that most men did not want an independent, career-woman wife, merely an admiring audience, and women were conditioned not to want to be left on the shelf – the ultimate resting place, they were sternly warned, of the woman who got career ideas above her station, or who became so independent she did not need a man to keep her.

In her 1952 autobiography *In the Mink*, pioneer journalist Anne Scott-James, mother of Max Hastings, says that when she was on *Vogue*, where she started as a secretary, lots of girls would apply for jobs, and then ask for Fridays off as Mummy liked them to be in the country at the weekends.

Scott-James found that most of them were simply not cut out for office life, and even *Vogue* was too tough for them. Although, as we now know from the book and film *The Devil Wears Prada*, working on a magazine such as *Vogue* can be pretty nerve-racking, a monthly magazine dealing with fashion and beauty is not at all the same animal as a major daily newspaper getting to instant grips with the fast-happening issues of the day, and where copy often has to be written at breakneck speed.

In any case, women did not fit the abiding cliché of a newspaper journalist which was, as we know from a hundred films, that of the tough, chain-smoking, dogged reporter in a Homburg hat with a ticket saying Press stuck in his hatband, wearing a belted raincoat and taking out a battered notebook from his pocket as he swigs whisky from a hipflask. In the early days, the standard picture of a journalist was always of a man – or if a woman, of a butch lesbian. Graham Greene's 1930s novel *Stamboul Train* has a female journalist character, Mabel Warren, a cruelly caricatured bull dyke. It was not a role model many women wished to emulate.

The first novelist to write about a woman journalist who was remotely like a woman was Penelope Mortimer with her character Muriel Rowbottam, and she took care to make her female journo spectacularly unsuccessful in her job. A successful female journalist – even a successful career woman – would not have been a character most readers could identify with, even as late as the 1950s and 60s.

However, it is worth noting that in 1940, Howard Hanks made a new version of the play and film *Front Page* called *His Girl Friday*, starring Cary Grant and Rosalind Russell, where the female character matches the guy for wise-cracking and journalistic expertise. But this was not often seen in reality, even during the war years.

The strongest images of women at the time were as simpering secretaries, downtrodden housewives, or women who kept having children such as the heroine of another Penelope Mortimer novel, *The Pumpkin Eater*, later made into a film starring Anne Bancroft. In Margaret Drabble's early novels, even very clever Oxbridge-educated women with Firsts take second place to their husband's big career, and this was considered quite normal. It seemed there was no encouragement from any quarter to have a serious career of your own, especially one that was exciting and that challenged every fibre of your being. A little 'jobette' that could be given up at any time, was all that women were socially allowed.

In fact the late Elaine Dundy, author of the abiding bestseller *The Dud Avocado*, and first wife of theatre critic Ken Tynan, wrote of the 1950s in her 2001 autobiography *Life Itself!*:

> Except for the screwball comedies, where women were allowed some equality in regard to jobs, professions and careers, we females were taught by endless example never to seem to have even the appearance of 'competing' in any way with our husbands.

Or with any man, she might have added. But there was more. Until the Second World War, married women were not allowed to have paid jobs in many industries and usually had to give up their career on marriage. Very often the job was relinquished without too much fuss as the prevailing wisdom of the time was that the pinnacle of every woman's ambition was to marry, settle down, have children and become a housewife. *Jeanne Heal's Book of Careers for Girls*, written in 1955 by a famous female television personality of her day, asks this:

> Since it is agreed that most girls want a husband, home and a family, and regard a job as a stop-gap between leaving school and getting married, what is the case for women entering the professions?

She answers:

> To me the basic feeling of being independent, of being able to earn my own income even given the nicest husband in the world to keep me, is an absolute essential. But I know that my outlook is far from typical. I know that most women prefer not to have a job, and I know there are intelligent reasons why being a housewife and a mother can be the most satisfying whole-time job in life.

Jeanne Heal does not go on to say what those 'intelligent reasons' are, though. Nor does she mention journalism in her list of careers for girls.

Many of these difficulties were, of course, general factors militating against women entering and succeeding in any profession at the time.

33

But when it came to Fleet Street, and national newspaper journalism, there were, on top of all of all the other problems facing would-be career women, still more peculiar, specialised conditions prevailing, even apart from those already mentioned, which made it almost impossible for women to gain and maintain a foothold there.

In the first place, there was no automatic route into Fleet Street, either for men or for women. For most men, never mind women, securing a rare, coveted job on a national newspaper was very difficult indeed. There were few jobs on offer at any one time, so you had to be tough and ambitious and talented with a steely core of unshakeable determination to succeed when dozens of talented hopefuls were applying for every single scarce job.

The trade unions made it even more difficult, as on many papers there was a policy that nobody could ever be sacked, except for 'gross professional misconduct'. If ever an employee, or 'brother', was threatened with the sack, the rest of the staff was liable to come out on strike. And no management wanted to risk losing a day's print run, with all the loss of revenue and presence on the street that entailed, especially in the days when daily circulations were measured in many millions.

If virtually nobody could be sacked, it followed that few new people could ever be hired. It was common to hire men in pubs, and very occasionally, women were recruited at parties. Jilly Cooper was a famous example of this, but until the 1980s at least, very few women would ever venture into a pub on their own.

For men, though, there was a time-honoured method of getting a foot in the door, and that was by first becoming an office boy, copy boy, teaboy or messenger on a local paper, often starting at the age of 14. Future editors such as Ernie Burrington of the *Sunday People*, Charlie Wilson of *The Times* and *Sporting Life*, Arthur Brittenden of the *Daily Express*, and Derek Jameson of a number of papers, started off in this way.

Hugh Cudlipp, eventually chairman of Mirror Group News, began his professional life as a junior reporter on the *Penarth News* in Wales. Mike Molloy, who would eventually become editor of the *Daily Mirror* and editor-in-chief of Mirror Group Newspapers, started his newspaper career as a holiday relief boy, sharpening pencils for the Art Desk. Molloy was at the time studying art at Ealing College.

Victor Knight, political editor of the *Daily Mirror*, also started his newspaper career as a copy boy at the age of 14.

Many of the male entrants to Fleet Street were self-educated people, often from working-class families, who nevertheless showed great drive, talent and ambition at an early age. In fact, Ernie Burrington has put in his *Who's Who* entry: 'self-educated'.

It was not so easy for a girl to get a job even as a tea boy or messenger on a local paper. In fact, there was even a job on newspapers known simply as a 'boy' – a lonely, menial, errand-boy job that could, nevertheless, give that initial chance to a clever, talented lad from a non-privileged background.

The route into jobs on the so-called quality papers was different. There, you more or less had to have an Oxbridge degree and if you had been editor of the university newspaper, or taken an active part in university debates, you could often walk straight into a job on *The Times, Sunday Times, Observer* or *Daily Telegra*ph on graduation. Until Oxbridge colleges became co-ed, few women even went up to university – let alone hankered after a job on *The Times*.

In the glory days of Fleet Street, there was a wide gap between the popular and the 'quality' press, and few journalists ever crossed the divide. The popular – that is, the best-selling – titles had the money to pay their staff highly, but they also had the most powerful unions and were the toughest employees. Life on the quality papers was gentler, less well paid, but just as masculine and even more like an exclusive men's club. In his book *Good Times, Bad Times,* former *Times* and *Sunday Times* editor Harold Evans wrote that before he arrived on the scene, the big-name correspondents and executives would grandly sweep out of the door at 6pm, to make way for 'the non-commissioned officers', the lowlier staff who took their place on the night desk.

In the main, staff on the popular, or downmarket, papers were recruited from the literate and ambitious sectors of the working classes and on the quality press, from the educated intelligentsia. No wonder women, of any class, were hardly able to get a look-in.

Yet a few, very few, did somehow manage it, in spite of the many stumbling-blocks stacked up against them. It was, even in the early days, not totally unknown for a bright girl who had been to Oxbridge (Anne Scott-James, Katharine Whitehorn, for example) to get jobs on papers such as *The Times, Guardian* or *Observer*, but for a woman to work her way up through the ranks without this privileged start was virtually impossible. In any case, there would have been places for only one or two women on such papers, not for droves of them. But the 'tall poppy' syndrome itself went against women even trying to get into Fleet Street. The small number of big female stars seemed so big, so unassailable, and they held on to their columns or pages for decades, often until they could hardly totter into the office.

Sunday Times film critic Dilys Powell, for example, one of these early women, was still struggling into the office in her 80s or 90s. It was as if you had to be extra, and extraordinarily, special to have even half a hope of getting in, and then staying there. Many of the early newspaper women themselves carefully cultivated this 'special' air of being a kind of Hollywood superstar and that also served to frighten off the more timid souls.

But there was still more. The papers themselves were, in the days of the powerful print unions before and after the Second World War, very small indeed. The endless sections, supplements, lifestyle pullouts and magazines of today simply did not exist, partly because of paper rationing, but also due to the restrictive practices of the print unions. So, one might ask, how did the unions become so very powerful? The short answer is that newspapers had to come out every day and there was often no time for the management to argue. When several editions were being printed throughout the night and literally every minute counted, no proprietor could afford the time to bargain with the print unions. This meant the unions won, every time.

Keith Waterhouse writes that when he first joined the *Mirror*, it was a 'pitifully small paper, grossly overstaffed, with half a dozen highly experienced feature writers fighting to fill one page a day.'

In the 1940s, newspapers were thin because of wartime and post-war newsprint rationing and this usually restricted them to eight pages, or two sheets of paper. Then, when rationing ended, the pitifully small papers could not be very much larger because the printers would not print bigger papers. Or, if they would, they demanded wages and overtime and extra staff often beyond the ability of even the richest proprietors to pay, for doing it.

There was no chance then of a 'Polly Filler' or a 'Philippa Space' as *Private Eye* has it, mouthing off inconsequentially so as to fill acres of otherwise empty newsprint; quite the reverse.

Vitally, most men did not believe women were an equal sex. Few relished the idea of women earning as much as they did, or maybe more. Jean Rook was known as the 'first Lady' of Fleet Street, not the first person, and was billed (or billed herself) as the highest earning *woman* on Fleet Street; again, not the highest earning *person*.

Many of the women who made it have stories about how they were paid a pittance in comparison to the men, even when they were supposed to be in an equal position. It was common for male, but not female, reporters, to be given staff cars. The idea that a man, any man, was always worth more than a woman even when that women was doing the same job, took a long time to disappear.

In her autobiography, *Memoirs of an Unfit Mother*, Anne Robinson admits that we simply didn't know how bad it was, or how strewn with huge obstacles was the path.

But once a few brave women paved the way and established themselves, more wanted to follow in their footsteps because journalism sounded such fun. Yes, women were also at the same time fighting their way into medicine, into the law and to some extent, into politics. But these were serious occupations that needed serious-minded women, and not all women had the determination, or indeed the academic ability to grind away at a subject for years on end, in order to enter these professions.

Yet in journalism – in theory – there was always a place for people who, while not necessarily being formally educated, had quirky minds, a witty turn of phrase or a unique way of looking at life. And journalism was, above all, a career where women with a curious or offbeat way of viewing the world could eventually make a unique contribution. Here, they could have a voice of their own, and a voice that was quite different from that of the male.

And once given the opportunity to express themselves through newspaper columns, women soon showed the reading public that they had exciting and provocative things to say that had never been said before – at least in the popular prints. Once they had their feet firmly under the office desk, women began to write about, and give a public airing to, subjects that had remained taboo or hidden before, such as how to stop unwanted babies from coming or how to cope with an unfaithful husband, down to apparently trivial subjects such as what kind of gloves to wear to church, or whether your handbag should match your shoes.

Whereas men tended to write about 'big' subjects like politics, international affairs and sport, women started writing about subjects of particular interest to women. Many early female newspaper journalists, great names such as Ernestine Carter, Alison Adburgham, Felicity Green and Iris Ashley, wrote about fashion, a subject of little interest or concern to the average man, but of abiding fascination to many women.

Although fashion was the first 'female' subject to be given serious space in newspapers, before long, women were writing on subjects that had been kept firmly under wraps before, such as abortion, childbirth, single mothers, contraception, sexual satisfaction, the problems of combining a job with looking after children and states of mind such as depression, anxiety and stress.

Now as we know, anything goes, but in the 1950s, subjects such as menstruation, female orgasms and the mysteries of female plumbing generally were completely taboo and previously, nobody, not even women, had written about them. Before women came to journalism, the only place you could read and find out about personal medical matters was in medical dictionaries or inaccessible journals such as *The Lancet* or *British Medical Journal*.

None of the men in newspapers was then writing about such things but even if they had, they would not have been from a female perspective. For the pioneer women in journalism, all the minutiae of everyday life, and anything that might be of interest to readers, became valid subjects, and soon started to go into print. First of all, papers such as *The Guardian*, where the redoubtable Mary Stott was the first woman's editor, commissioned articles on these subjects and then the middle market and tabloid papers followed suit, each gradually amassing women journalists to write about women's issues.

They – that is, women journalists – contacted psychologists, sex experts, doctors, to talk candidly about previously forbidden subjects, for a large and grateful readership. Women led the way in what later came to be called lifestyle, writing about health, particularly alternative or complementary health, and trailblazing articles about cancer, money, relationships, affairs, sex before marriage, often from a personal viewpoint.

Katharine Whitehorn has said that she was one of the first female journalists to be given the opportunity to write like a woman, rather than a man. Now men are following suit trying to write like women with their articles about fatherhood, single parenting, grooming and the difficulties of attracting a partner. Men are now writing articles about their emotions, whereas in the old days of newspapers, men didn't officially have emotions; they just got angry and hot under the collar.

But at the same time as women were firmly establishing specifically female voices on newspapers, some women journalists wanted the chance to enter strongly-guarded men's worlds to become political or foreign correspondents, science correspondents, news reporters, news editors, sub-editors, photographers and even editors.

In all these areas, success would finally, if belatedly, be achieved.

Three

The pioneers

Even though it took women a long time to start to make serious waves in Fleet Street, nobody can say that they were never given an early chance. In fact, the first female editor of a national daily newspaper was Mary Howarth – in 1903.

That was the year that newspaper proprietor Alfred Harmsworth had the bright idea of founding a daily newspaper especially for women. He had already established a women's section in the *Daily Mail*, the newspaper he founded in 1896, and this was so popular that he thought there was room for a newspaper aimed entirely at the female half of the population.

Women's magazines, both weekly and monthly titles, were rapidly taking off and establishing respectable circulations in all sectors of the market, so why not go the whole hog and start a daily paper for the gender so far more or less ignored by newsprint?

This new project was to be called *The Daily Mirror*, and would contain news about the latest Paris fashions, cooking hints, how to treat your servants, dress for Ascot and all the other burning topics of interest to women of the day. And so, in November 1903, the *Daily Mirror* began life as the first daily newspaper for gentlewomen. It burst onto the news stands with a massive £100,000 promotional campaign, plus the offer of a gilt mirror, free with the first issue, and cost one penny.

The reason it was named the *Daily Mirror* in the first place was undoubtedly because it was generally thought that women looked at themselves in the mirror all the time. *And if we call it the Mirror they'll be obliged to look into it*, won't they? And this point was rammed home by the free gift of the gilt looking glass.

There were ads on the front page, as was usual for newspapers in those days, and little actual news, but titbits about fashion, royalty and interior decoration, and such topics, inside. The very first edition had advertisements for dress shops and department stories such as Paquin ('mantles and gowns'), Redfern Creations, Debenham and Freebody, Peter Robinson of Oxford Street, jewellers Tiffany and Co and Victory's Furs – all noticeably upscale stores and products.

Page 3 had 'To-day's news at a glance' and contained, in very short paragraphs and sentences, births, marriages and deaths of society people, information that cheap furs were 'doctored' to make them look more expensive, and international news snippets such as that the entire Chilean cabinet had resigned, and that 48 people had died as a result of a Japanese ship colliding with a Russian steamer.

The paper, which came out a full 15 years before women got the vote, was to contain 'everything from the arrangement of flowers on the dinner table to the disposition of forces in the Far East' and was to be 'entertaining without being frivolous and serious without being dull'.

It was a brave and worthy aim, and on November 2 a total of 265,217 gentlewomen bought this exciting new publication as it hit the streets. By the end of January 1904, though, they had stopped looking into the *Mirror*, sales had dropped alarmingly to 25,563 copies a day, and the newspaper was haemorrhaging £3,000 a week.

This would never do so Harmsworth, ever the astute businessman, quickly changed tack and replaced the editor, Mary Howarth, with a man, Henry Hamilton Fyfe, whose brief was to turn the publication into a picture paper for women – and men. The cover price was immediately cut to a halfpenny. Within a month, sales of the new, improved unisex and picture-led *Daily Mirror* had increased sevenfold and the failure of the first newspaper aimed entirely at women was quietly forgotten. Harmsworth wryly observed:

> Some people say that a woman never really knows what she wants. It is certain she knew what she didn't want. She didn't want the *Daily Mirror*.

Harmsworth later said that the women-only *Daily Mirror* was the only journalistic failure with which he was associated. He had a theory that women wanted a daily paper of their own but soon learned to his cost that they did not. Or, at least, they did not want *his* women-only paper. He also said that the experience taught him that women can't write and don't want to read – an observation that reverberated down

Fleet Street for decades, and justified keeping women out wherever it was possible to employ a man for the job instead.

Henry Hamilton Fyfe had the nasty business of sacking all the women and paying them three months' wages (about half what the men were getting anyway) instead of notice. He has said in his book *My Seven Selves* that the women tearfully waylaid him in the corridor, left little presents on his desk and begged to be allowed to stay. Hamilton Fyfe then wrote that sacking these women 'was a horrid experience – like drowning kittens ', a horrifically memorable phrase that has ever since enshrined itself in the language and lore of The Street.

The revamped *Daily Mirror* with its emphasis on 'exclusives', then a new idea, soon became a highly successful downmarket newspaper, an easy read, but ever mindful of its total failure as a women-only paper, was to develop an aggressively masculine image, underlined perhaps by its long-running strip cartoon of unregenerated Northern man, Andy Capp, and the sexy cartoon pin-up, Jane.

But although Mary Howarth was the first female editor of a national daily, and has gone down in history as such, she was not actually the first woman editor of a national British newspaper.

That was the remarkable Rachel Beer, aunt of the war poet Siegfried Sassoon; she was editor of two Sunday papers at the same time: *The Observer* (1891 to 1904) and the *Sunday Times*, (1893 to 1904) both of which were owned at the time by her husband Frederick. While she was at the helm of *The Observer*, the paper secured one of its greatest exclusives, which was the admission by Count Esterhazy that he had forged the letters that had condemned the Jewish officer Captain Deyfus to Devil's Island. The story led to the pardon of Dreyfus and the court martial of Esterhazy.

But Rachel Beer, who was a member of the Institute of Journalists and the Society of Women Journalists, was a complete one-off, and after the failure of the women-centred *Daily Mirror*, it was to be some years before women found their way back into Fleet Street in any sizeable numbers or could make any sugnificant contribution, and who would pave the way, in their unique fashion, for subsequent women to carve out a career for themselves in The Street.

Xenia Field was a truly remarkable and versatile woman who wrote on gardening for many years for the *Daily Mirror*, in spite of not having a garden of her own and, as one of the very first career women writers, also championed prison reform and wrote plays. She was born in 1894, as Xenia Lowinsky, and died in 1998. Small and light, she was an 'old lady' at the paper for as long as anybody could remember. One *Mirror* journalist remembers the following exchange:

She was once standing behind features sub-editor Vic Mayhew while he was subbing her copy.

'Do you want something, Mrs Field?' he asked.

'No, young man, I am just watching what you are doing to my article.'

'Mrs Field,' said Mayhew, 'do you want me to treat you as a greatly esteemed and very elderly lady, or do you consider our relationship as one between fellow, professional, journalists?'

'Oh, we are both professional journalists, I'd say.'

'In that case, Xenia, fuck off.'

She got the message, but would occasionally appear late in the evening, usually around edition time and presumably after dinner in the West End, with friends to whom she would show the editorial floor of 'her' newspaper. For years people would recall the night when she appeared from the lifts and staff looked up to ask: 'Who's that old woman Xenia has brought in, this time?'

She approached the night news desk and said: 'May I introduce Lady Churchill?'

She had FOUR plays running concurrently in the West End at one time during the war. In addition to her regular column in the *Mirror*, Xenia Field wrote gardening books, and her sympathetic study of women in prison, *Under Lock and Key*, was published in 1963.

She wrote a Saturday gardening column for years but without ever getting the space that she felt she deserved. But her column supported a great deal of advertising, from seeds to watering cans and garden sheds. She asked for a pay rise on the grounds that her column was extremely popular with readers but was told that, instead of an increase, she would be paid half a crown (around 13p) for each reader's letter that she handled.

A few weeks later, Xenia wrote about a rose she had discovered called *Lachryma Christi*, which was supposed to have sprung from the tears of Christ at the foot of the cross, and preserved down the centuries by a succession of monks. Seeds were available, she wrote, for every reader who wrote in for them.

So many bags of mail arrived as a result that extra staff had to be taken on to cope with them, and letters kept coming for weeks afterwards. Xenia made so much money from handling all these letters at 2/6 a time that the management quickly worked out a pay rise would be cheaper.

The story about the rose came at about the same time – the mid-1950s – as the famous story about virgin births which ran for weeks in the *Sunday Pictorial*, and took the circulation to well over six million. This was, maybe, the era in which people believed that if it was in the papers, it must be true.

The Labour politician and secretary of state Barbara Castle was also an early journalist on the *Daily Mirror*. As Barbara Betts, she ran an advice column for servicemen and their wives during the war, handling questions about pay and complaints about social support and children's welfare. She was also an ARP (Air Raid Precautions) officer during the blitz. She married journalist Ted Castle in 1944, and was elected to parliament as Labour MP for Blackburn in 1945, after which she left journalism for a famous career as a Labour politician.

One of the first women to make a significant mark in women's journalism, and to give a platform and outlet to many women writers, was Mary Stott, the first woman's editor of *The Guardian*, originally the *Manchester Guardian*.

Mary Stott was born in Leicester in 1907, the youngest child and only daughter of local journalists Robert and Amalie Waddington. She always thought of herself as a plain, disagreeable child, but she had an early feminist example in her mother, who not only had a career, but took her daughter to meetings of women liberals and charity fundraising events during the first world war. In fact, one of Stott's earliest memories was of being driven around with a green ribbon in her hat (the then colour of the Liberal party), campaigning in the 1911 general election. At the time women were not allowed to vote, but they were encouraged to campaign.

Mary Stott was educated at Wyggeston grammar school in Leicester which she left at the age of 17 to go straight to the *Leicester Mail* as a 'temporary copyholder'. As a woman, she was not allowed to join either the Typographical Association or the Correctors of the Press Association, so could not progress in her ambition to become a news reporter. Instead, she was asked at the age of 19 to take over the woman's page of her paper, as for this job she did not need to be a member of either union. In her autobiography, *Before I Go*, Stott recalled that her heart sank at this offer, which she felt to be a demotion and as if her chances of ever becoming a 'real' journalist were lost for ever.

This early setback started her thinking about women's causes and injustices and she realised that in the important area of discrimination against women, she had a chance to make a difference. Her next job was at the *Bolton Evening News* and in 1933 she moved to the Co-Operative Press in Manchester, where she edited the weekly *Co-Op News*. This consisted of news of the women's co-operative guild, and

43

children's publications, and was still not really what she wanted to do. She married fellow journalist Ken Stott, of the *News Chronicle* in 1937 and in 1943 they had a daughter, who would become the journalist Catherine Stott. They lived in Heston Moor, Cheshire until Ken died suddenly in 1967 at the age of 56.

Stott determined from the first to be a working mother and by 1945 she was on the staff of the *Manchester Evening News* as a sub-editor. At last, she felt like a real journalist. However, the privilege of being in a 'man's job' did not last long and she was sacked in 1950 apparently solely to prevent her rise through the ranks with the audacious ambition to become chief sub – a job that was designated for men only, and operated by a kind of dynastic male succession.

Stott had little choice then but to 'retire' and spend time looking after her daughter, but her background in 'real' journalism, however brief, stood her in good stead when in 1957 *Guardian* editor Alastair Hetherington asked her to edit a new women's page he wanted to start on the paper. Because she had acquired subediting and page make-up skills during her brief stint as a sub, Stott could both commission articles and edit the page, so Hetherington got two journalists, as it were, for the price of one.

In any case, Mary Stott was ideally suited to this job, and she instantly began to establish a new kind of woman's page that would be challenging, controversial and exciting, giving a new and upcoming generation of women journalists and writers their head. This policy was quite different from the situation that obtained at the *Daily Mirror* and *Daily Mail*, for example, where copy and views were strictly controlled by the proprietor and the editor, and had to fit the paper's existing stance in both style and content.

Stott actually invented the type of pages that are still going in *The Guardian G2* section today, where new, previously untried or highly controversial subjects are often given their first public airing. And *The Guardian* is still pre-eminent at giving a public platform to women with unusual, minority, or uncomfortable views and experiences – so long, of course, that they will either resonate with or interest, the paper's typical female reader. This free and easy approach is never an easy furrow to plough and Mary Stott did not always get it right but the content of her pages was always unpredictable, and set in motion a number of big careers.

As Women's Editor Stott championed such outspoken journalists as the young Jill Tweedie, Polly Toynbee and Liz Forgan, and let them say what they liked. They were, after all, writing for an educated, forward-thinking, liberal-minded readership. Mary Stott's page, in her own words, was to depend mainly on 'warmth, sincerity and personal involvement.' By 1964, she had been editing the page for seven years and it now began to reflect, and sometimes be in the vanguard of, the up and coming feminism that at the time the other women's pages, concentrating as they did mainly on beauty, fashion and cookery, were ignoring.

By now the word '*Manchester*' had been dropped and the paper became simply *The Guardian*, establishing its main base in London rather than up North. One of Stott's early writers, the ex-deb Fiona McCarthy, who had her own Monday column in *The Guardian* in the 1960s, says that Mary Stott established an 'influential and idiosyncratic female sub-state' on the paper.

All the topics that might be of interest to women such as abortion, sex before marriage, contraception, balancing working life with having children and a husband or partner, were written about on the woman's page with the result that a whole generation of young women owed their early feminist education and consciousness-raising to Mary Stott of *The Guardian*.

The only problem was that although writing for *The Guardian* was a wonderful showcase for idiosyncratic or avant-garde views and ideas, the paper never paid much for its women's page pieces. In fact, it was probably in those days the lowest-paying paper on the street, at least for its female contributors. On the plus side, the paper, although highly unionised, was never a closed shop, and this meant that untried and amateur correspondents could have articles accepted for publication. Mary Stott was a great one for picking unsolicited contributions from unknown authors from the huge pile that landed daily on her desk, and publishing them, at a time when it was virtually impossible for this type of contribution to be even remotely considered for publication on any other national newspaper.

One reason for this was that many papers in those days, especially those of the Mirror Group, operated a tightly closed shop which meant that the only acceptable copy was that written by full and fully paid up members of the National Union of Journalists, who were supposed to be 'trained' journalists.

The result of this was that nobody new and untried, however clever and talented, could ever get a start on a tabloid, as the union members would come out on strike if copy written by a non-union member was used. This policy of course made it even more difficult for women to get a foothold on the Street. It will be remembered that Equity, the actors' union, operated a similar policy, thus giving another parallel to the two professions.

Mary Stott was particularly concerned about women's isolation, and she was instrumental in setting up and promoting women's networks, then a very new idea. In fact, the prospect that women might want to bond together and establish solidarity was, in those days, quite startling. Men had their networks, their old school ties, yes, but not women. They were all marooned as if by a moat in their own homes, especially in the days when few women owned, or could drive, a car, or had a telephone.

The *National Housewives' Register*, an early networking organisation for women, began life with an article in *The Guardian* in 1960, as did, later, the Pre-School Playgroups Association. Such organisations as NAWCH – the National Association for the Welfare of Children in Hospital – the Single Woman and Her Dependents and the Disablement Income Group, all started with an article or letter in *The Guardian*. These associations, tiny at first, grew into national institutions and created solidarity and new movements among the new generation of thinking, professional, concerned women.

Fiona McCarthy, herself later the author of groundbreaking biographies such as the shocking story of Eric Gill, where she drew attention to his incestuous relationships with his daughters and his own sister, said that Mary Stott's *Guardian* pages 'operated as a community notice board on a giant scale.'

Eric Gill of course made a significant contribution to the print industry himself, with his neat, clear Gill Sans typeface, used in newspapers, on the London Underground, by Penguin Books and the BBC.

Some of the 'ordinary' women in the suburbs, whose first pieces were published by Mary Stott, later became journalists in their own right. Betty Jerman was one former housewife who later, thanks to an initial piece in *The Guardian*, became a national newspaper journalist.

Stott mixed unknowns with up and coming celebrities, and she also used such well-known names as Margaret Drabble, Lena Jeger, Marghanita Laski and Shirley Williams. Her weekly *Women Talking* slot became one of the most widely read and talked about features of the time. Household names, unknown housewives, teenage aspirants, elderly feminists such as Cicily Fairfield, better known as Rebecca West, who covered the Nuremburg Trials for the *New Yorker* – all were given a voice on these pages, making them varied, unusual, provocative and sometimes startling, but always interesting and, for aspirant young journalists of the time, required reading.

The *Guardian* women's pages under Mary Stott brought the burgeoning *samizdat* feminism of the late 1960s and early 70s out of the underground magazines such as *Suck* (for which the young Germaine Greer wrote a column) into full public glare and opened it up as a subject for serious national debate. Rebecca West herself gave the movement one of its most famous quotes:

> 'I myself have never been able to find out what feminism is; I only know that people call me a feminist whenever I express sentiments that differentiate me from a doormat.'

Stott is credited with inventing the genre of journalism special to women at the time, that of the 'unburdening'; a common enough (some may say too common) genre today, as the ever-rising tide of misery memoirs bears witness.

Although *The Guardian* was read mainly by educated women, there was no class bias or elitism to the pages and Stott also published articles by working-class women who were totally dependent on their husband's low wages. It was all new, heady, and exciting and at the time: no other newspaper was covering these issues. Mary Stott gave many women the confidence to talk about topics that had never been discussed before, and in doing so, to bring previously hidden or ignored issues out into the open.

Before long, men were listening to what the women were saying and, what is more, taking notice. Fiona McCarthy adds, in Mary Stott's obituary:

> 'The 1960s women's page was an onslaught on old-time suburban female values from within. The silence of women in those days was pervasive in a way incomprehensible to women living now.'

Mary Stott died in 2002, at the age of 95. Her 14 years as woman's editor at *The Guardian* was followed by such luminaries as Liz Forgan, Frances Cairncross and the thriller writer Jane McLoughlin.

Sheila Black, who died in December 2007 aged 87, was another pioneer, albeit of a very different type from the campaigning, concerned Mary Stott. Black was born in 1920 in Sri Lanka and came from a moneyed, educated background. Her father was a businessman, and Black was educated first in England, then at a finishing school in Switzerland. Determining to be an actress – and she had this aspiration in common with some other high-profile journalists such as Jean Rook and Lynda Lee-Potter – she went to RADA and for a time did indeed tread the boards. She married young, in 1939, and had a daughter and a son. The marriage did not work out and the couple were divorced in 1951. In that same year, she married Lee Howard, then editor of the *Daily Mirror* and that marriage also ended in divorce, in 1973. Lee Howard later became the partner of another pioneering journalist, the

Mirror's Italy correspondent Madelon Dimont, eldest daughter of novelist Penelope Mortimer.

Sheila Black never married again, although she had a long running and passionate affair in the 1950 and 60s with the then editor of the *Financial Times*, Sir Gordon Newton.

Gordon Newton had invited Sheila Black to his office after she had written him a letter in 1958, out of the blue, saying that the FT should expand its consumer coverage. At the meeting, he hired her on the spot, taking a great risk as not only was she a woman, but a married woman with children in tow. The *Financial Times* had been strictly a men-only newspaper and Newton's policy was to hire bright and very young men. Among his appointees was the future chancellor Nigel Lawson (perhaps now better known as father of Nigella), Christopher Tugendhat, later a European commissioner, and also the future editor of *The Times*, William Rees-Mogg.

Black was the first woman to be hired as a journalist at the *FT* but she quickly became a household name and proved herself a gifted, stylish and innovative writer. She started the popular *How to Spend it* section in 1967 and rumour has it that Newton would go to her office in the evening after official work, and there they would share a gin and tonic – and maybe more. Gordon Newton had a reputation for being a difficult, buttoned-up, remote kind of man but Sheila seemingly brought out his passionate side, and his affair with her humanised him, to a large extent.

Possibly partly influenced by her marriage to Lee Howard, Black was able to bring a touch of popular journalism to the staid *FT,* and she also wrote about non-business and non-city matters such as contraception, then hardly considered a topic for mass readership, especially in a serious newspaper.

She persuaded Newton, who was besotted with her, to carry a feature on the newly-discovered contraceptive pill, and this called forth the wrath of at least one reader, who wrote to say the article should have been called *How to be a Prostitute and Get Away with It*. Black replied to this reader that his suggestion of such a headline was interesting but unfortunately would not fit on the page.

Black's versatile journalistic talents soon became apparent. She was a chatty and amusing writer and soon amassed a formidable contacts list, which meant she was able to call on leading celebrities of the day for quotes to embellish her articles. She was also a sensible and level-headed commentator on personal finance and tax issues, always complicated subjects for anybody to get their head round, never mind trying to make them interesting reading matter.

The *How to Spend it* section that she founded is now a separate magazine and remains one of the most enduring and popular elements of the *FT*.

When Newton retired in 1972, Black left with him. She had already become famous in journalistic circles as 'Sheila Black of the *Financial Times*', and she provided a shining example of what could be possible for a woman writer. She worked for a time in public relations and later joined *The Times* where she instantly became 'Sheila Black of *The Times*', always writing about financial, business and consumer affairs, although often with a female, or feminine, angle. She also championed consumer groups and organisations, and to this day, she is remembered best by her first title: *Sheila Black of the Financial Times*.

The writer and academic David Kynaston, author of *Austerity Britain* and also of the official history of the *Financial Times*, says that Sheila Black was probably the most influential person in the paper's history in softening and relaxing the style of the paper, and giving it a wider appeal than just to City men.

Sheila Black contributed major input to Shirley Conran's *Superwoman* books, and also to the *Weightwatchers* books officially authored by Bernice Weston. All these books became bestsellers, but Black was never properly credited for her contribution to these volumes. Newton died in 1998, but nobody knows for how long – or whether – the affair continued after their professional relationship ended.

Another very different type of writer, Anne Edwards, was a columnist on the *Daily Express* in the 1950s and 60s. She was billed as one of the paper's star female writers, along with Eve Perrick, mother of Penny, in the days when the *Express* sold more than four million copies a day and many of its writers became household names.

Eve Perrick concentrated mainly on showbiz, while Anne Edwards wrote witty and irreverent light-hearted articles about fashion and current affairs. Born in 1909 and the youngest of three children, she was given the unfortunate first name of Lettice, which she quickly changed to the much more innocuous Anne. Printing ink was in her DNA as her grandfather was a war correspondent and later drama critic for *The Times*.

She graduated from Somerville College, Oxford, and first worked in an advertising agency where she met her husband Bill Crossley. They married in 1936, had two children and the marriage lasted until his death in 1976. After several jobs in journalism she landed the Anne Edwards page on the *Daily Express*, and this made her name. It became so popular that her face appeared in ads on the side of buses, and she was billed as one of the few female columnists who were just as eagerly read by men. Anne Edwards died in 2005, at the age of 95, leaving a book of childhood memoirs unpublished. But although she was so famous in her day, such is the ephemeral nature of the clever, witty, off the cuff column that few have even heard of her today.

If you want to be remembered as a journalist you really have to write books as well as entertaining articles, and Anne Scott-James certainly excelled in this.

Born in 1913 and again educated at Oxford University, Scott-James began her career on *Vogue* as a secretary in 1934, straight after leaving Oxford. She soon graduated to writing and editing, and joined the staff of *Picture Post* in 1941, where she met and married her second husband Macdonald Hastings. (Her first husband had been editor and publisher Derek Verschoyle, but that marriage lasted less than a year.) She was the *Picture Post* woman's editor from 1941 to 1945, and then became editor of the British edition of *Harper's Bazaar*. After that she joined the *Sunday Express* as women's editor and stayed from 1953 to 1957. Her last job in journalism was as a *Daily Mail* columnist, and in the late 1960s she left journalism to write books on gardening. Her marriage to Macdonald Hastings also ended in divorce and her third husband was the cartoonist Osbert Lancaster; that marriage lasted until Lancaster's death.

In her early autobiography, *In the Mink*, published in 1952, Scott-James writes about the problems women have in combining a career with bringing up a family, a predicament that has still not been satisfactorily resolved. When her son Max (the journalist and former editor Max Hastings) was born, she managed to carry on working in an office for a time with the help of 'Nannie'. But when Nannie left, the problem reared its head again. There was no possibility, in those days, that a husband would help out with childcare or housework, and children were seen as being entirely the woman's responsibility.

In Chapter 17 of *In the Mink*, titled: The Problem Unsolved, Scott-James writes:

> Should I go on putting my profession first? Or should I leave the job and do more for James [Max]? Or go on compromising indefinitely? The problem loomed larger in my life every month. And it isn't just my personal problem, but a more serious and important one, for most married professional women are facing it today – or those, at least, who have children and who have reached a point in their careers where their work is largely creative.

She goes on:

I decided to take three months' complete rest to see if I liked home life and leisure or not. My friends talked as if I were taking the veil, but if I didn't like it, there was nothing to stop me changing my mind again. I wouldn't, I felt sure, want another full-time executive job until James went away to prep school, but there are ways of compromising, even if none of them is quite satisfactory. You can take a part-time job .. or you can take an advisory job .. or you can work at home. Probably my own best bet would be to stay home and work as a freelance, avoiding the insipidity of a purely private life.

Scott-James ends the book:

I still haven't worked out how to combine a home and profession. One the one hand, it can't make economic sense that so many years of education, training and experience should be suddenly thrown away. ..On the other hand, I shall soon have two children and couldn't dream of going back to the full-time business rush. But I am a staunch believer in having one's cake and eating it, a principle I have followed greedily throughout my life. I know there must be a way of having an eating this particular cake, and somehow I shall find it.

Anne Scott-James did indeed find a way of eating her cake and having it. When the *Daily Mail* pioneered the female opinion column in the 1960s, she was chosen as its first columnist. She was the first First Lady, if you like. Scott-James has an enduring reputation for being formidable and frightening and her son Max Hastings has spoken publicly of his troubled relationship with her. Always rather grand, she used to holiday on the Riviera while Max went to Butlins with the nanny, so he revealed to Sholto Byrnes of the *New Statesman.*

Some pioneer women journalists, such as Veronica Papworth of the *Sunday Express* and Olga Franklin of the *Daily Mail*, were popular in their day, highly promoted by their newspapers, but have left too little trace of their lives and careers to be able to say much about their contributions now. Olga Franklin came from a Russian background and in the 1950s, covered the exploits about the famous Russian long-distance walker (and most peculiar person), Dr Barbara Moore.

Franklin wrote a disarming article in *The Spectator* in 1972 about the rise of the woman journalist:

She may make a quick killing and marry the editor; she may land Gregory Peck like the French girl reporter, or President Kennedy like Jacqueline Onassis, or end up with Anthony Crosland like Susan Barnes. Or perhaps, most unfair of all, she may rise straight from the top editor's bed into Fleet Street with hardly any qualifications at all as I did myself and as I know some of my colleagues also did (but I do not want to libel anybody).

(Anthony Crosland was a prominent Labour politician of the 1960s whose avowed intent was to get rid of 'every fucking grammar school' and replace them with comprehensive schools. Susan Barnes was an American journalist who wrote for the *Sunday Times* and later became a novelist writing as Susan Crosland)

Veronica Papworth had a popular personal column in the *Sunday Express* for many years and also did fashion sketches. But again, little trace of her work or life now remains.

The journalist Sandy Fawkes was another fashion artist, and quite a lot is known about her, rather too much, some people might think. Fawkes, first wife of Wally Fawkes, otherwise known as Trog, the cartoonist, was a talented artist and modern adventuress who not only held prominent jobs in her lifetime but lived a life full of excitement, incident and even extreme danger.

By the time Sandy Fawkes died in December 2005, aged 75, she had become a hopeless alcoholic and a more or less permanent fixture in the Coach and Horses and French pub in Soho, where she consumed simply astonishing amounts of whisky, according to onlookers. The surprising thing, wrote her obituarist in the *Daily Telegraph*, was not so much that she often appeared drunk, as that she survived so long, as she hardly ever seemed to eat anything.

Fawkes, born in 1929, had a most unusual start in life as she never knew who her parents were but was found, as a baby, in the Grand Union Canal. After this Dickensian beginning came a Dickensian upbringing, as she was sent to a series of foster parents and apparently suffered much abuse. She wrote about her early years in the 1970s, after the case of Maria Colwell, a child who had died at the hands of her parents, came to light, as she felt people ought to know how badly some children suffered during their early years. This was a topic, now aired everywhere, that had been firmly silenced until then.

Sandy Fawkes was intelligent and artistic and managed to get to Camberwell School of Art where she was encouraged by the Soho artist John Minton to become an artist herself. John Minton, who committed suicide at the age of 40, introduced Fawkes both to Soho and to drink, and these twin pleasures were to become the mainstays of her life as indeed they were to another talented Soho alcoholic, Jeffrey Bernard. Through John Minton, Fawkes, then rejoicing in the surname of Boyce-Carmichelle, met Wally Fawkes and they were married in 1949. They had four children, one of whom died in infancy, and in the 1960s she began working as a journalist, first of all doing fashion drawings for the
52

Daily Sketch and later becoming fashion editor of the paper. She then became a feature writer for the *Daily Express*, and covered the Yom Kippur war in 1973.

By this time she and Wally were divorced and she landed a job in America on the *National Enquirer*, where many British journalists have been employed, at least briefly. In 1974 she met a handsome, younger man in a bar in Atlanta, Georgia. She was immediately attracted to him and they began an affair, but he turned out to be a serial killer, having killed at least 18 people before meeting her.

His name was Paul Knowles and the car in which he and Fawkes embarked on a leisurely tour of Florida turned out to have been stolen from a missing person. Even the clothes Knowles wore had come from a murdered man. He was shot dead by police just one month after he and Fawkes had parted, and she later realised she had narrowly missed being killed herself.

The journalist in her knew that it would make a great story, however, and indeed, it was published as *Killing Time*. Fawkes harboured great hopes that this book would be turned into a film, thus making her lots of money but although it was optioned several times, the film was never made.

Sandy Fawkes in some ways epitomised, or maybe created, what became a stereotype of women journalists at the time, that of the loud, drunken, rackety, raucous, foul-mouthed but clever female who could drink any man under the table.

Another such was *Sunday Mirror* writer Ann Pacey, who also died of alcoholism, in 2006. After working on the *Yorkshire Post* Pacey started her Fleet Street career as film critic of the *Daily Herald*, and after the demise of that paper went to work at the *Sunday Mirror*, which did not greatly please the paper's existing film critic, Madeleine Harmsworth. Harmsworth wrote in the journalists' trade paper *Press Gazette* after Pacey's death that Pacey initially came across as unbelievably snooty, and was very much a man's woman in that she seemed to regard other women as dirt beneath her feet.

There was little female solidarity in Fleet Street in those days, as sisterhood was far into the future. In fact, many women journalists who had made it themselves tried to stop other women from getting to any position of power or influence. This came to be known as the tactic whereby women journalists would climb the ladder and then pull it up after them, thus preventing other pretenders to the throne from getting anywhere.

But Madeleine Harmsworth went on to say that after this initial *froideur* and suspicion of each other, a deep and enduring friendship developed. In the event, Pacey did not steal Harmsworth's patch but concentrated on writing TV previews, at which she often shone. When on form, according to former colleague Ray Setterfield, who usually subbed her material, Pacey could produce 'copy of sparkling originality that was a joy to read' and which would require no intervention by the sub-editorial pen. Sadly, says Setterfield, this was not always so. On bad days she could supply words 'that would leave the subs groaning in despair and notorious examples of Paceyisms were pasted on the walls.'

Contributing to her obituary in *Mirror Pensioner Online*, Setterfield went on to say that rewriting Pacey had its dangers as she could deliver a screaming torrent of abuse at the hapless sub who dared try to 'improve' her prose, and this tirade would be liberally littered with four-letter words. But then, just as unpredictably, the other Pacey could surface. Setterfield remembers one time when, after performing major surgery on her copy, he received a card with a picture of sunflowers and the message: 'Dearest Ray. Thanks a million sunshine flowers for rescuing my copy. I owe you a drink.'

She would often describe Setterfield, as she frequently described her tolerant bank manager, as 'a diamond geezer'. Pacey's abusive outbursts were almost always fuelled by alcohol and Madeleine Harmsworth recalls that the Mirror Group, in pre-Maxwell days, was always sympathetic to her plight, and frequently funded her drying-out periods or, as we should now say, rehab. Colleagues described her usual return from lunch (invariably liquid, and usually taken at a TV preview theatre, if not in the office pub, The Stab In The Back) as 'clanking down the corridor', referring to the vodka bottles in the shopping bag she always carried. She joked against herself, saying that if she ever wrote an autobiography, its title would come from the first words she heard in the office most mornings: *Shall We Just Hoover Round Her?* For she always backslid eventually, even when managing to keep off alcohol for long stretches. Pacey was by no means the only alcoholic on this particular newspaper group; far from it.

Many of the men employed there could probably easily outdo her considerable capacity. We are now used to female binge drinkers but in those days it was considered a shocking sight to see a woman so frequently under the influence of drink.

Madeleine Harmsworth believes that alcohol was both Pacey's undoing and her best friend as, when the worse (or better) for drink, she often sparkled as a writer and became witty, raunchy and irreverent.

In the end, though, the paper had to let her go as she started to drink even more furiously, making her behaviour wildly unpredictable. In any case, her health finally gave way under the prolonged alcoholic onslaught, and she retired to a bungalow in Surbiton, Surrey, where she tried to keep in touch with her former *Mirror* colleagues. Harmsworth gave Pacey a generous tribute: 'She was truly a one-off. Sometimes exasperating, always self-destructive, but never dull.'

A more serious, sober journalist on the *Sunday Mirror*, originally the *Sunday Pictorial*, was Audrey Whiting. One of her most startling stories appeared in 1955, about a supposed virgin birth. The story concerned a young German woman who claimed that she did not lose her virginity until she was married, two years after her daughter was born. She asserted that no man had taken part in the process – long before the days of IVF or any form of assisted conception – and after exhaustive investigation, her claim was believed by doctors and was reported in *The Lancet*.

This story was one of the scoops of the decade, and it was reprised on BBC Woman's Hour in 2001. The story ran in the *Sunday Pictorial* for five weeks and was the culmination of an investigation by Audrey Whiting and a team of doctors. The story also had the happy effect of doubling the *Pictorial*'s already large circulation.

Audrey Whiting was born in 1927 in Hull, Yorkshire, also Jean Rook's birthplace, and after leaving school, first joined the *Hull Daily Mail* and then the *Yorkshire Evening Post*. She joined the staff of the *Daily Mirror* as a reporter in 1948 and was appointed Paris correspondent in 1950. She became New York correspondent in 1952 and chief European correspondent in 1953, marrying the editor of the *Daily Mirror*, Jack Nener, as his second wife, in 1954.

Unusually tall for a woman – about six feet – her wedding to Nener was described by Cudlipp as The Night Of The Long Wives, and he thereafter referred to the couple as Jack and the Beanstalk. And when she took over the royal beat on the *Sunday Mirror* some office wag explained that it was 'because she's the only one who can see over the wall'. Whiting was not the only pioneer woman journalist to marry a *Mirror* editor: another was Sheila Black.

At the time, it was not encouraged for husbands and wives to work on the same paper, and this was why and when Whiting transferred to the *Sunday Pictorial*.

She rejoined the daily paper in 1970 and stayed there until 1985, when she retired. Nener had retired in 1961 and died in 1982. During his long retirement and ill-health, Whiting concentrated mainly on writing royal stories, but never went on a royal tour because she did not want to leave her ailing husband alone at home.

In common with so many journalists working for the Mirror Group after Robert Maxwell bought the company on Friday July 13 1984, Whiting had a disappointing end to her long career. In 1985, she met Maxwell in the lift and he said (or rather boomed) to her: 'You'd better watch it or you'll be out on your neck!' This gave her the courage to walk out, after nearly 40 years with the Mirror Group.

Nancy Spain is not much remembered nowadays but in her heyday she was a famous celebrity journalist, popular for her quick wit and also her cut-glass accent. Born in 1917 in Jesmond, Newcastle upon Tyne, Spain was educated at Roedean School near Brighton (a distinction she shared with Katharine Whitehorn) and first became a sports reporter on local papers in the North East, showing terrific determination at a very young age with getting her name in the paper.

National success soon followed, and by 1950 Spain was a popular and prolific journalist. Always lesbian by inclination, she had a long relationship with her 'soul mate' Joan Werner-Laurie, known at Jonnie, editor of *She* magazine. Spain became pregnant in 1952 and felt she had to pretend that Joan Werner-Laurie – who had been married but was also basically gay – was actually the mother, and the child was registered in Jonnie's name. The father of Spain's child was Philip Youngman Carter, then editor of *The Tatler* and husband of detective novelist Margery Allingham.

Nancy Spain's son Tom was given the surname Seyler, the name of Werner-Laurie's husband, and grew up believing that she, not Spain, was his birth mother. In Spain's autobiography, Werner-Laurie, who already had a son of her own, Nick, is referred to as the mother of the boy. By 1964 Spain was a famous columnist and feature writer on many leading newspapers and also a major star on radio and TV. None of this would have been possible in those days if Spain's lesbianism had come out in public. Spain and Werner-Laurie were later joined by the rally driver Sheila Van Damn and became a kind of threesome.

Their unbroken success story came to a dreadful end in 1964 when Spain and Werner-Laurie flew in a privately chartered plane from Luton Airport to Aintree for the Grand National. The plane crashed en route and both Spain and Werner-Laurie, as well as the pilot, were killed. To this day, nobody knows what caused the accident. Pamela Carmichael, who became the next editor of *She* magazine, says that just two days after the plane crash, literally hundreds of women had applied for the editorship of *She*. Nancy Spain had been a panellist on the popular radio game *My Word*, and after her death, her place was taken by Anne Scott-James.

Another Nancy, Nancy Banks-Smith, has made TV criticism her very own. Her dry, witty and insightful reviews have enlivened the *Guardian* television pages since 1969 (and, before that, those of the pre-Murdoch *Sun*) and, now in her seventies, she is still going strong. She did try to retire once, but was brought back by popular request, and has lost none of her sly bite.

She has said that she drifted into television criticism 'by chance' when on the *Daily Express*, as she was the journalist 'most obviously asleep in the office when Dennis Potter, the TV critic, went off his head and exited excitedly, saying he could write better stuff than that.' Which of course he did, magnificently.

At that time, the 1950s, nobody knew anything about TV. 'Everything about it,' Banks-Smith said, 'was surprising and exciting, like a new lover or a strange country. On the bus in the morning, everyone was talking about the night before. No one went out on a Wednesday in case they missed that dependable sensation, the Wednesday Play.'

When she started, because it was so new, TV itself was regarded as a lowly medium and television criticism was not considered a serious occupation for a proper male journalist. This left a great gaping hole, which women eagerly filled. At one point, says Banks-Smith, all the TV critics seemed to be women, as it was considered a 'nice little job for a woman' – something you could do from home and which didn't require very much effort.

This chapter ends with a tribute to the grand old ladies of film criticism. Iris Barry was successively film critic for *Vogue*, *The Spectator* and the *Daily Mail*, where she held sway from 1925 to 1930.

Caroline Alice Lejeune, always by-lined with just her initials, began her career on the *Manchester Guardian* in 1922, then joined the *Observer* as its first regular film reviewer, where she reigned for 32 years. She died in 1973. Because she always used initials, many readers did not even realise that C A Lejeune *was* a woman, which was, perhaps, what she intended.

Assiduous magazine readers in the 1950s and 60s may remember the name Freda Bruce Lockhart, the long lasting, apparently indestructible, film critic for *Woman* magazine and the *Catholic Herald*.

Showbusiness writer Ivan Waterman recalls a scene from the 1970s, when he was a film reviewer, and Freda Bruce Lockhart was, possibly, the oldest critic still working. Disabled for many years, she had to somehow manoeuvre her wheelchair into tiny preview cinemas long before disabled access had been invented.

Waterman recalls:

All was still and deathly dull at 127 Wardour Street W1 about 7pm one Tuesday. A mediocre thriller called *Spy Story*, by a mediocre director called Lindsay Shonteff was being shown to the assembly of tired, emotional and mostly jaded hacks. Freda Bruce Lockhart, the infamous, disabled and ancient *Catholic Herald* film critic, was in her wheelchair in the aisle of what used to the the Rank Preview Theatre. And, as always, she was fast asleep, snoring her head off.

Suddenly, Fergus Cashin, another legendary film critic, entered the cinema with what appeared to be a carving knife in his right hand. Already well tanked up, he staggered down the aisle until he collided with Freda's wheelchair. He fell onto the chair and as it began to move, shouted angrily: 'Why the fuck do the seats move in this place?'

Freda woke and began to scream while being propelled through the spotlight in her wheelchair, which eventually came to rest against the side of the cinema. By this time, Fergus Cashin was flat on his face.

Possibly the best-known and best-remembered of the early female film critics is Dilys Powell, a friend of Lady Ottoline Morrell and in her youth a member of what is now known as the Bloomsbury Group. Powell, born in 1901, was educated at Somerville College, Oxford, and first joined the *Sunday Times* as film critic in 1928. She left in 1931 but rejoined the paper in 1939 and was to stay until 1976, finally moving to *Punch*, although as late as 1994, a year before her death, her reviews were appearing weekly in the *Sunday Times*.

Dilys Powell is widely credited as being one of the first critics to spot the talents of Steven Spielberg and Clint Eastwood, when nobody else had heard of them. She was awarded the CBE in 1974, and her admirers say that she was always open to new directions in cinema and never snobbish about this art form which was so new in her day, and in this respect was quite unlike her great rival on *The Observer*, C A Lejeune.

Four

The fashion writers

Fashion is one of the few areas in journalism that women have made truly their own. And pretty much every male editor in Fleet Street has always accepted, however grudgingly, that fashion must have a prominent place in his newspaper.

Even the 'heavy' papers soon realised that, somewhere among the pages, there must be a light read and fashion coverage often provided that light read. But reputation-wise, fashion writers and editors have never had an easy ride with their fellow journalists of either sex as there has been a tendency to regard them as snooty airheads who would not recognise a real story if it hit them in the face.

This is not necessarily true as fashion has often provided stories as exciting and sensational as anything else considered worthy of being written up in a newspaper. However, the prevailing view of fashion writers was perhaps summed up by the photographer and all-round creative individual, Cecil Beaton, when he referred in his diaries to 'those appalling women journalists, Alison Settle and Mrs Whish.' The year was 1926 and the occasion, the Paris collections.

Nothing more seems to be known about the mysterious Mrs Whish, who apparently wrote for the *Daily Express*, but Alison Settle, born in 1891, was a prolific journalist who concentrated mainly on writing about fashion. She became the third editor of British *Vogue* and also wrote for several newspapers, but why that old queen Cecil Beaton should have taken against her is odd, as she is credited with discovering him.

After a long stint on *Vogue*, Alison Settle joined *The Observer* as fashion editor and finally retired in 1960, at the grand old age of 69.

Katharine Whitehorn took over this job, after it was originally offered to Anne Scott-James, who first accepted, then declined it. Whitehorn commented in her memoirs that writing about fashion was considered to be the 'Queen Bee' job of the women's pages in those days.

Fashion was one of the few jobs that was guaranteed to go to a woman, but there were very few openings as the fashion editors of the time tended to stay in their jobs for decades. This meant that an opportunity for new blood arose only when they retired, often when they were in their late 60s or early 70s, as with Alison Settle, who died in 1980.

Nowadays, we think of fashion as being mainly set and determined by the young, but in the early days of fashion reporting, it was quite a different story. From the 1920s to the 1960s, fashion meant, quite simply, Paris. That city's couturiers determined the 'look' each year and everywhere else it was copied slavishly. The job of the fashion journalists was to attend these collections in January and June, report reverently on them and inform their readers from a great height what the Paris designers – often predominently gay men – were dictating for next season.

These were the days when fashion, even for relatively casual occasions, was nevertheless largely formal and depended on wearing the right hat, gloves and shoes to complete the ensemble. Fashion was above all, class-ridden and the way it happened was that the aristocracy and very rich would wear the newest looks which were often made specially for them by the great couture houses. After these grande dames were seen wearing the new looks, they would gradually filter down the social classes.

The Duchess of Windsor favoured Mainbocher, who, like her, was originally American, and Jackie Kennedy and Audrey Hepburn were dressed by Givenchy. How do we know this? Because the fashion writers of the time told us so and now, how could we ever forget? Also, the celebrities of their day would be endlessly photographed in their latest Dior, Chanel, Balmain or Schiaparelli, while the ordinary mortals gazed at them in awe and wonder.

Couture was in those days a massive industry, even if only a very few women could actually afford to be dressed exclusively by these top designers, and the major fashion houses fought to dress the A-list celebrities, as this would bring them, the couturiers, fame and fortune. Manufacturers would have to pay huge sums to be allowed to copy their designs for the mass market.

The social class aspect of fashion meant that fashion writing itself was also very class and status ridden and came from the top down which is of course, just the opposite of today, when the couturiers tend to show expensive, upmarket version of fashions which have already originated and established themselves at street level.

Despite the fact that fashion writers concentrated hard on reporting 'the collections', obviously their writing had to go wider than this, as these exclusive shows happened only twice a year, and there was an empty page waiting to be filled each week. So for the rest of the year, fashion writers would advise their readers on what to wear and how to look good with, again, the information always coming from a great height, as if handed down on tablets of stone. In the early days, fashion writers would dictate good taste with a kind of snobbishness, certainty and aloofness that nobody would tolerate today.

They pronounced in hectoring tones on 'correctness', as this early example from the *Daily Mirror* in 1935, shows:

> It has been said so many, many times – I hate to rub it in – don't drape yourself for office hours like a haberdashery counter. Resist brooches, bows, necklaces. There is only one frivolity I won't deny you – feminine and unnecessary though it be – a buttonhole. A bunch of cowslips under one's nose somehow brings spring into the most unromantic office.

Katharine Whitehorn writes that when she took over *The Observer* fashion pages, she wanted to relate fashion to 'all sorts of other things' and not just pronounce in godlike fashion on hemlines and fabrics. But while Whitehorn wrote amusingly about such subjects as choosing suitable clothes to wear in freezing country houses and she divided hats into three types: offensive, defensive and shrapnel, one gets the feeling that fashion, as such, was not really in her blood. After three years of trying to get women out of their limp cardigans (as she put it) she gratefully gave up fashion writing to concentrate on the personal column for which she became a national institution.

Whitehorn was spectacularly unsuccessful in trying to persuade women out of their cardigans, as they are still going strong – if limply – half a century later. She did introduce an irreverent note to writing about fashion though, at a time when the big fashion writers were deadly serious about their subject. It is true that fashion has always had its silly moments, and is an easy target inviting instant parody, but readers need genuine information from those who know what they are talking about, not just a cheap laugh from a columnist trying (but not always succeeding) to be funny.

Ernestine Carter, born in 1906, was actually American but became fashion editor of *The Sunday Times* in the 1940s. She was at the famous

Dior show of February 12, 1947, to witness the notorious New Look, which after the austerities and clothes rationing of the Second World War, quite literally shocked the world. Yards and yards of material were used for the famous white grosgrain jacket with cinched-in waist, and accompanying billowing black skirt. This originally infamous but totally glamorous outfit, which has become one of the most instantly recognisable fashion images of the twentieth century, has since been in dozens of exhibitions all over the world and was given another airing at the popular V&A Exhibition, *The Golden Age of Couture*, in 2007. It still has the power to shock, even though we have become so used to it, and the curvy new totally feminine look – retro but somehow brand new – as loved by women all over the world and was to last until youth fashions hit the streets in the early 1960s, and changed haute couture once again.

In her *Sunday Times* column the same week the Dior New Look was launched, Ernestine Carter wrote:

> 'the models were arrogantly swaying their vast skirts, the soft shoulders, the tight bodices, the wasp waists contemptuously bowling over the ashtray stands like ninepins.'

Carter was still in situ at *The Sunday Times* when the next big fashion quake happened, in the 1960s, and she then wrote:

> 'It is given to a fortunate few to be born at the right time, in the right place, with the right talents. In recent fashion there are three: Chanel, Dior and Mary Quant.'

In fashion, hemlines went above the knee for the first time in 1961 and from then on crept up until the mini-skirt was hardly decent. Ernestine Carter pronounced 1963 'the year of the leg' and started to concentrate on writing about young fashion, even though she herself was in her late fifties by then.

Ever since the 1960s, there has been a big debate about who 'invented' the mini-skirt – surely one of the most enduring fashions of our time – and much friendly rivalry took place among fashion writers of the time as to who was the first to show this bold new fashion on their pages. The truth is that the mini-skirt invented itself, and both designers and fashion writers lagged far behind.

The first thing any trendy teenager did in the early 1960s when buying a skirt or dress was to shorten it by several inches. Manufacturers were way behind the teen scene at that time, and took time to catch up as previously high fashion had been mainly for the middle-aged. Girls copied their mothers until the sixties when suddenly it was the other way round, and before long women of all ages, even the now elderly Duchess of Windsor, were appearing in inappropriately short skirts.

This was the first example of street fashion leading couture, and it has happened ever since. Not since the days of Dior's New Look has a Paris couture house led fashion in such a dramatic way, and it never will again. Fashion, in common with so many other areas of life, was democratised in the 1960s and it was the job of the big-time fashion writers to note this, then write and comment on it. The best ones tried to nail down the change in society which the new young fashions heralded.

Ernestine Carter credited the French designer Courrèges with inventing the mini-skirt in 1964; in fact, what he did was to bring it into couture, as it was already in existence and being worn by the British teenager. Other countries were way behind, and for the first time young throwaway British street fashion led the world, rather than Paris haute couture. Older readers will remember the model Jean Shrimpton arriving in Australia in the mid-1960s in a mini-dress three inches above her knee and this shocking garment made appalled headlines all over the world.

The mini-skirt was the first truly populist look and was to usher in a completely new style of fashion writing. Whether the main newspaper fashion writers, then in their fifties and sixties, were the right people to comment on all this, is another matter, but nowadays fashion editors are mainly young themselves.

After reigning as Queen Bee at the *Sunday Times* for more than three decades, the tiny, birdlike and always elegant Carter finally retired in the 1970s and her place was taken by the loud, boisterous and quite different Molly Parkin. Carter wrote several books on fashion, was also a museum curator, and her name has become enshrined in fashion archives.

Alison Adburgham was fashion editor of *The Guardian* for a similar length of time and also wrote about Mary Quant. *The Guardian* was less concerned about 'the collections' and Adburgham, along with Carter a total fashion obsessive, concentrated more on British fashion and showed clothes that *Guardian* readers were more likely to wear. In October 1967, Adburgham talked to Mary Quant about the revolution in fashion, and the gist of the conversation went thus:

Adburgham: You would agree that a great designer is one who gives people what they want before they know they want it?

Quant: Yes, fashion doesn't really influence the climate of opinion, it reflects what is really in the air. It reflects what people are reading and thinking and listening to, and architecture, painting, attitudes to success and to society... there's a new climate of living now, which was started by the young in the 1950s and has been gathering momentum. We have taken the snobbery out of fashion.

A: Was it you who triggered off the fashion explosion?

Q: Not really. In the beginning I was just typical of the people who felt like that. Then the tickets followed. It was not happening because of me. It was simply that I was part of it... pornography is great if it's good.

A: What is good pornography?

Q: Good pornography is erotic but pleasing. Only ugliness is obscene.

A: Have you any theory to explain why fashion has virtually abolished the bust? At fashion shows the model girls appear to have bosoms as flat as two pancakes.

Q: The bosom is a motherhood symbol ..

A: You know James Laver's famous fashion theory of the erogenous zone which shifts the focus of attraction in different periods from ankles, to hips, to breasts and so on... what is the erogenous zone of our present period?

Q: The crutch. This is a very balanced generation and the crutch is the most natural erogenous zone. Clothes are designed to lead the eye to it.

One can sense Adburgham struggling with all this. But that's how it was in the 1960s, when all this sort of stuff seemed very new indeed. Down on the more popular papers, Deirdre McSharry, Barbara Griggs and Felicity Green were more in tune with young people and young designers.

Deirdre McSharry, then woman's editor of the *Daily Express*, is credited with discovering Twiggy and also creating the first daily newspaper fashion pages in colour. Magazine editor Sue Peart, who was given her first job, on *Cosmopolitan*, by McSharry, says: 'As fashion editor of the *Daily Express* in the 1960s, Deirdre had launched Twiggy onto the world after spotting her under the hairdryer at Leonard of Mayfair. Deirdre adored fashion, fine writing, amusing company. She treated every day like a performance, whipping us into action and making us believe anything was possible. She was a commanding presence and not without her volatile moments, but she was also fond of her team of flighty twenty-somethings.

'Deirdre was passionate about careers for women. She introduced the *Change Your Life in a Day* courses with the Industrial Society. She was a nurturing editor and proud of the training she gave.'

Deirdre McSharry later became fashion editor of *The Sun*, then went with Joyce Hopkirk to the new *Cosmopolitan* in 1972, where she eventually became editor. McSharry's place at *The Sun* was taken by the elegant and chic Jean Dobson, formerly of the *Daily Mirror*.

McSharry also had fashion deep in her system and after retiring from popular journalism, became a fashion curator. She still curates and also gives talks on fashion and costume. She is Irish, as her name suggests and was educated by nuns at the Dominican Convent in Dublin and later at Dublin University. In common with some other female journalists, McSharry first became an actress and it was while she was on tour that she began writing for newspapers. She went to New York in the 1950s where she joined *Women's Wear Daily* as a fashion reporter.

Jean Rook had a spell as a fashion editor, and writes in her memoirs *The Cowardly Lioness*, that when she was at *The Sun* (in pre-Murdoch days) she completely failed to notice the young teenage Twiggy as a major star in the making. She got into terrible trouble later with the formidable woman's editor, Amy Landreth, for this major mistake and generously paid tribute to Deirdre McSharry for launching Twiggy on her huge career.

As with Katharine Whitehorn, one gets the impression that Jean Rook was not really one of life's fashionistas. However, they both made it big in their own way, later. One problem was that the male editors of the time, dismissing fashion themselves, imagined that 'anybody' could write about it, and that you didn't actually need many brains for the job, either. In fact, the best fashion editors are steeped in fashion; it is a religion to them and they write intelligently and expertly about it. For the true fashion writer, fashion matters, and it is not just another journalistic assignment.

Barbara Griggs was also one of the new young wave of fashion writers in the 1960s. Griggs, born in 1932, graduated with a first-class degree in English literature from Birmingham University and after a gap year teaching English in Paris, more or less instantly landed a job on *Vogue*. She says: 'My family was friendly with Audrey Withers, then editor of *Vogue* and although I had always wanted to write, because of her I became interested in fashion.

'I don't know that fashion was deep in my DNA, certainly not as much as for many of the fashion writers, who would literally talk about nothing else. Even after a full day at the collections in Paris, they wanted to talk about fashion through the night.' Griggs spent a year working as *Vogue*'s Shophound but then wondered whether she actually wanted to write about fashion any more.

'A friend told me that Joy Matthews, woman's editor of the *Daily Express* was looking for an assistant so I wrote to her offering myself.

We met for coffee in Harrods on a Saturday morning and she offered me a job right away.' Griggs became fashion editor of the *Daily Express* in 1958 and says: 'Women were really interested in Paris in those days. It was very glamorous and remote from their everyday lives, and as well as reporting on the collections, we tried to make Paris-type fashion accessible to our readers.

'I wasn't initially sure I wanted to concentrate on fashion but as I could speak fluent French, and most of the fashion writers and women journalists couldn't, I got suckered into fashion again. But it was huge fun at the time.

'I remember when Paris introduced the Sack. It was clearly going to be a big look so I went to John Lewis for some fabric, got a pattern made, got my sister to make it into a dress and by six in the evening we had pictures of a sack dress with a pattern offer which was in the paper the next day.

'As the Sixties progressed, Paris began to matter less and less and couture was replaced by ready-to-wear. Then street fashion became the big thing. I used to go up and down Oxford Street looking in the chain stores for cheap new looks, while most of the Fleet Street fashion writers were showing pages of expensive frocks.' After the Express, Griggs went to the *Evening Standard* still trying to get away from fashion but in the event became fashion editor there, and stayed until 1969. She then went to the same job at the *Daily Mail*, leaving fashion finally in 1978.

Looking back, she says: '*The Daily Express* was great fun in those days, when Arthur Christiansen was editor and the paper really tried to encourage women. We had so many talented women writers – Joy Matthews, Eve Perrick, Anne Edwards – all of whom were writing from a woman's point of view. We had lots of talented female news reporters, as well.

'The *Daily Mail* was quite different, very tough and hard and not at all women-friendly. I remember going to a conference once to discuss women's coverage in the paper and I was the only woman there! All these men were talking about what women wanted, as if they were great experts.

'I had married in 1970 and my first daughter Bibi was only six weeks old when I became fashion editor of the *Daily Mail* in 1972. By 1978 I really was fed up with fashion but not only that, my husband Henri and I had written a book together which was successful, and I knew then I wanted to write books. I was becoming fascinated with herbal medicine, writing a book on it, and simply could not concentrate enough on it while still working full time at the *Daily Mail*.'

Griggs' daughter Bibi van der Zee is now a journalist on *The Guardian,* so what does she think are the main differences for a woman journalist then and now?

She says: 'I think it is much tougher now, partly because there are no secretaries or assistants, far fewer staff and so much more is expected of you. We had enormous fun and a far, far better time. The glamour of the job has gone in much the same way that it's no longer glamorous to be an air hostess. The other factor is that because of the power of the unions, the pay was vastly better in our day. I was earning £14 a week at Vogue and when I went to the *Express*, that immediately jumped to £25 a week which was total riches in 1958.'

Many fashion writers of the time were given picture by-lines and became stars on their newspapers. One of the biggest fashion leaders in the 1960s was Felicity Green of the *Daily Mirror*, whose pages were required reading for anybody remotely interested in what fashion was doing. Green did cover Paris fashions but she was always more concerned with featuring the kind of clothes that *Mirror* readers might actually be able to afford, and buy.

Felicity Green started her career as a secretary and worked her way through fashion magazines, eventually joining the Mirror Group as associate editor with a brief to promote women's influence in every aspect of the paper. *The Daily Mirror* had become extremely masculine after its early, false start as a woman's newspaper and now the management felt it was time to start feminising the paper again.

Her main sphere of influence was in promoting what we would now term 'street', or high-street fashion; the kind of clothes the readers might actually be able to afford. However, during the 1960s, when Felicity's fashion influence was at its height, there was a total fashion explosion anyway and London was its happening city. Names such as Mary Quant, Biba and Lee Bender of Bus Stop, ushered in the youthquake, with the kind of young clothes that had never been seen before and which would have been hard to ignore.

But it was Green who spotted and encouraged these young designers by putting their clothes in the paper, often to the dismay of the chairman, the very aloof, patrician Cecil King. After she had featured Mary Quant's mini skirts in her pages, King asked her: 'How long are you going to put those ridiculous clothes in my newspaper... how long do you propose to go on with this?'

Green's reply: 'As long as they are news. And what will you do if I do continue to put them in the paper?' Cecil King replied that he would arrange for her to be fired, and then walked out of the room.

'What I wanted to put in the paper were trends and news to inform and entertain. Our readers certainly couldn't afford Hardy Amies or Norman Hartnell, who were the designers being featured in other papers.'

Of course, Felicity Green's influence was huge because the *Daily Mirror* circulation in those days was also huge, and her fashion pages, headed '*Felicity Green on the fashion scene*' were highly promoted. She said: 'We had an overlap with *The Times* at one end of our readership and people who could hardly read at the other, so our readership was fairly broad. I felt I wanted to relate clothes to people, give advice on where you might wear them, how you might wear them and what kind of statement they made about you.

'At the time this was something new, as fashion was mainly presented as pictures with captions in those days. I made fashion into features, something readable and something that related to the lives of the readers, rather than just informing them from on high what Paris was doing this season with hemlines, collars or evening gowns.

'Before the sixties revolution, when clothes for young women became fun and cheap, teenagers used to dress exactly like their mothers. There was no youth culture at all and I think we were the first newspaper to embrace it on our pages. This meant that there was a schism right through the world of fashion as until then it had been a deadly serious business with beautifully made clothes that lasted for years. Now, for the first time ever, we were into throwaway clothes which cost hardly anything, and young clothes now looked very different from the ones the older generation were wearing.'

The always elegant and stylish Felicity Green, another of nature's true fashionistas, struck it big when she recognised and championed Barbara Hulanicki, the former fashion artist and founder of Biba. She says: 'When Barbara worked as a freelance fashion artist, she did sketches for me at the *Mirror*. I noticed that she herself always dressed beautifully and asked if she could design something we could put in the paper as a very simple mail order offer. She said yes, so we got together and designed the famous A-line dress which went into the paper at £3 and it immediately sold 21,000.

'The dress itself was sleeveless, made in pink gingham and had a little pink headscarf to go with it. I was absolutely enchanted with Barbara's design as it was so new and fresh and I wanted to put it on a double-page spread in the paper. The advertisement director immediately sent for me and asked, who is this foreign person you are giving all this space to in the *Daily Mirror*? I replied that whether or not she was foreign didn't matter because she was an extremely clever designer and this offer would be a big hit with our readers.

'He gave me the go-ahead, and I was asked to estimate how many we might sell. I put it at 3,000 and thought this was hugely optimistic. In the event, we kept running out of pink gingham and Barbara's husband Stephen Fitz-Simon had to scour the country for more. In those days not many *Mirror* readers had bank accounts, so they sent in postal orders which caused a problem as Stephen's bank wouldn't accept them. But anyway, the whole thing was a stunning success and certainly launched Biba as an up and coming fashion house for the young.'

The Biba style became etched into public consciousness, and it is all thanks to Felicity Green. However, Biba might have made it big anyway as Stephen Fitz-Simon was, like Mary Quant's husband Alexander Plunkett-Greene, a formidable entrepreneur. Both double-barrelled husbands died young but at the time of writing, Quant and Hulanicki are still very much alive.

Felicity Green also chalked up another first during her days as fashion supremo at the *Mirror* when she appointed a men's fashion columnist and sent him to Paris wearing a Pierre Cardin space suit. She says: 'He never spoke to me again! But it was the fun element that mattered; serious tailoring would never have shown up on our pages and we had to have something of world-shattering interest to our readers.'

After Felicity Green was promoted to the board of Mirror Group News as the first woman ever to be appointed to such a position, her place as fashion editor was taken by Lesley Ebbetts, but the 1960s fashion explosion was over. The 1960s fashion writers and editors were lucky as they were handling genuine stories, and that the 60s was the most influential decade in fashion history ever, either before or since.

Green resigned from the Board on learning that the newest recruit, Mike Molloy, was earning almost twice what she was: £26,000 to her £14,000. She then joined the Vidal Sassoon hairdressing empire, later working in executive positions at the *Daily Telegraph* and *Daily Express*, and later still as founding editor of the *Marks and Spencer magazine*, which was published by one of her protégées, Christopher Ward, founder of Redwood magazines, and a former editor of the *Daily Express*, who had been sub-editor of her fashion pages at the *Mirror*.

For young women, there was suddenly an exciting choice of fashion clothes available and many hot new designers, several of whom were trained at the Royal College of Art's new fashion school, were setting up their own labels. The 1960s ushered in mods, rockers, hippies and what we now call vintage, or retro, clothes also became fashionable.

This was the era of Carnaby Street, with exciting young fashion for men as well as women, of the King's Road and the Portobello Road, each with their own distinctive style.

Clever writers and journalists such as Felicity Green, Deirdre McSharry, Barbara Griggs and also the young Janet Street-Porter, were around to put all this exciting stuff into their papers, and readers eagerly lapped it all up.

The way in which fashion got into the papers in the old days was very different from now. Mainly, it was a matter of the writers and editors slogging round the wholesale warehouses – or sending their assistants. Models were booked up directly and there were no such creatures as fashion stylists. Today, the fashion PR industry makes sure all the fashion editors get to hear of anything new, and there are make-up artists, hairdressers and accessory experts to ensure that every look is just right. In Felicity Green's day there were no PR girls so, as she says, contact was a problem and getting hold of the clothes in the first place was a problem as well.

Lynne Franks, who has become almost a household name thanks to her appearance on *I'm a Celebrity – Get Me Out of Here*, started off her professional life as a fashion PR with a vast untidy warehouse type of office in Covent Garden.

But somehow, with or without PRs and the whole complement of auxiliary workers considered so necessary today, the fashion writers managed. There were also considerable perks from being a dedicated fashion writer or editor. In the first place you got the first privileged peek at the new clothes and new lines, way before your readers – and if you liked anything, you could often get it wholesale, or for almost nothing. If you were of model size, as many fashion editors were, even if not of model height – Felicity Green was five foot nothing – you could often 'borrow' clothes out of the fashion cupboard in offices to wear to functions such as smart lunches, weddings, dinner parties or other smart occasions, thus giving the appearance of having a constantly changing, up to date, designer wardrobe.

Fashion writers and editors were assiduously courted by manufacturers and designers as, after all, a favourable write-up in a leading paper could practically guarantee thousands, maybe tens of thousands, of sales.

All this applied from the earliest days of fashion writing and it still applies. There are not, nowadays, many fashion writers who are as long-lasting or as intimately associated with one newspaper as the old guard of Carter, Settle, Green and Adburgham.

But mainly, instead of remaining on one paper all their working lives, today's fashion writers tend to flit around from magazine to newspaper and back again, or branch out into consultancy or PR work. This means that the era of 'big name' fashion writing is more or less over, with only that of Suzy Menkes remaining a household name, and she has not written for British newspapers since the late 1980s.

Fashion writing is also no longer exclusively a totally female area. Men now write about and style women's fashion, whereas in the old days they were always the photographers. Now, it is as common for a woman to be the fashion photographer. Even so, fashion coverage remains what it has always been, a female-led field.

But there is fashion writing and fashion writing. When I joined the *Sunday People* as fashion writer in the early 1970s, I soon realised the requirement wasn't to write about fashion at all, not really. Grand notions about being the next Ernestine Carter, Alison Settle or Felicity Green flew quickly out of the window as it became clear that, week after week, all the men wanted was an excuse to put a picture of a scantily-clad female in the paper.

At least we could afford the top models and top photographers; anything else would have looked unacceptably sleazy, but it was hopeless to try and get any real fashion into the paper. My brief, as it were, was to get knickers, bras, suspenders, corsets, boob tubes and halter tops into the paper masquerading as serious fashion. We were very grateful in those days for Janet Reger, whose sexy but always upmarket underwear saved many a tabloid fashion editor's neck.

Funnily enough, you never see pictures like that any more on the fashion pages of newspapers; instead, they tend to have line-ups of what they consider the best high street looks, or compare a cheap high street outfit with its upmarket equivalent. There is also no movement in fashion pictures, as in the early days when Felicity Green's models were photographed in some very athletic poses. Everything is very static and the models always look haughty. The main reason for this change is the advent of colour. Until the late 1980s, fashion pictures in newspapers were always black and white; there was no colour at all, so photographers had to be more inventive with poses.

Another major change is that older models are used. In the 1960s, all fashion models were young or very young, with few over the age of 25. In 2008, fashion writers and editors think nothing of using models in their 40s, 50s or even 60s. The advent of bigger women has ushered in the 'plus' model and plus-size clothes are featured, even if high fashion still uses ultra-thin teenagers.

But on newspapers, fashion coverage has become more of a service than an excuse for a sexy picture. After a long absence, fashion drawings are making a return, as exemplified by Lucia van der Post's Friday fashion advice column on *The Times*.

In journalism, it has often been a case of where women lead, men follow and this is particularly exemplified in fashion coverage

Whereas in the old days it was only female fashion that was featured – with the exception of the Cardin space suit of course – now men's fashion gets, if not equal billing, at least a reasonable showing. *The Guardian* Weekend Saturday magazine has a line-up of men's fashion at least once a month, and the ever- increasing newspaper space given over to men's fashion has ushered in a new career for beautiful young men: that of the male model.

Five

Agony and ecstasy

Another area of journalism that women have made particularly their own is that of the advice column, or problem page. The major contribution of the clever and often outspoken 'agony aunts' has been to put information and knowledge into the public domain that was formerly jealously guarded by the medical and allied professions.

Before the agony aunts brought previously unmentionable subjects into newspaper columns read by millions, most people grew up in almost total ignorance about their own bodies. Then, through the advice columns, grateful women readers gradually learned about orgasms, contraception, whether they were 'normal' in their desire for sex or lack of it, and what exactly happened during such times as puberty and the menopause.

Men, too, started to learn more about female plumbing and also about how their own systems operated. Many agony aunts continually pushed back the boundaries of what it was acceptable to put in a family newspaper, and we may forget that in the 1960s, for example, one could not use the words vagina, menstruation or penis, or talk about oral sex. Marjorie Proops, one of the most high-profile agony aunts ever, reckoned she was the first person to use the word 'masturbation' in print.

Now, of course, as we know, anything goes. There is a popular drama called *The Vagina Monologues* which has toured the world, and no daily newspaper ever thinks twice about mentioning periods, pre-menstrual syndrome, erectile problems or, indeed, masturbation.

We have got used to certain bed-hopping politicians and celebrities being referred to as 'cocktail sausage' or 'five times a night', yet before

73

the frank and fearless agony aunts came on the scene no newspaper would have dared refer to sexual prowess or lack of it involving a public (or, indeed, any real-life) figure.

The agony aunts also had to deal – and still do have to deal – with thorny relationship problems experienced by their readers, such as whether to have an affair, how to cope with falling in love with somebody totally unsuitable like a schoolteacher, your sister's husband or boss at work, or with a husband's incessant and unwelcome demands for sex.

Moral issues such as abortion, pre-marital sex, homosexuality and incest have all been tackled over the years and between them, the agony aunts helped to usher in the permissive society, often in the face of ferocious opposition from those considering themselves moral arbiters. The aunts have also advised on debt problems, death and bereavement, dating after divorce and when – or whether – you are too old or too young for sex.

They additionally have to advise on complex issues such as anorexia and bulimia, self-harm, inappropriate sexual contact – and they have be confident that their advice and information is correct, otherwise they would never be forgiven or trusted again.

So being an agony aunt is a highly responsible job, an important newspaper service, which needs a very special type of person to do it. In an article in *The Independent* in 2000, agony aunt Virginia Ironside lamented the recent tendency to employ celebrities as agony aunts, rather than wise, compassionate, knowledgeable journalists. Ironside wrote:

> The agony column had traditionally been the soft underbelly, the heartbeat of women's magazines and newspapers. True, it's always been a journalistic exercise because if the agony column isn't interesting nobody will read it, but readers will usually find quite a bit of medicine in the jam. Not only is there illumination, explanation and compassion, but almost more important, there is information. Most agony aunts have reams of addresses of specialists, self-help groups, titles of books, contacts – and masses of knowledge about rights and services that the ordinary person doesn't know exist... While the agony column may sometimes be entertaining, the people who write into it aren't entertainers.

Although many of the newspaper agony aunts have carefully fostered a reputation of being wise, all-knowing, kind and caring, they have often had agonizing lives themselves, and their knowledge and prowess has sometimes been bought at a very high price. Claire Rayner, for

74

example, had one of the most horrible childhoods imaginable and Marje Proops hardly had an easy ride in life, either.

Rebecca Marjorie Rayle (anglicized from Israel) was the elder of two daughters born to a Jewish East End publican and his wife. Her mother had longed for a pretty, blonde daughter which she certainly did not get with Marje. Their younger daughter Josephine fitted the parental bill slightly better but Marje was always large and awkward and considered herself completely unattractive to men – a belief she was to share with a later agony aunt, Claire Rayner.

The family grew up pretty much on the edge of survival and after leaving school at 15, Marje, who had shown early signs of artistic promise, went to Hackney Technical College where she learned drawing, including how to draw nude bodies. She said later: 'I think my art training was the most useful grounding for anybody because my familiarity with the human body was ingrained very early on.'

Her first job was in a fashion drawing studio above a butcher's supply shop and she later rented a tiny studio of her own in Wine Court Office, off Fleet Street. She was soon selling fashion drawings to the *Daily Express, Daily Mail* and women's magazines for 7s 6d (about 35p) a time.

Her lack of attractiveness (as she saw it) to men totally blighted her early life but in the event she married Sidney Proops, known as Proopsie, in November 1935. Her first experience of sex when she married as a virgin at the age of 24 was a hideous shock, more like being horribly tortured than being made love to, as she was to write later.

She said of her wedding night:

'When it got to bedtime I was confronted by this great big ugly penis which terrified the life out of me when I saw it. And Proops was dressing it up with a condom before pushing it into me. It was a tremendous intrusion, and it was frightening, disagreeable.

'And I think if you are introduced to sex like this, you feel from very early on that you are victimised. You don't think about a man loving and wanting you... the whole thing was such a hideous and very very painful experience. And it really did hurt terribly every time.'

They had a son, Robert, in 1941 after which Marje gave Proopsie an ultimatum: she would stay married to him but she would never, on any account, have sex with him again. Surprisingly, Proopsie agreed to the no-sex ban which stayed in place for the rest of their 40 year marriage. She publicly perpetuated the myth that they were blissfully happily married and few people, apart from her close colleagues at the *Mirror*, ever suspected anything different.

Marje was determined to carry on her career as fashion artist rather than becoming a little Jewish housewife, and in the late 1930s she was summoned to the offices of the *Daily Mirror*, where the woman's page editor, Esme Zelger, was leafing through the fashion portfolio Marje's agent had sent her. Zelger introduced Marje to the features editor Hugh Cudlipp who immediately commissioned her to represent the paper as its fashion artist at Ascot. Her first drawing appeared in the *Mirror* on September 4, 1939 signed by 'Silvaine'. Cudlipp, who chose the name, considered that 'Marjorie Proops' could not possibly be a suitable name for a glamorous fashion artist.

At this time she was still freelancing and her big break into journalism came when she was writing captions for her illustrations for the magazine *Good Taste*. The editor, Julia Cairns, realised that Marje Proops was a real writer and commissioned her to write a piece on what it was like being a young wife and mother in wartime Britain. This led to other writing commissions and Marje was on her way.

In 1945, just after the war ended, and Proopsie had returned to civilian life as an engineer, Marje was appointed fashion editor of the *Daily Herald*, the mouthpiece of the trades union movement, at £23 a week. She was writing and illustrating at the paper under the editorship of Hugh Cudlipp's brother Percy, and began writing a column called *Womansense*, which gradually widened out from fashion coverage to writing about other issues. Her big – accidental – break came when the *Herald*'s advice columnist, Mary Marshall, died suddenly of cancer and her letters began landing on Marje's desk.

Marje started reading them and said: 'I was horrified. Absolutely horrified. It never occurred to me that people were writing letters like this. And I decided I must make an effort to answer them, to give whatever little bit of comfort I could – and it was really comfort more than help, because I knew nothing.'

She rejoined the *Daily Mirror* in 1954, and was to stay there until she died in harness in 1996. At first she was a general columnist, being sent all over the world to report back with the popular, warm touch for which she quickly started becoming well known. Her picture, at first a cartoon and then a photo, depicted Marje with a long cigarette holder (later replaced by a more PC ballpoint pen) in her mouth, a 'wise' expression and short, curly hair.

There was a story told by Marje that when Hugh Cudlipp introduced her to the then editor of the *Daily Mirror*, Jack Nener, 'he stood up like the gentleman he wasn't and said: "Fucking glad to meet you".' Nener was known for his foul language but his wife, journalist Audrey Whiting, insisted that Jack would never have said anything like that to Marje. Whether or not this is strictly true, everybody who knew Nener agreed that such a comment was certainly in character.

Marje first started writing an advice column in the new *Woman's Mirror*, another attempt by the Mirror Group to attract women readers. The magazine was edited by Jodi Hyland who became Hugh Cudlipp's third wife and although it was successful this time in terms of readership, it never attracted much advertising and it folded in 1967. But it gave Marje the platform she needed and launched her career as an agony aunt. The advice she gave was considered very outrageous for its day and championed extra-marital intercourse, contraception, abortion and sex before marriage.

Meanwhile, Marje was enjoying her own extra-marital intercourse, with *Mirror* lawyer Philip Levy, a bachelor in his fifties when the affair started.

From the start, Marje consulted professional advisers, doctors, psychiatrists and other counsellors, to make sure her advice was always well-informed and up to the minute. At the same time, she was always entertaining and amusing, and this called forth the wrath of self-styled guardians of public morality such as the Salvation Army, who considered her advice 'frivolous' and irresponsible.

Marje was made an OBE for 'services to journalism' and also Woman Journalist of the Year in 1969. At the presentation one of the judges said: 'She has the power to write about emotionally disturbing issues with a disarming common sense. She never moralises, but is always on the side of tolerance and humanity.'

Marje admitted later that with her private life, any moralising would have been extremely hypocritical. In May 1971 she became the official advice columnist of the *Daily Mirror*, with much pre-publicity and a huge, glamorous new photo. The new page was called *Dear Marje*, and very soon the page tackled subjects that were just coming to public light, such as baby-bashing, wife-beating and domestic violence generally.

She campaigned hard for more liberal attitudes towards divorce and abortion but found lesbianism, brought into public focus by the film *The Killing of Sister George*, extremely disturbing. She argued for equal pay for women and called for the Pill to be made available to young girls without the doctors telling their parents. She wrote big features on faking orgasms, male impotence and wife-swapping while always maintaining that she was against promiscuity. And remember that Proops herself was 60 years old when this column was launched; a fact she kept a very close secret.

Over the years she had to change her advice to move with the times. In 1962, for example, she had written that divorce was an unmitigated disaster, saying she knew a lot about the stresses of divorced women and the devastating loneliness, as well as the social stigma it could cause but later came to understand that divorce could be a blessed release from an unhappy marriage.

In the 1970s and 80s the *Dear Marje* column was getting around 45,000 letters a year but this went down to 25,000 as circulation of the once mighty *Mirror* plummeted after Maxwell arrived. In 1984, when Maxwell bought out Mirror Group News, Marje was already 73, had tin hips from her severe arthritis and seemed as if she might not last much longer. So the canny Maxwell, aware of the column's popularity, approached her to buy the name Marjorie Proops for the paper.

Marje refused, saying she couldn't let her beloved Proopsie's name go to the paper, and she also refused, unlike Claire Rayner, ever do to any advertising. Marje was however, like so many journalists on the *Mirror* including Anne Robinson, totally taken in by Maxwell and for all her wisdom and perception could not, or maybe would not, see what he was really like.

In 1986 Marje became mentally ill and had a nervous breakdown. Although she lived to be 85 and worked right up to her death, she had suffered much serious illness in her life; a horrific 56-hour labour with her son Robert which meant she could never have any more children (even if she'd wanted them); an early hysterectomy, crippling arthritis and bouts of mental illness. Her awful initiation into sex – an experience replicated in Ian McEwen's best-selling novel *On Chesil Beach* – gave her lasting compassion with all her women readers who had suffered similar traumas with something widely touted as enjoyable.

In 1994, two years before her death, Marje was still working in her office even though she could hardly hobble about owing to her arthritis. She was still game, still witty, still sexy and still totally up to date with all the issues that most concerned her readers. She kept a very special book, *The Joy of Sex* by Alex Comfort, locked in her drawer in case anybody should steal it. It was her most thumbed volume and in her view, the best sex book ever written. She was also at the time having a relationship with an (unnamed) 'toyboy of 70'. Both Proopsie and Philip Levy were long dead by then.

Marje was a true professional, an entertaining and trenchant journalist down to her fingertips and just the right person for the *Mirror* in its heyday. Felicity Green has called Marje's prose 'liquid gold' and envied her facility and speed. Marje's cartoony appearance definitely helped, and she played up to her image for all she was worth.

Anne Robinson maintained that Proops did not advance the cause of women on the *Mirror* and that all she was interested in was the preservation of her own empire. After her death her place was taken by Dr Miriam Stoppard but Stoppard, already famous in her own right, has never made anything like the impact of Marje in the paper. Stoppard, a qualified medical doctor, gives sensible and expert advice but has never had the kookiness that made Marje so popular for so long.

One of the reasons Proops was so successful in her day was because, one has to admit, the *Daily Mirror* was then a big-selling and influential paper. Now, it is not.

Claire Rayner, born in 1931, was a very different kind of agony aunt from Marje and not so much a journalist as a kind of 'big nurse', dispensing advice as if to a patient. Claire is a State Registered Nurse and qualified midwife, so she came from a completely different professional background from Marje.

Rayner has written about her horrific childhood with her feckless, mendacious parents, and also about her long-lasting, completely faithful and monogamous marriage to her husband Des. She has asserted on many occasions that she has never had a sexual partner other than Des and that she has never wanted anybody else, which must make her something of an oddity in the days when 30 or more partners is considered the norm, married or not.

She may be very different from Marje but Claire Rayner, also Jewish, was an equally big talent. Rayner first began to be noticed when she was an agony aunt on the young woman's magazine *Petticoat*. She stood out as a potential, or actual, star, and her column became a weekly must-read for the nation's youth. There was something very outspoken and straightforward about Rayner's advice, in the days when most advice columns were decidedly mealy-mouthed.

Her column on *Petticoat* attracted the attention of Katharine Hadley, then woman's editor of *The Sun*, and Rayner was hired in January 1974 after the existing advice columnist, Dr Wendy Greengross, left.

From the start, Rayner was uneasy about *The Sun* and wrote in her 2003 autobiography, *How did I get Here from There?*

> I hated what the paper was doing. It had been the old *Daily Herald*, a lovely, honest, working-class paper, keen on left-wing politics. Now that it had been transmogrified into a cheap nudge nudge leer leer scandal sheet it really was the pits.

Rayner maintains she took the job only because Wendy Greengross had insulted her at a Marriage Guidance Council meeting (later Relate) by referring to Rayner's husband giving up his job to be kept by his wife writing rubbish. She felt that Dr Greengross – a qualified medical doctor – was arrogant and elitist, especially when she called *Sun* readers 'barely literate'.

One of the three editors who interviewed Rayner for the job said: 'We liked your column in *Petticoat* and we think you could beat Marje into a cocked hat.' Rayner never took to the paper's editor, Albert (Larry) Lamb, who she said was 'never cuddly, never curly, never kind, never sweet' but she acknowledged he was a gifted editor.

Lamb informed her that he did not want any rubbish about people finding their inner selves or any suggestion that the great British working man was anything other than super-virile all the time. Rayner insisted that every reader's letter should be answered, as a service, not as a money-making endeavour, and she took the column deadly seriously, whereas she felt that Lamb just saw it as a sop to daft women readers, and as a way of getting more sex into the paper.

Rayner says that she herself saw her column as an extension of her nursing career and she campaigned for freedom of choice in all sexual and personal matters.

She got into trouble with those notorious self-styled moralists Mary Whitehouse and Valerie Riches, of the Responsible Society, for her response to a reader's query: What is wanking? Rayner's answer that masturbation can be enjoyable set Whitehouse off in full cry, and got her into trouble with Lamb, who did not approve of such words being used in the soaraway *Sun.*

Larry Lamb would, says Rayner, take her out to an expensive lunch at the Savoy Grill when she would far rather have had a pay rise and after a time she began to feel angry and exploited at the paper. Matters came to a head in 1980 when she discovered she was being paid much less than the other journalists and asked for a pay rise. She had asked for 35% to give her parity with the other journalists but Lamb offered her 10%.

At that she resigned and went to the *Sunday Mirror*, which she found very different: '*The Sun* had been pushy, noisy and go-getting. *The Mirror* made itself comfortable. The place was full of journalists who never seemed to get a word into the paper, which puzzled me... and the paper was known as The Velvet Coffin.'

Rayner was marked out to succeed Marje but in the event it never happened. Not long after Maxwell arrived, Rayner went to the short-lived *Today* newspaper, since when she has never again had a regular agony column, even though she is still best known as an advice columnist. She asks what right she had to do the job and answers herself by saying: 'none, I suppose, except being asked to do it and finding more and more people wanted me to.' Rayner also says she found herself becoming deeply embroiled in her readers' problems and that although many miseries are certainly self-inflicted, many more arise from the way the state is run, with its built-in injustice (as Rayner sees it) to the poor and helpless.

Like Marje, Claire Rayner continually pushed back the boundaries of what it was acceptable to say in print and shocked the nation by advertising sanitary towels on television, in the first campaign that was not mealy-mouthed and coy about this essential female product.

Now, of course, there is no such coyness and much of this is due to Rayner. She feels that much of her success is due to her willingness to use direct language in medical and sexual matters rather than euphemisms.

She has also been on many committees, president of the Patients' Association and a long-standing supporter of the National Health Service. Rayner is not only a journalist but a prolific novelist, radio and television broadcaster and public campaigner. She has had no formal training as a journalist and picked up the tricks of the trade by first writing for small-circulation nursing magazines and gradually extending her range after giving up nursing when her first child Amanda was born.

Rayner, like Marje, has been a gift to cartoonists and both have exploited to the full their easy recognisability. But even if they may come over in some circles as jokes, both agony aunts have been ferociously ambitious career journalists who found their natural metier advising others. Few journalists, men or women, past or present, have possessed their sheer staying power and Rayner, along with Marje, has had much illness in her life including, in her youth, being sectioned in a mental hospital in Canada.

Rayner has suffered breast cancer, overactive thyroid, arthritis, severe post-natal depression and hormonal problems, as well as malfunctioning vocal chords which are responsible for her distinctive breathy voice.

Claire Rayner was replaced at *The Sun* by Deidre Sanders, a daughter of the Manse, who has been in situ ever since. Much more serious-minded and less cartoony as an advice columnist than Marje or Rayner, Sanders, who is a trained sex counsellor, has dispensed responsible, informed advice along with her team of advisers and consultants, maintaining a kind of calm centre at the heart of *The Sun*.

Sanders was recruited from *Woman* magazine, where she wrote on consumer issues. When Claire Rayner resigned from *The Sun*, the woman's editor, Kate Hadley, was instantly overwhelmed with applications for Rayner's job. In the event, Sanders was exactly the right person, less volatile, less publicity-minded than either Marje or Claire Rayner, and a solid, hardworking journalist.

Sanders, now in her 60s, works with a team of eight counsellors who all meet regularly to try and keep up with the latest sexual trends – at least as far as answering readers' letters goes. Sanders' column is, apparently, one of the most-read items in the paper, and now includes texting. For a while, it was put on *The Sun*'s website but had to be taken off as it was so popular it was feared that people would just read it online and not bother to buy the paper.

Over the years Sanders has had to cope with answering letters on ever more bizarre aspects of sexual behaviour and nowadays, her 'casebook' includes quite explicit photo strips to illustrate sex and relationship dilemmas. Sanders believes that porn is now ubiquitous and it is pointless to try and stem the tide. Much has changed since Marje pronounced that pre-marital sex was not to be encouraged, and large numbers of sexual partners, for both men and women, is now the norm. Drugs are universal, and the internet has changed everything.

Virginia Ironside, the *Independent* agony aunt. comes from quite a different background from the working-class, barely-surviving origins of Proops and Rayner. Her mother, Janey Ironside, an early career woman, was the first professor of fashion at the Royal College of Art and also, as her daughter revealed later, a hopeless alcoholic. Ironside's parents were divorced and Virginia was their only child.

Working as a journalist from a very early age, Ironside, like Rayner, has been all over the place professionally.

She first came to public attention when she wrote a book, *Chelsea Bird*, at the age of 19. This made her immediately famous and led to a rock column in the *Daily Mail* in the 1960s. Ironside's move from frivolous rock chick to serious agony aunt arose out of her own long experience of clinical depression and also coping with a mother who was, although chic and soignée and much in the public eye, often secretly completely incapable from alcohol. Virginia Ironside herself was also a divorced single mother which, again, provided valuable personal experience.

She was one of the many journalists who applied to take over Claire Rayner's column at *The Sun*, but in the end remained at *Woman*, where she had taken over from Anna Raeburn who left to become a radio presenter. Ironside stayed at *Woman* for 10 years, then worked for a time at the *Sunday Mirror*, (after Claire Rayner left) but she was eventually replaced by an older woman. This was none other than Marje herself, who was by this time about 80.

Ironside has been advice columnist at *The Independent* since 1994, where she introduced a new concept with *Dilemmas*, a now much-copied idea in which readers themselves give the advice to a problem posed at the top of the page. Plus, of course, it is cheaper to have readers providing copy than using teams of professional advisers and writing replies to every single reader.

Ironside also writes the 'Grannie Annexe' column in *The Oldie*, apart from which she is the author of many books, including novels, biography and autobiography and children's books.

In common with Claire Rayner, Ironside has never been coy about sharing harrowing details of her private life with the reading public, and she has most recently written about her colostomy. She is known for reporting from the front line of her own experience, whether this is illness, alcoholism, bereavement, childbirth or depression and she approaches the reader on an equal level, rather than as somebody coming at them from an all-knowing and saintly great height.

Ironside has also written much about the purpose and changing content of agony columns over the years. She considers that agony columns have always been regarded as lightweight, 'women's stuff' because they deal with emotional problems, traditionally the province only of women. Writing in the *British Journalism Review* in 2006, Ironside paid tribute to Marje who, she considered, read market trends brilliantly, and who was a true one-off, the like of which we will never see again. Times have changed, trends have changed and the agony column itself has changed, Ironside believes, from giving information about sexual matters to discussing the difficulties people have in forming good, lasting, honest relationships with each other.

Ironside considers that, though agony aunts still have a useful part to play, they are no longer handing down advice on tablets of stone, in the same way that we no longer regard doctors, nurses, teachers and lawyers as automatic god-like repositories of wisdom. In the past, she says, agony aunts were one-woman search engines, with leaflets, lists of helpful organisations, telephone lines and useful books readers could consult.

Nowadays we have the internet, many self-help groups and health charities and in any case, women's magazines and the women's pages of newspapers are full of real-life misery stories sent in by readers more than happy to have their names and pictures displayed all over the paper. All this could make the traditional agony column redundant but it thrives – so long as the columnist chosen is the right one.

Until the 1990s, the agony column was the province of downmarket newspapers, as if only working-class women had problems. Mass-selling magazines such as *Woman* and *Woman's Own* always had their advice columnists such as the long-serving Evelyn Home and Mary Grant. Both pseudonyms became household names, but such columns were never a feature of glossy or 'aspirational' publications until British *Cosmopolitan* came on the scene in 1972, and the American writer Irma Kurtz was hired as agony aunt – a position she holds to this day.

But after *The Independent* introduced its *Dilemmas* in 1994, other upmarket papers began to introduce advice columns. Vicar's wife Anne Atkins wrote a very moralistic problem column in the *Daily Telegraph* for a time, and then *The Times* employed the versatile journalist Bel Mooney – another person never shy about putting her private life on public view – and the *Daily Telegraph* hired Lesley Garner. *The Guardian* has copied the Independent's *Dilemmas* page by getting readers to answer knotty personal problems and the *Daily Mail* later hired Mooney as advice columnist.

The very upmarket Katharine Whitehorn has an advice column in *Saga* magazine, even though she says she is constantly met with the question: but surely old people don't have problems?

Indeed they do, and these days their problems are just as likely to be about sex and relationships as preparing a will or getting ready to go into an old people's home. Old people are people too, these days and ever more sectors of society are getting an advice column in a suitable publication. There are now versions of the advice column in most publications including *The Spectator*, whose witty, deadpan and apparently authoritative *Dear Mary* column is, at least since Jeffrey Bernard's death, one of the best-read columns in the magazine.

Which brings us to the agony uncle: why has there never been one? Well, actually there has. As early as the 18th century, the *Athenaeum Gazette* had an advice column which at one point was edited by Daniel Defoe, author of *Robinson Crusoe*. There was an agony uncle in the London *Evening News* in the 1960s and 70s, now long-forgotten, and psychotherapist Philip Hodson has had a few goes at an advice column.

Hodson, though, like Anna Raeburn, comes over best on radio. But agony uncles have always been few and far between, and the genre is not exactly thriving. Women seem to do it best.

Will there ever be another Marje? Virginia Ironside thinks not. The days of the highly promoted household names are over, there is ever more proliferation in the media and no one publication stands out as being huge, as the *Daily Mirror* (with more than 14 million readers every day) did in its heyday. 'But,' Ironside says, 'agony doesn't go away, and nor does the need for newspapers to provide succour and information for thousands of wretched and unhappy people. And if the columns give a few people a laugh along the way, frankly, who cares?'

In more recent years there has been a tendency to hire celebrities, such as Mariella Frostrup, Margaret Cook (ex-wife of the late Labour politician Robin Cook) and the ubiquitous Ann Widdicombe as agony aunts. But really, the agony aunt aspect should come first, and the celebrity, later. The celebrity agony columns rarely work as the celebrities never have time to attend to them properly and in any case may see them as just another ego-boosting outlet, rather than as serious journalism.

Six

Politics and war

The two areas of journalism where men tried hardest to keep women out were those of political and foreign reporting. For many years they succeeded but, as ever, a few brave women fought their way past the formidable mental and physical barricades that were set up to deter them – never mind the actual barricades of war fronts.

And today, there are probably just as many women reporting in these areas as there are men.

The struggle began as long ago as 1890, when *The Women's Penny Paper*, a suffragette publication of the time, applied for permission to have a female parliamentary reporter in the Press Gallery. The request was summarily turned down by the Sergeant at Arms, who warned that the 'consequences were too difficult to conceive'.

The supposed consequences were not explained and in the event it was to be another 29 years before women even tried again, although this time they were slightly more successful. But only slightly. This time, two female journalists sought, and won, permission to sit in the Press Gallery to report on a truly momentous event: Nancy Astor taking her seat as the first woman MP, in December 1919. The pioneer journalist Marguerite Cody, from the *Daily News,* and another, unnamed, woman journalist from the *Central News* were issued with a pink ticket each and allowed to write up the event, so long as they remembered to describe every detail of the new MP's outfit.

After the session was over, the two reporters were obliged to give up their pink tickets and the privilege was withdrawn. In 1925 a parliamentary sketch writer got into trouble for bringing a female typist into the gallery and it was to be another quarter of a century before a woman was allowed to have a permanent reporting job in the gallery.

This woman was Eirene White, later to become a well-known MP herself. She was political correspondent for the *Manchester Evening News* from 1945 to 1949 after which she contested, and won with a majority of only 20, the seat of East Flint for Labour. By this time women reporters were granted access to the same bars and facilities as the men, even though these privileges were not widely taken up.

At the time Eirene White (then Jones) was a journalist on the *Evening News* her sub-editor was that other pioneering woman, Mary Stott, who normally handled her reports, in her words, 'pepping them up a bit' to provide her with a suitable headline.

White came from a prominent intellectual and socialist family. Her father was the deputy cabinet secretary to four prime ministers, and Eirene was educated at St Paul's Girls' School and Somerville College, Oxford. After becoming an MP, she held her seat for 20 years after which she went to the Lords as Baroness White of Rhymney. In 1948 she had married another journalist, John Cameron White, and she died in 1999 at the age of 90.

Although White was the first political correspondent of a leading newspaper, she was not really a career journalist unlike another pioneer, Nora Beloff, who became the first woman political correspondent of a national newspaper.

Beloff, who held the post at *The Observer* from 1964 to 1976, is remembered as a tough and combative personality and dogged journalist. She had a reputation for being extremely outspoken, and while very skilled at getting good stories, would write her copy in what came to be called 'The Ladies' Lounge' on scraps of paper which she would then phone over to her paper. Despairing sub-editors often said that her copy had to be 'snowploughed' into clarity, although Prime Minister Harold Wilson reportedly read her stories to discover what his cabinet was up to.

Beloff came to amused public attention when she sued *Private Eye* for stating that she had slept with a number of senior politicians. She won her case but *Private Eye* was to have its revenge, as for ever afterwards she was referred to as 'Nora Ballsoff' – the name by which she was remembered.

Single for most of her life, Beloff made a surprise late marriage to fellow journalist Clifford Makins, who in common with Max Hastings' father Macdonald, used to write for the popular boys' comic *Eagle*.

Those whose memories go back far enough may recall that the young Bernadette Devlin, who became an Irish MP at the age of only 21, was told off for wearing trousers in the House. She replied in typical spirited fashion that she would remove her trousers if all the male MPs did the same. Nowadays, when just about all female MPs wear trousers all the time, it is perhaps salutary to recall that trousers were forbidden for all women entering the House until 1974.

That went for female political correspondents, too. And trousers or not, women in the Press Gallery were lone figures in skirts until such journalists as Julia Langdon and Elinor Goodman came along, and changed the face and look of parliamentary reporting for ever.

Langdon, in 1987 the first woman to chair the parliamentary lobby group, became a journalist through a happy chance.

Unlike Eirene White and many other early women journalists, she did not go to Oxbridge, or even to any university. Instead, she left school at just 16, immediately after taking O-levels.

Born in 1946, Langdon came from a forces family and was educated at the Royal Naval School. She says: 'I came from a section of society which didn't then believe in educating girls, and I certainly didn't come from an academic family. I think I am from the last generation of career women who didn't go to university but might have trained as a secretary.

'Instead of that, just as I was about to leave school I started reading a pile of career booklets somebody had dumped in our classroom. One was about journalism and I was immediately intrigued. The result of reading this booklet was that I marched straight to the *Portsmouth Evening News* a day or two after leaving school and asked for a job.

'They told me to go away and take A-levels, so I went to Portsmouth Technical College and passed three A-levels. I was interviewed by the editor who asked me if I knew who wrote *The Decline and Fall of the Roman Empire*. I said Gibson – instead of Gibbon – but he didn't notice. And I got the job.'

Langdon was hired in 1964 as a junior reporter at £7.14.6d a week – with an extra £1 a week for her A-levels. 'In those days only 350 people a year were taken onto the journalism training schemes which had just got going, and I was indentured for three years, after which I got my National Council for the Training of Journalists' proficiency certificate. I was running the women's pages as cheap labour and spent a very happy four years on the Portsmouth paper.'

She then felt it was time to move on and applied to Fleet Street. At the time, only those journalists who had the NCTJ certificate and were considered 'trained' were eligible for Fleet Street jobs, although exceptions were sometimes made for Oxbridge graduates (see Ann Leslie, later this chapter)

Langdon continues: 'I had an interview at the *Daily Express*, but the very nice man who saw me and took me to the pub next door said he thought I was much too young for the *Express* and I would do better to try an evening paper.

'I had to fill in a form to see the news editor and I was taken on the staff of the John London Diary, at the *Evening News* at the amazing – for those days – salary of £32 a week! I had a great time there interviewing famous people and I was still quite young, only 22. I was living a heady girl life in London when I met my first husband, Peter Cole, who had come straight from Cambridge and who was on the same paper.

'Peter's girlfriend before me had been Valerie Grove, who also became a journalist. In those days there was a certain snobbishness about Oxbridge graduates who tended to look down on people like me.'

It was not generally considered a good idea for husbands and wives to work on the same paper, and Langdon went back to the *Sunday Express* where this time she was given a job on the diary there, known as Town Talk. 'This job was lots of fun too: the diary team was Peter McKay, Robert Fisk, Lady Olga Maitland and me.'

Olga Maitland, the daughter of an earl and thus granted the title of Lady, had earlier worked on the *Sunday Express* diary under the editorship of Michael Watts. Watts says that many people imagined she had just waltzed into the job on a gossip column because of her 'silver spoon', but actually she was a serious journalist who had done time on local papers and also a Fleet Street news agency before joining the *Express*. In 1992 Lady Olga successfully fought Sutton and Cheam for the Conservatives and was a high-profile MP until she lost her seat in 1997 when Labour swept into power.

Back to Julia Langdon: 'I was at the *Express* for two years when I had a row with the editor John Junor about unwelcome intrusion into people's lives. I said that I did not want to do this sort of work and I found it destructive. Junor asked me what I wanted to do instead and I didn't really know, except that I didn't want to pry into people's lives, so I walked out.'

Soon after this, Peter Cole was sent to New York as the *London Evening News* correspondent there, and Langdon went with him, where she was the *Daily Sketch* correspondent and wrote for the Sydney *Daily Telegraph* group as their New York columnist. The *Evening News* then closed its New York bureau, the *Daily Sketch* folded and the Coles came back. 'By this time I wanted to do more than gossip columns,' Langdon said. 'I wanted to write about more serious subjects, and I saw a job ad for a political correspondent on *Labour Weekly*. I applied for this, got it and stayed there for a wonderful six years while Labour was in opposition.

'This job turned out to be a brilliant career move as a new generation of up and coming Labour politicians, Neil Kinnock, Roy Hattersley, David Owen, all had to read the party paper and in opposition I was very useful to them. I covered Westminster and got a lobby ticket. Then in 1974 Labour came to power. I was very involved in Labour politics – I was a councillor in Kensington and Chelsea – but I also got to know the Tory party.'

Langdon believes it is essential to be a political animal if you want to be a political journalist, and she herself has been a lifelong socialist. 'I got to know the House of Commons extremely well when I was at *Labour Weekly*, and also started doing some broadcasting. Then I was appointed political correspondent at *The Guardian*.'

When Langdon was number two at *The Guardian*, Elinor Goodman, almost exactly the same age as Julia Langdon, was also number two on the political staff at the *Financial Times*. 'It was extraordinary,' recalls Langdon, 'as we kept being mistaken for each other. The MPs couldn't tell us apart, solely because we were the only two women lobby correspondents. We both got very used to people coming up and mysteriously continuing conversations they had previously been having with the other one of us. We both have long faces and were both working on broadsheet newspapers, but that's as far as the resemblance goes. But in those days, there were very few female political journalists, and they didn't bother to differentiate between us.'

After leaving the *Financial Times*, Elinor Goodman went to Channel 4 News, where she became a highly popular and visible political correspondent, and where she was to stay for 23 years before retiring. Langdon got used to MPs saying: You're on television a lot these days.

Langdon's first 'first' came in 1984 when she became political editor of the *Daily Mirror*, the first woman to hold this position on a major national title. 'Maxwell hired me and I must say that we got on very well together. Maxwell thought I was wonderful and I attempted to reciprocate... I got to interview some of the great dictators of the time and I was the only member of the *Daily Mirror* to be sent everywhere Thatcher went. I went all over the world in that job and it was fantastic. I was massively well paid, as well.'

By this time Langdon's first marriage had broken up and she was married again, this time to fellow political journalist Geoffrey Parkhouse, of the *Glasgow Herald*. 'For most of the time I was at the *Mirror* I didn't have children, so it was easy enough for me to travel. The job was not easy to combine with bringing up a family as the evening and night time hours were too tough.' Langdon's daughter Georgia was born in 1987, by which time she was political editor of Maxwell's short-lived 24 hour newspaper, the *London Daily News*.

She says: 'Sometime in the 1980s, newspaper editors realised that it was an advantage to have women as political correspondents. For one thing, a woman is more visible – even if wearing trousers these days – and for another, it's much easier for women to get the good stories, I think, as male MPs like talking to women and you are always being asked out to lunch and dinner where, over wine, the best stories often emerge. Anyway, by the early 1990s, most newspapers had a woman in the Press Gallery.'

Her next job after leaving the *Mirror* was as political editor of The Sunday Telegraph where she took 'a massive pay cut' in order to show that she was not Maxwell's creature and still a serious journalist. She was sacked after three years by the then editor, Trevor Grove, second husband of Valerie Grove, for being a 'leftie'.

'I had just had my second baby when he fired me and that could have looked bad, but it was not the reason for the sacking. He was a pinkish Tory with little understanding of the political world and he couldn't comprehend why he inherited me when he became editor of what was a right wing paper. He actually fired me for spending New Year in Venice – without realising I was staying with the Tory Party Treasurer, Alistair McAlpine and hot-bedding with the Thatchers.' In the event, Langdon fought her dismissal and won a year's pay from the paper.

Since then she has been freelance, writing and broadcasting widely on political issues. She is the author of an unauthorised, but very detailed, biography of the former Secretary of State for Northern Ireland, the late Dr Marjorie (Mo) Mowlam.

What is the attraction of writing about politics? 'Of all the jobs in journalism, I think this gives the biggest buzz,' she says. 'You are piecing things together, finding out, interpreting events and you are on intimate terms with Cabinet members. You are right at the heart of what is going on and in many ways more relevant to the political process than many backbench MPs.'

Langdon was asked, twice, to stand as a Labour MP, but refused. 'I never had ambitions in that direction and much prefer writing about politics.'

Mary Holland, who wrote for *The Guardian, Observer* and *Irish Times*, and who also had a major career as a television presenter, was another distinguished political correspondent.

Holland made reporting on Northern Ireland her particular speciality and saw it as her mission in life to hear and report on all sides in this complicated issue in the clearest and simplest way possible. She felt that otherwise readers simply would not understand what was going on.

She was born in 1935 in Dover, of Irish extraction, and educated at convent boarding schools. She went to London University to read law but did not complete her degree. Instead, in common with many of the pioneering journalists profiled in this book, she went to work for *Vogue*, in her case after winning one of their young talent contests. Holland joined *The Observer* in 1964, firstly writing about social affairs and later specialising in politics after being sent to Ireland. She had briefly reported for *The Observer* from Indonesia, where she went with her then husband, diplomat Ronald Higgins.

This marriage broke up soon after Holland was posted to Ireland in 1968, where she covered the political violence then just erupting. At first, Mary Holland was the only British journalist specifically covering the troubles, even before the civil rights marches of 1968. On Bloody Sunday, in 1972, she was standing right behind the Catholic priests who pulled two demonstrators from the crowd as they were dying.

In her private life, Holland began a relationship with Belfast journalist Eamonn McCann, eight years her junior. He was the father of her two children, Kitty and Luke, and had been Bernadette Devlin's election agent.

Holland realised that it was always difficult to get at the truth of what was happening in Northern Ireland and wrote in 1994, after the IRA bombing in Canary Wharf:

> There are many forms of censorship and, from personal experience, I know that self-censorship by journalists of what they write and report is the mosr corrosive, at least in a democracy, where theoretically there are few restrictions on the freedom of the press.

> One saw this over and over again in Northern Ireland. Most journalists who reported on the conflict came to understand that they were working within serious, if unspoken, constraints – political disapproval, fear of offending public opinion, the denial of access to certain sources. To deny these realities, to insist on making waves, meant running the risk of being branded as 'unreliable' or a 'Provo lover' – but what this meant was that the public was not given the information to enable it to understand what was happening.

Holland herself risked being attacked from both sides and found herself labelled a 'Provo lover' for much of her career at *The Observer* and then, when she worked for the *Irish Times*, was called a 'Unionist apologist'. Her bipartisan coverage of the troubles got her into trouble with the Irish politician Conor Cruise O'Brien, who became joint editor of the *Observer* in 1979. Holland's coverage of Northern Ireland did not start and stop with political events, as she also wrote about the everyday lives of the ordinary people there.

In particular, she campaigned for modernisation of Ireland's abortion laws and in support of her campaign confessed that she herself had undergone an abortion. She was rewarded for this candour by having excrement pushed through her letter box.

Many people now consider that Mary Holland contributed greatly to the peace process by enabling all sides to have a better understanding of the situation, and that she was the first journalist in Britain to give genuine coverage to the complex nature of the problems in Northern Ireland.

In doing this, she forced the British government to sit up and take notice of what was really going on, thanks to her close analyses of the situation. Mary Holland died in 2004, aged 68.

All these women – and at the time of writing Julia Langdon is still going strong in her 60s – paved the way for successive generations of female parliamentary reporters and editors, so that today it no longer seems strange to have a woman in the job.

Far from it. Among today's younger political correspondents, Anne McElvoy, Rachel Sylvester and Alice Thompson all stand out.

The only related area which women have not so far penetrated much has been that of parliamentary sketch writer, where a wry, throwaway wit is required just as much as political acumen and understanding. The late Frank Johnson was a brilliantly humorous and trenchant sketch writer and journalists such as Quentin Letts and Simon Hoggart are carrying on that tradition with their highly readable and amusing accounts of what is going on day by day in parliament. Is this skill, one wonders, something closely allied to the male chromosome, as most female political writers have been extremely serious minded?

The only female parliamentary sketch writer who has made any impression is Ann Treneman, of *The Times*. She is sardonic, in the best sketch writer tradition, but far gentler than her male counterparts.

Julia Langdon's cousin, by the way, is married to Simon Hoggart and, in the relationship merry-go-round that characterises both modern politics and journalism, Mo Mowlam's husband Jon Norton was previously married to journalist Geraldine Bedell and is now the partner of another high-profile female MP, Clare Short.

In much the same way as female political journalists have broken through into a previously jealously guarded all-male world, so have female foreign and war correspondents come into their own.

Just about every television channel now has a highly visible female war reporter and women are no longer so rare in this position on newspapers, either.

The first female foreign correspondent of note was the American Margaret Fuller, who reported on England and Italy for the *New York Tribune* in the 1840s.

However, the most prominent American war correspondent was Martha Gellhorn, who became equally famous for two events in her life: marrying Ernest Hemingway, and entering Dachau in 1945 to report on the atrocities there to a shocked and horrified world.

Gellhorn, considered by many to be the first female war reporter of any profile at all, paved the way for later correspondents such as Marie Colvin and Christina Lamb of the *Sunday Times,* and television reporters such as Kate Adie and Christiane Amanpour of CCN, by concentrating on the stories of the sufferings of real people caught up in horrendous conflict, rather than just the hardware of war and close analysis of military campaigns.

Refused official permission to join the forces invading France, simply because she was female, Gellhorn tricked an official into letting her board a hospital ship where she locked herself in the toilet until the ship had set off for Normandy, by which time it was too late to offload her. On her return to England, she was arrested by the military police and sent to a nurses' training camp.

Born in 1909 in St Louis, Missouri, Gellhorn became an accredited war reporter for the American *Collier's Weekly,* for which Hemingway also worked. She spent her last years in England, giving numerous interviews to fascinated journalists who always, always – in common with the present author of this book – insisted on mentioning her five-year marriage to Hemingway. Gellhorn died in London in 1989.

The first serious female British foreign correspondent was Shelley Rohde, who died in 2008 aged 74. Rohde was born in London, the daughter of a scriptwriter and an actress and attended a total of 13 schools. She was expelled from three, which possibly gives some indication of her independent spirit.

She left school at 16 with no qualifications and her first job in journalism was on the *Notts Free Press* in Sutton Ashfield. Her next job was on *The Star* in London, then one of three London evening papers and she joined the *Daily Express* when barely out of her teens. The editor, Arthur Christiansen, a noted champion of women journalists, sent her to Moscow as its first woman correspondent there when she was just 21. Rohde learned Russian and became the official interpreter when Communist leaders Nikolai Bulganin and Nikita Krhuschev made their famous visit to Britain in 1955.

After this she joined the *Daily Mail* in Manchester and also became a television presenter for Granada. Rohde was seen as a strong role model for younger journalists working in Manchester such as Angela Neustatter, who remembers the 'mega-macho' world of newspapers in those days. Rohde was always, says Neustatter, 'elegantly feminine' and never tried to be one of the boys.

Rohde brought up her four children as a single parent after her divorce and is perhaps now best remembered for her biography of the painter L S Lowry. This book came about after Rohde went to interview him, and he told her he had given up painting as he was now too old. Rohde, however, noticed that the paint on a canvas they were looking at together was still wet, and so began a friendship which resulted in a bestseller.

It can, of course, be dangerous to cover wars as a journalist and women are by no means immune. Eve-Ann Prentice, another pioneer war correspondent, herself nearly died in a Nato bombing when she was covering Kosovo for *The Times* in 1999. Prentice also covered the Serbian conflict and reported from Poland, Romania and Russia.

The journalist Gloria Stewart, who became famous not so much for her journalism as for being the mistress of writer Paul Johnson and going public on his spanking proclivities, also reported from Moscow for a time in the 1970s. Stewart was married at one time to John Knight, assistant editor and chief feature writer on the *Sunday Mirror*.

Eve-Ann Prentice was born in Bury, Lancashire, the daughter of a Labour MP, Derek Page, who became a life peer. She was sent to a Catholic girls' boarding school in North Wales, and it was the nuns' insistence on communism being a sin and evil, a blind prejudice arising out of no knowledge whatsoever, that decided the young Eve-Ann to become a journalist, with the intention of finding out the truth for herself.

At the age of 17 she started to train on the *Lincolnshire Free Press*, and after stints on several other local newspapers she joined *The Guardian* as a sub-editor on the foreign desk, a job that also included reporting on Eastern Europe. She met her first husband Pat Prentice on the Lincolnshire paper and together they went to work on the *China Daily* in 1984, although they soon returned as they discovered they hated living in a compound. They also found the insistence on observing strict political correctness all the time stifling.

Prentice returned to *The Guardian*, later joining the *Sunday Telegraph* as one of the paper's first female production editors. She was interested in joining the new *Sunday Correspondent*, billed as a completely new type of Sunday paper and one of its founders, Peter Cole – first husband of Julia Langdon – took her on as production editor. The brave attempt at a new Sunday paper never really got off the ground, for all that it had a full complement of Fleet Street's finest working on it, and it sank just a year after launch, in 1990.

Prentice's next job was at the foreign desk of *The Times*, where she became diplomatic and Balkans correspondent. She gave evidence at the Slobodan Milosevic hearing at The Hague and secured the last interview with him before he died.

She rejoined *The Guardian* in 2004 but she was already becoming very ill with the bone cancer which was to kill her in 2007, not long after marrying her second husband Aidan Morrin.

Clare Hollingsworth, of the *Guardian* and later the *Daily Telegraph*, was one of the first female defence correspondents. She later went to work for the *International Herald Tribune* in a similar capacity.

Female war correspondents first came to the fore in significant numbers during the Vietnam war but in those days they were completely overshadowed by their male counterparts. The first challenge for some of these women, in the 1970s, was in trying to get there at all and in 1971 the foreign editor at *Associated Press* simply refused to let women work on his desk, considered essential training before you were allowed to be sent abroad.

The second major challenge for women in the early days was being able to get remotely near the action. Many military officers thought that women would prove a serious distraction and often, possibly with a misguided but no doubt well-meaning sense of protectiveness, refused to give permission for women reporters to get into combat areas.

Maggie O'Kane of *The Guardian*, who has covered the Balkans, Afghanistan, Burma and Northern Ireland, believes that female war correspondents are often perceived as a lesser threat than men, although this does not mean that they are necessarily less at risk. The story of Yvonne Ridley being captured by the Taliban while reporting for the *Sunday Express*, is widely remembered for the inherent dangers of the job.

On the plus side, O'Kane says that female reporters can establish a greater degree of intimacy than men with casualties of war such as rape victims, and in many cases such women would never have been able to speak to a male reporter. Women, says O'Kane, can bring a certain empathy to this kind of reporting, where a delicate touch is needed, and another war reporter, Ann McFerran, always makes a point of using female translators and interpreters. Male interpreters, she says, often do not convey the subtleties 'that turn a good story into a special story'.

When reporting on war, do female reporters have to go out of their way to prove that they are courageous, fearless and brave? O'Kane says that she has never felt any particular pressure from the newspaper's foreign desk to be brave, in fact quite the reverse as editors at home frequently worry more about the wellbeing of the reporters than do the reporters themselves.

Another positive effect of women reporting war is that what was for a long time regarded as 'soft news', such as overcrowded hospitals, food and water shortages, child casualties and civilian victims, is now seen as an essential aspect of reporting on conflicts. In modern warfare, it is civilians who often suffer the most and it is mainly the female reporters who have highlighted this aspect for the benefit of readers or viewers at home.

Because there is not so much of a 'frontline' in today's conflicts, those who suffer most tend to be the innocent civilians, and female reporters are there to record this for the rest of the world. Female war reporters particularly concentrate on examining the effect of war on society, and how people caught up in it could easily be your sister, cousin, parent or child. This brings faraway conflicts home to people and allows readers to put themselves in the position of those caught up in the war.

The profile of female war reporters was particularly high in Iraq and some commentators believe that women reporters add a 'wow' factor which increases readership of the coverage in newspapers, and encourages people to watch if on television. And while few people notice what male war reporters are wearing, there is constant discussion from other branches of the media on the women's outfits, hairstyles and make-up, if any. So, for the moment at least, female war reporters are more noticeable than their male counterparts, even if they are, nowadays, almost as numerous.

BBC South Africa correspondent Hilary Andersson, based in Johannesburg, said that at the British Divisional Headquarters in Iraq, there were, for the first time, as many female as male war correspondents present. She said: 'It was to this evenly matched group that the British high command revealed the top secret war plan on the eve of the ground war.' The soldiers, though, were intrigued to see so many women reporters and could hardly believe it as they all had to jump into World War One-style trenches and shuffle along during a Scud alert.

97

Things have moved on a lot since the 1940s, when women journalists and reporters were banned from attending military briefings. Hilary Andersson does not believe, though, that the fight for female equality in war journalism has been completely won, and wonders whether women will continue to provide such a 'wow' factor when the novelty value of having women reporting on wars dies down.

Women were highly visible as reporters during the Iraq war but they were not actually at the front line, but far away at the rear where they had access to satellite dishes. 'On the real front line,' says Andersson, 'the military embed positions were completely dominated by men.' It was considered that the troops would not take kindly to having women as embeds, although there were a few notable exceptions.

'The fact is,' Andersson points out, 'there are still deeply entrenched social attitudes, the legacy of humanity's entire male-dominated history, that weigh heavily when it comes to levelling the playing field in the arena of war. It is, of course, an arena that epitomises everything male – danger, conflict, dirt, guns and machinery.

'Also, many people, men and women alike, cannot figure out why women want to be on the front line in the first place. We played a high profile in this war because of real social change but partly because, on television at least, a vast number of viewers will watch us simply because they are amazed we are there.'

Hilary Andersson agrees with Maggie O'Kane that women bring something different to war reporting, which is the human side as they tend to be less interested in the 'boys' toys' aspects such as the latest fighter jets and artillery power. But, she says, many men report on the human side as well, especially these days and the main argument for having women reporters is that it 'massively expands the pool of talent.'

The ancient dilemma of how best to combine such a job with family responsibilities has not been solved. Maggie O'Kane has said she desperately missed her young son when reporting faraway conflicts, and some women, but not many men, do give up this kind of reporting when they have a family.

For this reason, Channel 4 correspondent Lindsey Hilsum has made a conscious decision not to have children, a decision she says she has never regretted.

One of the most high-profile foreign correspondents of modern times is Christina Lamb, of the *Sunday Times*. She has said that it was her love of adventure, and also reading books by Hemingway, V S Naipaul and Kipling, which got her into this kind of journalism in the first place.

When at Oxford, she wrote to the Asia editor of the *Financial Times* and got a place as an intern for the summer. 'This was very exciting,' she says, 'although in those days of liquid lunches I was never sure how the paper ever came out.' She found the foreign correspondents by far the most exotic of all the journalists there, and this fired her ambition to become one herself. While at the *FT*, Lamb found herself interviewing the late Benazir Bhutto, the result of which was to receive a gold-embossed invitation to her wedding some months later.

She attended the fairytale wedding, and became fascinated by Pakistan then was sent to Afghanistan by the *FT*, which resulted, she said, in 'all the adventure I could wish for. Caring passionately about injustice, I thought I could change the world, and being a journalist is a wonderful excuse to talk to anyone, from presidents to the most destitute, to go inside prisons and be behind front lines.'

Perhaps the most feted foreign correspondent of all is Ann Leslie, one of the few working journalists to be made a DBE. Former *Guardian* woman's editor Liz Forgan has also been made a DBE, but she moved on from journalism into management and public affairs in the early 1980s. The soon-to-be Dame Ann faced a cruel dilemma when she went to receive her gong from the Queen as to whether she should wear a skirt for the occasion. Like many women these days, she said, she always wears trousers and wearing a skirt now feels like being in drag; a far cry from the days when women were not allowed to wear trousers in the House of Commons.

It would be hard to imagine a woman reporting from a war front in a skirt these days, but the matter of correct dress for female war correspondents is still a vexed issue, and endlessly commented on in a way that does not happen with male reporters. Maybe it always will; there is a fashion element with all female journalists which looks as though it will never go away.

Ann Leslie was born in north-west India, and was sent to a hill station boarding school at the age of four. Straight after Oxford, she landed a job at the *Daily Express* in Manchester and only a year later moved to Fleet Street where she was given her own column, headed: 'She's young, she's provocative and she's only 22!' Leslie said later that she was regarded with extreme suspicion and even hostility in Manchester, that mega-macho world, for being both educated and female.

'Such was the culture of hostility to female journalists," she said, "that I came to resent the way my superiors did all they could to make a young male journalist training with me feel at home, while taking every opportunity to leave me in the dark as much as possible.'

Although she managed to pick up some rudiments of journalism, Leslie says that mostly what she learned was how to 'see off assorted sexist, bullying men such as news editors.'

Her big break came when the northern editor in Manchester asked her to write a column for teenagers, about pop music, fashion and 'things like that'. When Leslie protested that her teenage years had been spent overseas, that she knew nothing about fashion and had a tin ear for music into the bargain, she was told that she was the youngest person in the office, so she'd better just get on with it.

The column brought her to the attention of the then editor, Bob Edwards, who transferred her to London to write a young, jazzy, upbeat column.

She specialised for a time in showbiz but made her name when she moved to the *Daily Mail*, where she has remained ever since, and for whom she has reported from more than 70 countries. Leslie has put on disguise to meet dissidents in Tehran, interviewed people in forbidden North Korea and been shot at in Bosnia. She has been an eyewitness at some of the most dramatic events of the twentieth century such as the fall of the Berlin Wall, the famine in Ethiopia and the walk to freedom of Nelson Mandela.

Throughout all this, she has suffered bouts of severe illness, and has also managed to lead a family life, being married to the same man for many years and bringing up a daughter. Ann Leslie, perhaps the most high-profile of all foreign correspondents, has also enjoyed a parallel broadcasting career where she is in much demand as a panellist.

All journalists are adventurous and curious people, otherwise they would not be journalists, and the best thing about the job is that there is something for everybody. Although reporting from war fronts sounds particularly exciting and glamorous, and one of the main attractions is that you are there, recording important, dramatic and globe-changing historic events as they happen, it is not something that all female journalists wish to do. Some women writers may wonder: where would I plug in my hairdryer? Will I be able to get my highlights done? What about my nails?

Reporting about war from the front line is possibly not for those consumed by vanity, but the major breakthrough is that this kind of reporting is no longer a forbidden or no-go area, and you are no longer just barely tolerated in war zones on sufferance or as a kind of token. Of course, at the same time, girl soldiers are no longer such a rarity either, and so it seems that women have taken their place on more or less equal terms with men when it comes to fighting in or writing about wars.

100

Seven

The editors

Until the mid-1980s, when it first happened, it seemed totally impossible that a woman would, or could, ever become the editor of a national newspaper. Since that time around 15 more women have become editors; who were they and how have they fared?

Wendy Henry made journalistic history when she was appointed editor of the *News of the World*, the biggest circulation Sunday newspaper in the country, possibly in the world, in 1987. She was the first of a line known in some circles as the 'red-top totties', which was to become a long line of women tabloid editors.

It is true that Henry was not technically the first female editor of a national paper; that was Mary Howarth, of the *Daily Mirror*, in 1903, but both her tenure – and the paper itself –lasted only a matter of weeks.

Female newspaper editors have always been more cruelly under the spotlight than their male counterparts, partly because they were until recently a brand-new phenomenon and partly because women are always more highly scrutinised than men anyway, when in high-profile positions, where they are often regarded by men as some kind of illogical, freak occurrence – like having a woman Prime Minister.

For example, media commentator Bill Hagerty derided Henry's editorship as 'increasing circulation with a non-stop diet of sex and savagery'. Even Rupert Murdoch's far from delicate stomach, according to reports, started to churn at some of the content Henry was putting out for public consumption. Her editorship at the NoW did not last long, and she defected to the *Sunday People*, by now losing circulation very quickly indeed. Here, according to Hagerty, himself

101

briefly an editor at the *People*, her 'house of horrors' editorial policy continued.

She proceeded, he says, to turn this long-established and not noticeably squeamish newspaper, into a newsprint bloodbucket, printing pictures of the remains of some of the victims of the Sioux City air crash in America, and a picture of Sammy Davis, Jr, with his throat ravaged by cancer, both in the same issue.

There was also a notorious picture of the young Prince William in his school uniform, peeing into a bush. This picture gave a good, if obvious headline: *The Royal Wee*; nevertheless it was too much for Robert Maxwell and he promptly sacked his new female editor.

But who is Wendy Henry? An identical twin, she was born in the north and educated at the Queen Mary School, Lytham. Her first staff newspaper job was as a junior reporter on the *Daily Mail* in Manchester in 1975, from where she went to the *News of the World* in a similar capacity, and stayed from 1976 to 1979.

Peter Reece, then running a news agency in Manchester, has this story about Wendy Henry in her days as an 'innocent at large' (not to last very long).

> I admit with enormous pride that I was the first to recognise Wendy's talents as an aspiring reporter when many of my colleagues thought I was mad to employ a chubby little rag-tag, ill-dressed, militant Trotskyite who had once been arrested for throwing a bottle of milk at the prime minister of the day, Edward Heath.
>
> And despite dire-warnings from various influential news editors (as in 'influential' to my income) that one day soon she would get me into serious trouble, I kept the faith even until she became Fleet Street's celebrated first female editor of a national newspaper.
>
> However, on the day in question she was a raw and untutored talent and I should have known better than to send her to chronicle the royal progress of Princess Michael of Kent on a visit to Manchester.
>
> Wendy came back with some fabulous quotes. From a task that was nothing more than a routine diary job she turned in an exclusive and very saleable tale. The story was being dictated to any number of national news desks when my telephone rang.
>
> It was my friend Charlie, the city's CID chief, with a curt and bellowed summons: 'My office... NOW!'
>
> I sprinted across the city to Bootle Street as fast as my frightened little legs could carry me. There I was given the biggest bollocking of my life.
>
> On Charlie's desk was Wendy's Special Branch file which looked the size of a modest telephone directory, and he thumbed his way through it angrily.

Charlie's authority was on the line and he was determined to give me a tongue lashing at least equal to, or in even greater measure than, the one he had just suffered at the hands of Scotland Yard, his own Chief Constable and the Royal Protection Squad.

What the f*** did I think I was doing employing Wendy Henry as a reporter in a responsible news agency serving all the nationals, radio and television? – was the gist of his wrath.

He left me in doubt as to why. Wendy, then an innocent at large, had stepped through the crowds, dodged the grasping hands of the royal protection men, grabbed the Princess by the sleeve and clung on until she had answered any number of impolite questions on Princess Anne's private life.

'She was perfectly charming,' said Wendy in her own defence and naive innocence. I knew she was lucky not to have been arrested for assault.

I gave Wendy a good bollocking too – much of it second-hand from Charlie, after solemnly promising the CID chief I would never allow Wendy on another Royal visit, or embarrass him again.

But then I retired to the pub to lick my wounds, throw down some Boddingtons and muse on one very satisfying thought: 'That's my girl!'

Henry then went to *Woman* magazine as assistant features editor and later became assistant editor at *The Sun*. It was here that she first became notorious in newspaper circles as she was responsible for the infamous headline 'Gotcha!' when the *General Belgrano* was sunk during the Falklands War, torpedoed by a Royal Navy nuclear-powered submarine with the loss of 323 lives. This headline became the most notorious in newspaper history and in later editions was toned down by editor Kelvin Mackenzie to 'Did 1,200 Argies die?' She was then promoted to the editorship firstly of the *News of the World Sunday Magazine*, and a year later, to the *NoW* itself.

Henry edited the *NOW* for less than two years, after which she became deputy editor of *The Sun*, not really a demotion as editorships or near-editorships of daily newspapers are always considered more prestigious than top jobs on the Sundays.

After a very brief spell as editor of *The People*, Henry went to America where she became editor in chief of *The Globe* in Florida, returning to the UK to help launch a publishing company, Parkhill Publishing, with Eve Pollard. This company soon folded and Henry decided on a total career change. She left journalism altogether to go quite literally to the dogs. She became a 'foster dog co-ordinator' at Battersea Dogs' and Cats' Home, and has said she loves every minute of her new career.

In this, she is not the first *News of the World* editor to go to the dogs; a previous editor, Stafford Somerfield, became editor of *Dog World* when sacked from his NoW editorship.

Whatever the media commentariat – a mainly male enclave – may think about Wendy Henry's editorships and journalistic career, she tried to give the readers and proprietors what she imagined they wanted: increased gore and sensation for the readers and, importantly, increased sales for the owners. Rupert Murdoch reportedly told her that sales weren't everything, but most red-top and tabloid editors, male or female, since the 1980s, have decreased sales rather than put them on.

Media commentator Roy Greenslade has a 'revisionist' attitude to Wendy Henry, saying that when she was at *The Sun*, she was bubbling with loads of fresh, new ideas and ingenious headlines.

Henry was replaced at the *News of the World* in 1988 by another female editor, Patsy Chapman. Chapman, who hung onto this editorship for six years, worked her way up from lowly journalistic beginnings, starting as a tea girl. Born in 1948 and educated at Rochford Secondary School in Essex, Chapman's first job was on *Boyfriend* magazine, a title that has long since hit the dust. From 1964 to 1967 she was a reporter on the *Romford Times and Havering Express*. She then became a sub-editor, always a traditional route for red-top editors.

Chapman's sub-editing career progressed fast, and this was in the days when very few women were sub-editors at all. She worked at the *Western Daily Press* in Bristol from 1967 to 1971, then got her break into national newspapers when she became a sub on the *Daily Mirror*. Her first mid-executive job was as assistant night editor on the *Daily Mirror*, after which there was a mighty leap up to becoming deputy editor at *The Sun* in 1986. After two years, she was appointed editor of the *News of the World*, the first woman to work her way up through the tough and often thankless route of sub-editing.

One of the reasons very few women became sub-editors of daily newspapers was that hardly any, in the olden days, even wanted to be subs and even fewer wanted the graveyard shift of the night editorship. The fact that Chapman was prepared to do all this meant that she truly earned her spurs before being handed the top job. Chapman was a much quieter presence on the *NoW* than Wendy Henry, at least so far as the product was concerned, and since she left the paper in 1994, her career has also gone very quiet.

Chapman married in 1970 and has one son.

One of the most flamboyant and high-profile of female Fleet Street editors has been Eve Pollard, who for several years edited the *Sunday Express* while her husband, Nicholas Lloyd, was editing the *Daily*. For this double-act they were satirized as a cartoon couple, the Gambollards, in *Private Eye*. The Gambols, older readers may remember, was an extremely unfunny cartoon strip by Barry Appleby, which unaccountably ran for decades. Eve had been known for a long time in *Private Eye* as Eve Bollard.

Pollard, who these days is probably just as famous for being the mother of TV presenter Claudia Winkleman, has had a glittering career mainly at the tabloid end of the newspaper world. Starting off, in common with many female journalists, in fashion, Pollard went from being fashion editor of the young magazine *Honey* to fashion editor of the *Daily Mirror* magazine. She briefly joined *The Observer* as woman's editor, then had a long stint as woman's editor of the *Sunday Mirror*, from 1971 to 1981.

It was while she was in this job that she and the ambitious, Oxford-educated Nick Lloyd fell in love and divorced their first spouses to marry each other to become one of the most powerful couples in newspaper history. The marriage to Lloyd lasted, produced one son, Oliver, and when Lloyd was knighted by Margaret Thatcher, Eve Pollard of course became Lady Lloyd.

After 10 years as woman's editor of the *Sunday Mirror*, Pollard was appointed assistant editor of the *Sunday People* when her husband, Nick Lloyd, became editor. By this time, the idea that husbands and wives could not, or should not, work on the same paper, had long disappeared.

Pollard's ever-upward career then took her to television, where she became a presenter at TV-am for a couple of years after which it was back to print journalism to be editor of the American edition of *Elle* magazine for a year. She returned to the UK to become editor of the *News of the World's* Sunday magazine and in 1986 was appointed editor of *YOU*, the *Mail on Sunday* magazine. She became editor of the *Sunday Mirror* and *Sunday Mirror* magazine in 1988, and was editor of the *Sunday Express*, newspaper and magazine, from 1991 to 1994 after which she and her husband Nick were swept out by a new ownership. Nick Lloyd had by then been editor of the *Daily Express* for a decade.

Since leaving executive roles on newspapers, Pollard has enjoyed a varied career as founder of a publishing company and several magazines, and as a novelist. Her debut novel was written as a threesome with two other long-standing journalists, Joyce Hopkirk and Val Hudson.

Hudson and Hopkirk went on to write other joint novels as Val Hopkirk and Pollard branched out on her own, with her latest (to date) offering being a novel based on the life of Jacqueline Kennedy Onassis.

Eve Pollard has said that she never experienced any particular problems being an editor but that being a woman in an executive position was a definite advantage in the days of old technology, when printers had to be cajoled into making changes, and when editors totally depended on them to bring the paper out. Pollard said: 'In those days I was the only female assistant editor in Fleet Street and so I was the one who always had to go down to the stone and say, please, I know it's getting near edition time but could you ever manage to make this change on page one? I had to try to charm the head printer into making the change. At that period it was a definite advantage to be a woman,'

And those who know Pollard might add that she had two such advantages in being a woman, with possibly the biggest bust in Fleet Street, a twin advantage she never tried to hide.

She continued: 'But it's all changed now, it's a different world. And in a sense, we are pioneers, we women who have managed to get to the top in Fleet Street, and we can't afford to show any sign of weakness now.' Pollard said that she wanted to go into journalism originally because she had always wanted to be a writer, and this seemed to be one way of achieving this ambition, but that she never harboured any fantasies or ambitions to be an executive. 'It certainly never occurred to me that I would ever become editor of a national newspaper. I don't think it would have occurred as a serious possibility to any girl in those days.

'Fleet street was still very much a man's world when I came to the *Mirror* in 1969. But by the time the editorship of the *Sunday Mirror* came up things had changed so much that I wasn't really surprised that the paper was considering a woman editor, although I was surprised that they asked me.

'I've always thought, though, that women journalists worked harder than men and I've always thought they were every bit as good as men, not only as reporters but as executives. I think I am a good deal more approachable than many editors but it's only fair to add that on a Sunday newspaper there's much more time to encourage people to drop in and have a chat about things.'

When you are an editor these days, she says, you have to know about the business, marketing and advertising side of the business, and it's not enough just to have a flair for picking the sort of stories that will appeal to your readers. You have to know about things like the price of newsprint, the printing side, everything that could affect the circulation.

As to making up stories, of which many newspaper editors have been accused down the years, Pollard says: 'Why make up stories when there are so many fascinating true stories around? Why make up stories and then have to pay out a quarter of a million pounds in damages when you could spend the money on a television campaign or on sending a journalist to America or Russia or somewhere to get a real story.'

Eve Pollard was awarded an OBE for services to journalism and broadcasting in the June 2008 Honours.

Those who are familiar with journalism's trade paper *Press Gazette* may enjoy the male chauvinistic ramblings of a grumpy old columnist known as Grey Cardigan, who, posing as a chief sub-editor, has to contend with a (fictitious) female editor he calls Crystal Tits. She has a deputy, a stooge named Alistair and the names are taken from the TV cartoon characters, Crystal Tipps and Alistair. This female editor, a supposed amalgam of all the women newspaper editors Grey Cardigan has known personally or by reputation, spends her time at the nail salon, having massages and being undelightfully vague about the mechanics of actually getting a newspaper out and onto the streets.

It has to be said that many male commentators have not taken kindly to female editors, and have tended to write about them with sly disdain and biting sarcasm. Female editors and senior executives also face the ancient prejudice of: you appoint her and she'll just go off and have a baby. Grey Cardigan has written about this:

'I honestly cannot afford to appoint a senior subeditor who's promptly going to piss off pregnant for a year instead of settling down for the five years it takes to set or change a newspaper's agenda.'

In fact, few if any female newspaper editors have 'pissed off' and had a baby while in the top job. Mostly, they have either had their children before getting to the top or have decided not to have children anyway.

Tabloid newspapers led the way in female editorships, and the non-publicity shy Rosie Boycott was the first female editor of a 'quality' paper, *The Independent*. According to Bill Hagerty, she 'zipped through *The Independent* like a high-velocity bullet on her way from the *Independent on Sunday* to the *Express*. But in doing so, she established a numerical track record that outstripped the female heavy hitters who, in the late 1980s, threatened to make what was then Fleet Street into a feminine enclave.'

In becoming successively the editor of three national titles, Boycott became the most successful woman editor in history, even if none of these editorships lasted long.

One of the more interesting personalities to become a female newspaper editor, Boycott has had a chequered newspaper and personal history. Educated at Cheltenham Ladies' College, she studied pure maths at Kent University. This in itself is a rarity and possibly unique as most women in journalism, even those clever with words, can hardly add up two and two.

Jean Rook wrote of her '12 per cent' in maths exams, a percentage possibly shared by most of Fleet Street's finest females. However, this mathematical ability would mean that Boycott would easily be able to count up the wheelbarrow of money she received when ousted from the *Daily Express*. Most editors these days, male or female, hardly expect their editorships to last very long, and the thumping great pay off is often one of the attractions of the job.

Boycott first came to public attention in 1971 as one of the founders of the feminist magazine *Spare Rib*. Although *Spare Rib* never made any money and was always on the verge of closure, it brought Boycott to media attention, an attention she has enjoyed ever since. After leaving *Spare Rib*, she entered the more conventional, traditional (and moneyed) publishing world, to become deputy editor of *Honey* magazine, and successively, if fleetingly, an executive on the *Daily Mail, Sunday Telegraph* and *Harpers and Queen*.

She was editor of the men's magazine *Esquire* from 1992 to 1996, editor of the *Independent on Sunday* from 1996 to 1998 and of the *Independent* in 1996. Her editorship of the *Daily Express* lasted three years, from 1998 to 2001. Boycott has been married twice, firstly to journalist David Leitch, who died in 2004, and then to Charles Howard. She has one daughter.

Rosie Boycott has made her battle with the bottle very public and, in common with many ex-editors, has had a complete change of direction since leaving the *Daily Express*. She established an organic farm and promotes this highly, with books, television and radio broadcasts and appearances at literary festivals, where she has become a huge draw.

Other female editors of tabloid Sunday newspapers have included Bridget Rowe (*Sunday People* and *Sunday Mirror*, early 1990s), Tessa Hilton (*Sunday Mirror*, 1996 to 1999) Sue Douglas (*Sunday Express*, 1996;) Amanda Platell, acting editor, *Sunday Mirror*, 1996; acting editor, *Sunday Express*, 1998) and Tina Weaver (*Sunday Mirror*, from 2001.)

Hilton and Douglas have both enjoyed long lasting and varied careers in journalism and their editorships seemed but a blip in their high profile but rapidly-changing executive roles. After their brief editorships ended, both went into the less frenetic worlds of magazines, Hilton as editor-at-large on *Woman and Home* and Douglas to a top job at *Conde Nast*. Both have made lasting marriages, Hilton to fellow journalist Graham Ball and Douglas to celebrity historian Niall Ferguson, and both have three children. In 2007, Douglas had another career change and became chief executive of a leading literary agency.

Amanda Platell, originally from Australia, has remained single, living with her cat Jim, and since arriving in the UK has had a highly visible career in journalism and television. After her brief stints as an editor ended, Platell returned to journalism and writes Glenda Slagg-type columns, mainly for the *Daily Mail*, where she can, it seems, turn out an instant and highly readable opinion on just about anything.

Platell's career began in 1978 as a junior reporter on the *Perth Daily News* and she stepped off the plane to conquer London in 1985. She started by freelancing for *The Observer* and *Sunday Express*, and then became deputy editor of the new newspaper *Today* in 1987. In 1993 she was appointed managing editor of the Mirror Group but after a very short time moved to *The Independent* as marketing director and managing director. Her two stints as acting editor were interspersed by her appointment as William Hague's head of communications when he was fighting for the Tory leadership. Her Morgan and Platell political chat show, with Piers Morgan, began on Channel 4 in 2004.

Tina Weaver, at the time of writing the longest-lasting female newspaper editor in the business, was appointed editor of the *Sunday Mirror* in 2001. Weaver has come from a tabloid background, working her way up gradually since joining the *Sunday People* as a reporter.

Female editors of broadsheet (or so-called quality) papers, often last an even shorter time than their sisters on tabloids. Sarah Sands was appointed the first female editor of the *Sunday Telegraph* with great fanfare in June 2005 but was sacked just eight months later.

Sands, sister of musician and television scriptwriter Kit Hesketh-Harvey (The Vicar of Dibley is among his successes) started her journalism career as a junior reporter on the *Sevenoaks Courier*. She moved to the *Evening Standard* as editor of Londoner's Diary where she became successively features editor and assistant editor. She joined the *Daily Telegraph* as deputy editor under Charles Moore, with responsibility for the Saturday section.

A 'deeply talented career journalist who has got to the top through long hours and hard graft' according to media commentator Jane

Thynne, she wanted to 'feminise' the *Sunday Telegraph* but this approach did not go down well with either the core readership of the paper or the exclusively male executives above her.

Nor did it appreciably attract more female readers. Sands was appointed, as indeed are all editors, to try and stem the paper's declining circulation. It was thought that she might be able to feminise and 'sex up' this crusty old title, and when appointed, she said the wanted the paper to be 'like an i-Pod, full of your favourite things'.

After she was sacked, she complained that her plans for modernising the paper were 'strangled at birth' because they did not appeal to men such as Andrew Neil, chief executive of Press Holdings, the company owned by the Barclay Brothers. The brothers had acquired the *Telegraph* titles after previous owner Conrad Black was accused of embezzling funds.

Andrew Neil claimed that Sands had to be removed before she completely destroyed the *Telegraph* franchise, and he claimed she was concentrating on daft hug-a-tree features rather than proper, serious content. This accusation was hotly denied by Sands, who argued that she had spent 11 years at the *Telegraph* building up the franchise, and had largely succeeded.

Her contract was abruptly terminated after she refused to take orders from Fleet Street veteran John Bryant, appointed editor-in-chief over her head by the *Telegraph* chief executive, Murdoch McLennan.

Neil said later in an interview that it had been a mistake to hire Sands as editor and the only thing to do was to 'draw a line' under that mistake as soon as possible. In the spat between Sands and Neil that followed her dismissal, Sands argued that circulation had increased under her editorship and that her hug-a-tree features were in fact 'beautifully written examinations of the human condition.'

She admitted that the introduction of a new magazine, *Seven,* might have upset readers in their 80s and 90s, and added: 'I am sure that the low opinion held of me by Piers Morgan (a former editor of the *Daily Mirror* and later a media celebrity) and Andrew Neil has nothing to do with the fact that I have made fun of both of them in print – the only unpardonable sin in journalism.'

After being ousted from the *Sunday Telegraph* editorship, Sands became a consultant editor with the *Daily Mail* and a columnist in the *Independent on Sunday*. In 2008 she was appointed editor-in-chief of the UK edition of *Readers Digest*. She was first married to the actor Julian Sands and subsequently to journalist Kim Fletcher, and has three children, one with Sands and two with Fletcher.

After Sarah Sands another woman, Patience Wheatcroft, was appointed editor of the Sunday paper but again she did not last long and was out less than a year later. Wheatcroft came from a serious business journalism background, which probably appealed to the new owners but her appointment did not manage to halt the inexorable slide in circulation, the overriding challenge for any editor.

Patience Wheatcroft was born in 1951 and gained an LLB degree at Birmingham University, though she never practised as a lawyer. Instead, she started to specialise in city and business journalism, where she had a rapid rise, becoming deputy city editor of *The Times* in 1984, assistant city editor of the *Daily Mail* in 1986 and editor of *Retail Week* from 1988 to 1993.

She then went to the *Mail on Sunday* as deputy city editor and in 1997 became business and city editor of *The Times*, where she stayed for nine years.

The ubiquitous Janet Street-Porter, satirized as Janna Stray-Pawer for her Cockney-ish accent, became editor of the *Independent on Sunday* in 1999, but by the following year she had been replaced by a man, being honoured instead with the title, editor-at-large. This sounds grand enough but in effect meant she was to write a weekly 'Glenda Slagg' type column. Janet Street-Porter's brief editorship of the *Independent on Sunday* called forth the memorable comment from former *Sun* editor Kelvin Mackenzie that 'she couldn't edit a bus ticket.' Roy Greenslade has said that despite the fact that Street-Porter was hired for her outrageousness, the *Sindy* actually became more traditional under her editorship.

Born Janet Bull and brought up in a working-class home in Fulham, Street-Porter has held many jobs in newspapers and television, appeared in *I'm a Celebrity, Get me Out of Here*, and published two books of autobiography. Not known for her ladylike language, she exhibits a kind of brash confidence and certainty which gets her noticed – and appointed to senior jobs. She has been married four times, firstly to photographer Tim Street-Porter, secondly to publisher Tony Elliott, thirdly to film producer Frank Cvitanovitch and fourthly to somebody not in the public eye. None of her marriages or subsequent partnerships has produced issue.

At the time of writing, there are three female editors of daily newspapers remaining: Rebekah Wade at *The Sun*, Veronica Wadley at the *Evening Standard* and Dawn Neesom at the *Daily Star*. Each has held onto their job for a respectable length of time, Neesom since 2004, Wade since 2003 and Wadley since 2002.

Dawn Neesom initially made a success of the *Daily Star*, part of the Express Group, by taking it as far downmarket as it was possible to go and still be called a newspaper. She is entirely unrepentant about this as *The Star* bucked the general downward trend of newspaper circulations and actually increased as she took over. When Richard Desmond acquired the Express Group, the *Daily Star*'s circulation was just over 600,000; Neesom took it, for a time, to nudging a million.

Neesom started her career on the *Newham Recorder* and worked first for *Woman's Own* and then *The Sun*, arriving at the *Star* in 1997, where she has been ever since. Her newspaper philosophy was simple: give the readers what they want. And what they want, or at least what readers of *The Star* want, is fun, froth, celebrities and big tits.

But... they can probably get plenty of that in other publications. Where Neesom and *The Star* really scored was in decrying the government's policy over asylum seekers.

The Star's message which, put simply, comes down to: send 'em back where they came from, appealed so much to 'white van man' that he kept coming back for more. It worked for a while.

Neesom's explanation for putting on circulation when its main rivals, the *Mirror* and the *Sun*, were still losing was: 'Don't bore the readers. We have a light and frothy diet of celebrity and fun and we cover the big stories too but I'm not going to bore readers. That's where the *Sun* and *Mirror* go wrong.

'One day you'll get a picture of a baby in Africa covered in flies and the next, a picture of Beyonce in a glittering frock.'

Well – even *The Guardian* nowadays might do that.

Over at *The Sun*, Rebekah Wade, the youngest of the female editors, has been in charge since 2003. Wade was born in 1968 and educated at Appleton Hall, Cheshire and the Sorbonne. She first showed her mettle when she started to do undercover work for *The Sun* and soon progressed through the ranks to become deputy editor of the paper in 1998, at the age of 30.

Four years later she became the first female editor of the paper after being the third woman to edit the Sun's sister paper *News of the World* from 2000 to 2003. Wade has had a particularly high profile as editor, partly because of her flaming red hair and partly owing to her headline-producing marriage to soap actor Ross Kemp. Their private domestic life made headlines too, when Wade allegedly attacked Kemp who, as soap-watchers know, played a particularly hard, nasty character in *Eastenders*. The marriage later ended in divorce.

Wade was also one of the founder members of the campaigning organisation Women in Journalism.

Veronica Wadley, born in 1952, was educated at the expensive private schools Francis Holland and Benenden. Her first job in journalism was with the Conde Nast organisation and in 1978 she joined the *Telegraph Magazine*. She was successively features editor of the *Mail on Sunday* and the *Daily Telegraph*, and in 1989 became assistant editor of the *Daily Mail*, rising eventually to the position of deputy editor.

She is married to the author Tom Bower, as his second wife, and they have two adult children.

So, briefly, these are the pioneer female editors of Fleet Street. They are all very different people, with very different backgrounds – and foregrounds, come to that.

What, collectively, have they achieved and have they blazed a trail for future women at the top? In the first instance, they have demonstrated that it is perfectly possible for a woman to edit a national title, whether this is a daily, Sunday, tabloid or quality paper.

Although some of the women have only lasted a few months in the editor's chair, others have kept going for years and have continued to change and improve the titles they are responsible for. And these days, many men as well have lasted only a short time before being rudely tipped out of the chair and into the street, so gender is not a factor in editorship longevity, or lack of it.

There have been female editors of national newspapers now for more than 20 years and it no longer seems strange, or a token gesture. The question as to whether women have added anything particularly womanly to the titles they have edited is a more difficult question to answer as, mostly, the women concerned have been out and out professionals who could just as well edit the *Boilermakers' News* as a fashion or style magazine.

The secret lies in being able to take responsibility, being able to take the buck and to manage a large staff of disparate people; also, being able to make dozens of lightning decisions in a single day in the knowledge that not all will, with hindsight, be the correct ones.

The greatest newspaper editors, male or female, are those people who know, by sheer gut instinct, what will appeal to their existing readers and, with any luck, attract more.

Being a successful female editor is not just a simple matter of adding more 'feminine' content to newspapers, such as columns about bringing up baby or how to get this summer's look. Editors, above all, have to know what makes a great story and although this is a learned skill to some extent, it is the extra factor that makes a newspaper or, indeed, any publication, irresistible reading.

There has to be an innate understanding of politics and what are the most pressing issues of the day, and at least a smattering of affinity with business and financial affairs but most of all, the best editors are talent-spotters. The former *Daily Express* editor Arthur Christiansen possessed this ability as did *Sunday Express* editor John Junor. The late *Daily Mail* editor David English also recognised and rewarded up and coming talent. The finest editors are those who will put their talented writers and reporters in the foreground and be content themselves to operate behind the scenes.

Very high profile editors such as Piers Morgan are fun, but those editors who put themselves forward at the expense of their newspapers or their staff, are unlikely to last long.

One important area of newspapers to which few women editors are attuned is that of sports coverage. Many men buy newspapers for sport, more than anything else, and stand-alone sports sections are probably greater circulation-grabbers than any amount of lifestyle, tree-hugging or celebrity features. The *Telegraph* titles have always been known particularly for their sport and tabloid titles such as *The People*, have always sold – and still do – on the sports coverage.

Sensible non-sports minded editors, whether male or female, just leave the sports sections to highly competent sports editors, but it may be that all too many women editors have simply failed to see the importance of the sports content when redesigning or revamping a tired title.

Some commentators believe that in spite of the ever-increasing infiltration of women into top jobs, newspapers retain an overwhelmingly masculine image and one reason for this is the long hours, punishing deadlines and intense pressure of the job.

The *Financial Times,* where Sheila Black pioneered a softer touch back in the 1960s, has a woman, Marjorie Scardino, as chief executive of its parent company Pearson, but in 2008 only 17% of executive positions – none of these at the top rank – were held by women. The *FT* once brought in job-share schemes to encourage more women, but these did not seem to work as the schemes did not last long.

One reason for the continuing paucity of women at the top in newspapers, believes media commentator Peter Wilby, is that many companies, including newspapers, pick out senior executive potential between the ages of 28 and 35, the very ages when most women are either starting their families or looking after young children. Another reason, he says, is that most editors come from the newsroom and the backbench, and these positions are still overwhelmingly held by men. Women, he states, tend to find a news environment hostile and opt to write for lifestyle sections or contribute features from home on 'soft' subjects which do not need them to go out on the road or be in an office.

Wilby believes that in future women will be squeezed out even more from top jobs as staffing levels keep being inexorably cut and the most highly-prized journalists are those who never seem to go off duty but who are available to be sent on stories at any hour of the day or night. A part-time worker or job-sharer is, by definition, less committed than somebody who is not only in the office full time but who can also socialise or go out on stories after hours.

There is of course some truth in this but female editors and executives have historically rarely taken much time off to have their families. Eve Pollard, Tessa Hilton, Sue Douglas, Wendy Henry, Veronica Wadley, Patsy Chapman, Sarah Sands, Patience Wheatcroft and Rosie Boycott have all had children while hardly missing a beat in their big careers.

The fact that some of their editorships ended after a short time was nothing to do with 'juggling' but because circulations did not rise to the expected levels, there was a change in ownership, or a situation where nobody knew what they wanted and a change of editor seemed the easiest way of attempting to solve the problem.

Some female editors such as Rebekah Wade, Janet Street-Porter and Dawn Neesom have decided not to have children but the correlation that Wilby refers to, whereby significant promotions are being made when the women are away having babies, is simply not there.

In the past some proprietors, such as Maxwell, may have appointed women as editors simply for the look of the thing, to be seen as a champion of the fairer sex, but in general newspapers are too tough and competitive a game to risk appointing a woman just for novelty value. And don't forget that most of Maxwell's male editors didn't last long, either.

At least it no longer looks odd or eccentric to have a woman as a newspaper editor and it seems extremely likely that female editors will increase and multiply, however derided by the male media commentariat.

In the 1970s, Felicity Green made newspaper history as the first woman to be appointed to the Board of Mirror Group News. The company, now known as Trinity Mirror, has a blonde woman chief executive, Sylvia (Sly) Bailey, and although nobody regards Bailey in any way as 'token', it is noticeable that her picture appears more often on city and business pages than that of a male CEO probably would.

Sylvia Grice, the daughter of a freelance financial journalist and a housewife, was born in 1962 in Dulwich. She attended St Saviour's and St Clare's, a Church of England Girls' Grammar School in Tower Bridge and left at 16 with six O levels. Her first jobs were working in shops and temping, then she replied to an ad to sell advertising space on *The Guardian* – and discovered what she wanted to do. She became an advertising manager, stayed three years and then went to the newly-launched *Independent*. From there she went to IPC, joining the board in 1994 at the age of 31. She became chief executive after IPC broke away from its parent company, Reed Elsevier, where she presided over the closure of six old-established titles and the loss of 200 jobs.

These ruthless decisions were highly profitable, and AOL Time Warner took over the company. Grice – now known as Sly Bailey after marrying businessman Peter Bailey – became a bit-player in a giant global company, so when the chance came to run Trinity Mirror in 2003, she took it.

Since her time at Trinity Mirror, its three national titles, the *Daily Mirror, Sunday Mirror* and *Sunday People* have suffered serious circulation losses, with *The People* suffering most. Some critics of Trinity Mirror maintain that the problem lies not so much with Bailey as with the fact that the company's main interest is in cheap giveaways and ultra-local papers full of ads, rather than with national newspapers trading in exclusives and big stories.

Although Bailey has worked in print media for most of her life, she has never been a journalist and in fact, when working at *The Independent*, she became impatient at the management's championing of serious journalism rather than concentrating on making money from selling advertising space.

In 2008, Bailey collected a personal bonus of just under £800,000.

Eight

Working Girls

When the evening newspaper on which she was working folded beneath her, Maggie Hall wrote a job application to Bill Freeman, northern news editor of the *Daily Mirror*. It said simply:

Dear Mr Freeman,
Help. Help. Help.
Yours sincerely,
Maggie Hall, *Yorkshire Evening News*

Bill Freeman said later: 'I could hardly refuse to invite her for an interview. When I met her I decided that she deserved a job.'

She had started work as a reporter on the *Dewsbury Chronicle* in 1959. She now says: 'I loved my newspaper career and can't imagine, to this day, why anyone would want to do anything else! Also, I must stress that I never allowed the 'guys only' mantra to get to me. It just made me more determined to get stuck in and if I'm to be perfectly honest, I loved being one of the few women in an otherwise male cast of hundreds.'

Hall decided she wanted to be a journalist after O levels, even though the headmaster of her school was horrified. 'Girls don't do that!' he told her. And that was the end of any help she had from school. Her father made some enquiries, and learnt from a journalist on the local *Spenborough Guardian* that the best thing was to learn shorthand and typing, after which she could apply for a job. A year later, armed with her new qualifications, she shot back to the local paper, only to be told: 'Sorry, but we've already got a girl.'

She got a temporary job at Marks and Spencer, then went for an interview at the *Dewsbury Reporter*, only to be told there was no job available. But the editor remarked on her green hair, and said he wanted to write about a young woman who turned up at an interview with her hair in camouflage colours. He explained that the women's editor was away that week and he was holding the fort. Hall says: 'I replied that if my hair was going to be written about in the paper then I should be allowed to write the story.

'The editor went away to consult with the accountant and reappeared to tell me I would only get £2.5s if I was to work at the paper. I had been getting £7 a week at Marks and Spencer but I didn't hesitate and started the very next day, although I had to change my name as there was already a reporter called Margaret. So I became Maggie, which I have been ever since, even though my father hated the abbreviation.

'My very first byline read: *By a Staffman*. It never occurred to me to get upset. I was just so delighted to be in and yes, to be one of the boys.'

As Hall progressed, she was supposed to cover monthly Rotary Club speakers but women were not allowed to have lunch with the Rotarians. She declared that she would not cover the speaker without having the lunch first, and an agreement was worked out whereby she would be allowed to have lunch with the men but had to move round the table sitting next to different members, so that (presumably) none of the chaps would have to go home and tell their wives they had lunch once a month with a 19-year old girl.

In 1961 she landed her second job, with the *Lynn News and Advertiser*, Kings Lynn, because she had court experience – and many men who would otherwise have been given the job were away doing national service.

As well as court work, she also covered a male-only area, that of going to the Corn Exchange on market days to get the sale prices. After two years she felt it was time to move on and applied for a job on the *York Evening Press* only to be told: 'If we'd wanted a woman we'd have advertised for one.' At the next job she applied for, the London office of the *Argus* group of Cape Town, she was told there was no point in her being interviewed as they could not hire her as a woman and therefore pay her passage out to South Africa.

So she joined the *Yorkshire Evening News* in Doncaster, again as the only woman. In 1963, Hall landed a job at the *Daily Mirror* where she soon ran into a crowd of veterans on a pub crawl. One of the 'vets' came up to her and said: 'Now my dear, who did you sleep with to get this job?' She threw her Scotch in his face and he was not amused. 'After that I never had to put up with any such nonsense,' she says.

At the *Mirror*, she kept coming up against restrictions on women reporters. 'The 3 to 10 shift was the latest we were allowed to work; women were never allowed anywhere near the newsdesk, anything approaching a war zone was off limits, as was anything to do with sport. I wanted to get to New York but was repeatedly told: stop thinking about it as you will never get to New York. We can't possibly send a woman there.'

It was after being excluded from reporting on the World Cup Rally, organised by the *Mirror*, that Hall exploded. She was told she would never get a rally assignment, not even to check the progress of the drivers as they drove off the ferry in Calais, but as some kind of compensation was told she could work on the news desk for three weeks. Before that, she was not even allowed, as a woman, to answer the news desk phone.

'It wasn't so much that I was burning with ambition to work on the desk,' Maggie says, 'but because I wanted to find out how that mysterious part of the office, which pretty much ruled my life, worked. After three weeks, I was asked to be on the newsdesk permanently and felt that if I said no, the desk would be off limits to women for ever. So I said yes, and was the first woman on the *Mirror* desk, although not quite the first woman to sit on any newsdesk. That was Jean Stead, of *The Guardian*, I believe, who later became news editor.'

The Press Club was also at that time a men-only institution. The first woman member was the Queen Mother and Hall became female member number two, although it was not full membership as she was banned from the snooker room. Hall soon realised that membership had been opened up to women only to raise revenue – in much the same way that women were 'allowed' to join golf clubs, although not on the same terms as men – and Hall made such a fuss that she was banned from the Press Club for life.

It was also made clear to her that she would never progress upwards from the newsdesk or ever be made news editor, 'being a woman and all that...'

She wanted to report on Northern Ireland, which she had covered for the *Mirror* in Manchester but when the troubles broke out, was informed that the *Mirror's* insurance didn't cover women in war zones. The *Mirror* later had a change of heart and Hall did go to Northern Ireland several times until 1979 when she finally got her longed-for posting to the United States where she has lived ever since.

For years she had been fobbed off, with the bureau chief telling her that New York was much too dangerous for a woman and that it was so unsafe men had to go for a pee together…

Maybe the executive at the *Mirror* did not know, or had forgotten, that Audrey Whiting had been a New York correspondent in 1952, although her appointment had lasted only for a year. But a precedent had been set.

Maggie recalls: 'After I finally got my way the last 'men-only' section of the paper opened up to me: that of sport, where my first assignment was to cover a football game between Manchester United and the New York Cosmos. After I filed my story I was urgently bleeped by the sports desk who said: 'Maggie, we know you're over the moon about reporting a soccer match, but we need to know the score…'

Hall left the *Mirror* in 1983 but stayed in the US to freelance, and she retired in 2001.

Clare Dover was science correspondent of the *Daily Telegraph* for 13 years and science and medical correspondent of the *Daily Express* for 17 years. But she never set out to be a journalist at all. Born in 1938, she went to Ulverston Grammar School in the Lake District, then Liverpool University to read Chemistry.

'I think I first realised I was in a man's world when I went to university,' she says, 'as there were hardly any girls reading chemistry but at our co-ed grammar school the girls were encouraged to be independent and so I never thought I was in any way an odd one out.

'After graduating in 1959 I taught for three years, first in a girls' grammar school in Liverpool and then in horrible blackboard-jungle schools in London. I was supply teaching in some really terrible places wondering how long I could stand it when I saw an ad in the *Times Educational Supplement* for a science writer for a new magazine.

'I applied for the job, went for an interview and three days later got the job of assistant editor for *Understanding Science*, one of the first part-works to be published. I knew nothing whatever about magazines, couldn't type and it was a true baptism of fire, especially when the editor became ill and I had to stand in. This magazine company, weirdly, also published Enid Blyton's Noddy books and started up a pirate radio station.

'After three years I started looking for another job and saw an ad in the *Daily Telegraph* for a science journalist. I applied, along with 140 other applicants and thought no more of it until I got a letter calling me for interview. At the interview I had to write a quick piece in *Telegraph* style and by the time I got home there was a telegram offering me the job. This was 1965.

'I had to go and see the managing editor, a Mr Pauley, who was truly horrified at getting a female dumped on him and he told me I would be on a month's trial and after that if they didn't like me I would get the sack. I told him I had been offered a far better paying job – which I had, with a PR company – and it seemed aggression paid off.

'He said, well you seem to think you can do the job and so I was taken on as science correspondent. Every night a different sub would come in with a query, and I wondered how I could write stories without getting all these queries all the time. Then I discovered why all these subs had queries – they were coming to look at this young dolly bird writing about science. They didn't believe women could actually write about science. Writing about science, they thought, was strictly a man's job.

'Apart from the women's page writers, there were just two other women journalists on the *Telegraph* at the time. I stayed there for 13 years and I was getting a fraction of the wages the men were getting. When I left, they had just taken on a chap as number three in education, and he was getting far more than me as number one in science.

'The owners of the *Telegraph* at the time took the attitude that a woman could work for pin money, whereas a man was entitled to a proper wage. When I went to the *Daily Express*, I got the proper rate and it didn't matter whether you were male or female.

'I absolutely loved my job at the *Express* and would have stayed longer but I was booted out after 17 years as part of a cost-cutting exercise by the editor, Nick Lloyd. I am sure it was because my name began with D and they were sacking people in alphabetical order. In the event, they got through five different people before a proper science correspondent was appointed. Obviously, they had to have one – it's an essential job on a newspaper.'

Does she think women bring anything special to science and medical writing? 'Women like reading about health and women journalists like writing about health, so I suppose it was always going to become a popular female area. Women have made health and medical writing their own but I would not like to see it as an exclusively female area.

'Most of the actual science correspondents are still men, but health is very definitely female-dominated these days and all newspapers have greatly expanded their health coverage.'

The old Fleet Street, says Clare Dover, was a wonderful place which has no absolutely equivalent in today's national newspaper offices. 'You couldn't walk down the Street without bumping into a friend or colleague. There was something very special about Fleet Street and although the days were long, we had wonderful long boozy lunches. Nowadays everybody eats sandwiches at their desks, nobody ever goes out for lunch or meets anybody and all the newspapers cover exactly the same stories.

'It seems to me that modern newspaper offices have all the charm of an electricity board call centre. They are just word factories now.

'The atmosphere has gone and it was all to do with greed. I am totally in favour of computers as they have put an end to the endless typing and retyping we had to do to get a clean-ish copy, but greed meant that all the proprietors moved out to vastly cheaper places as the City wanted to expand, and the obvious place for it to expand was into Fleet Street. To think we were flung out to make way for merchant banks!

'Both of my old newspaper offices are now banks, all the lovely pubs have gone and all the greasy spoon cafes have been Starbucked. I am also against all these media studies courses as there just aren't the jobs for the kids when they graduate and the rates are going down all the time. Since newspapers moved out of the Street, the unions have not protected their members one little bit.'

Since being unceremoniously fired from the *Daily Express,* Clare Dover has been freelancing, specialising in science and medical subjects.

Another female journalist who managed to secure a posting in a New York office was Anthea Disney, for the *Daily Mail*, in 1974.

Here is what fellow journalist Tony Delano wrote about Disney in his book *Slip-Up:*

A lot of women have done well in Fleet Street. But only, until very recently, in specialised jobs such as columnists and editors of women's pages. They were never encouraged to work on the tactically powerful night staffs of the national papers. And when they were reporters considerate news editors tended to 'spare' them the big stories which, almost by definition, were gory, ghastly, lubricious or rough-and-tumble. They often found themselves looking after a protagonist's nonparticipating wife or being sent along to barter off sex appeal for entrée. Only a very very few ever got to be foreign correspondents.

But Anthea Disney had managed to build most of the roles she had played in her ten ferociously ambitious years of reporting into star parts. And by the time the phone rang to despatch her to Rio she could almost have made it on the power of pure umbrage. Who needs Pan Am?

Later, Disney rocketed into the media stratosphere as an editorial trouble-shooter in the Rupert Murdoch organisation and in 2008 was News Corporation's executive vice president for content.

Disney became world-famous as a journalist when she took a drug to darken her skin and pose as a young Indian woman facing racial prejudice in the Britain of the early 1970s.

Born in 1944, she attended a girls' boarding school and wanted to be a journalist from the age of 12. 'I have no idea where this desire came from as there were no journalists in my family but I had this mental picture of Rosalind Russell as a journalist in the film *His Girl Friday*, and it seemed such an exciting life. I suppose my mother must have taken me to see the film, the image stuck, and grew as I got older.

'It seemed that as a journalist you could ask anybody anything and have permission to be as rude as you like. I always knew from an early age that I wanted to be independent, have a big career, earn my own money and not marry a lawyer or a doctor and just be a wife and mother.'

Disney dropped out of university and got a temporary job as a shop assistant at the department store Swan and Edgar, now Tower Records. 'While working there I met a film producer who wanted somebody to translate a script from French into English. As I spoke reasonable French I did it, and made enough money to pay my rent for six months.

'I then banged on every door in Fleet Street but everybody told me to go away as they didn't take girls. Eventually I got accepted onto the IPC training scheme at *Woman's Own* as I didn't want to go onto a provincial training scheme. The executives I saw when going round Fleet Street told me I would get nowhere without a union card but going to the provinces was not what I had in mind.

'I thought that if I worked for a magazine I could then translate that into working on a national newspaper. I saw it as a way in, which is what happened.'

After Disney finished her indentures she went banging on doors in Fleet Street again and this time, in 1968, one door opened. 'I was taken on to the *Daily Sketch* diary for holiday relief for three weeks but in the event was offered a permanent job and became a diary reporter.

'I noticed that the feature writers all left at six o'clock so I used to hang around on the off-chance I would be offered a feature to write. *The Sketch* closed in 1971 and I became a feature writer on the *Daily Mail*, with David English as editor.'

Disney's big break came in 1972 when David English gave her a book to read called *Black Like Me*. It was the story of a white American man trying to expose what it was like to be black, and he took a drug that changed the colour of his skin. 'I read this book, figured out what David English was thinking and asked him if he wanted me to have a go at a UK version of the story.

'At the time,' says Disney, 'there was huge prejudice against Indians who were, it seemed, storming the UK and taking jobs away from British people. I was terrified and excited in equal measure at the prospect of doing this job, and had to do a lot of research.

'I first spoke to an Indian friend, the writer Dom Moraes, who told me that no young Hindu woman would ever live alone, so I would have to be a Christian, from the South of India. He helped me to invent a background so as to be authentic. I took voice lessons to learn to speak like an Indian woman, and also had to alter my body language to be more submissive, and cast my eyes down when talking. I then went to Puerto Rico to meet the doctor who had developed the skin-darkening drug.

'It was used to treat a condition where the skin goes blotchy, and I was told it could cause liver damage so this doctor who had invented the drug had to monitor my liver. In order to make my skin dark enough I had to lie naked on the roof of the clinic in 100-degree heat. The drug did start to work although it took some time until it went dark enough for me to pass as an Indian woman. I was lucky that my hair was long and dark already, but I had my hair and eyebrows dyed even darker to get that blue-black look of Indian hair.

'I had to change the soap and shampoo I used, everything, really as my usual cosmetics and toiletries were all wrong for the culture. Then I had to learn how to put on a sari and wear kurta pyjamas, both of which were unusual dress at the time. Even then I was an oddity for the time, a young Indian woman on my own.'

She went to Birmingham where there was already a large Indian population, and secured digs with an Indian family. 'I first got a job in a factory putting door handles on cars and later in a shop as an assistant in a department store.

'I kept up this persona for a month and did encounter dreadful prejudice. People used to move away from me on buses, avoid me in the street and I had a very bad experience when skinheads tried to attack me. Mostly, though, white British people just tried to pretend I wasn't there and I had the strange experience of being completely invisible. When I asked for directions, people simply wouldn't answer me or made out they couldn't understand me.

'I was living in a ghetto with recent immigrants, and found people just looked at me as if I was from another planet.

'But after a month the colour was starting to fade and I was no longer looking so authentic so I had to wrap the story up. It made a fantastic series and really exposed colour prejudice in Britain at the time. The colour took

124

a year to fade completely and I had horrible blotches on my skin as it didn't fade evenly. I went through a time of being bright yellow but I'm glad to say there were no lasting ill effects. And after the story, any Indian restaurant I went into would gladly give me a free meal, as they were so thrilled with the story.'

After the success of this story, Disney went to New York as the *Daily Mail's* first woman in the bureau, came back for a brief stint as features editor, then returned to the US in 1977 as head of the New York bureau.

She has worked in America ever since, later freelancing for the *Daily Express* and the *Observer* magazine where her reports on America hit a big chord with readers. 'It was a wonderful time to write on American culture, but I wanted to move into American journalism. Also, after being in the US for a few years I had lost touch with what was wanted on British newspapers and felt I could no longer tell what a good story was.'

In the event, Disney has enjoyed a big career in America, first working as editor of the *Sunday Daily News*, then editing magazines and finally in executive positions for Rupert Murdoch. She joined his News Corp in 1990, became president and CEO of HarperCollins publishers and later executive vice-president of content for the News Corporation.

What does she think are the main differences between British and American journalism? 'In America, it's more fact-based, and there's less wrapping stories round with verbiage. Also, you can never recycle quotes on American publications; everything has to come up fresh and new all the time.

'In America, the reporting is more important than the individual voice of the reporter, although personalities are now starting to become important.'

So far as women journalists go, Anthea Disney believes that since the demise of Fleet Street in 1986, nobody even notices whether you are male or female. 'I've worked in print, books, the internet and have been on the business side since the mid-1990s, and if you look around, nobody even thinks of you as a woman any more, or treats you any differently. That is the biggest change.

'I was almost impossible for a woman to get in the old Fleet Street. We knew it was going to be a mighty struggle and in truth, the struggle was half the fun. The specialness went when the papers decamped all over the place and now, Fleet Street is such a sad, empty street to go down. It's too depressing for words, all banks and coffee shops. There is no atmosphere at all.'

Long ago, Disney took a decision not to have children and has never regretted it. 'I didn't feel I could do my job in the way I wanted to with children, and I definitely wanted to give the job my undivided focus. She married fellow journalist Peter Howe in the 1970s.

Rita Marshall was the first woman to become home news editor of *The Times*, in its particularly masculine days. She was born in 1934, and had an early introduction to Fleet Street as her father was one of the uniformed doormen at the *Daily Express* building, known as the Black Lubyanka. She grew up in Lambeth and was educated at the Greycoat and City of London Schools. She took a course in shorthand and typing and then started as a reporter at the *Stratford Express* in 1954.

Her next job was at her father's paper, the *Daily Express*, where she ran the *Junior Express* as practically its only staff member. In 1956 she went to the *Daily Express* as a feature writer and reporter. Eleven years later she moved to *The Times* at a time when the paper was trying to become more 'popular' and starting to come down from its former great patrician height as an upper class publication. Marshall was brought in as one of a fresh new team to liven up the often deadly news coverage, and soon learnt that the only real difference between the tabloids and the broadsheets in those days was that you had to put semicolons instead of commas, and have two sentences to a paragraph instead of only one.

Longer sentences were also permitted, but Marshall always maintained that the skills were identical and it was only a few niceties of grammar and punctuation that made the difference. She was appointed news editor in 1974 and considerably livened up the news content of the paper to include human interest stories as well as politics and foreign affairs.

She did insist, though, that all reporters came into the office in formal clothes in case they had to be sent to Buckingham Palace or Downing Street at short notice. Marshall liked her reporters to get out on stories and not sit around the office all day long.

It was when Marshall was working as home news editor that she met her life partner, science correspondent Pearce Wright, who was then married to another. Although they tried their best to keep their affair secret, all the other reporters knew about it and would note the number of times Wright and Marshall would disappear into little private phone booths to talk to each other.

This was of course before the days of mobile phones, computers, emails or other technology which nowadays makes communication easier – or at least one assumes - when embarking on an office affair. Eventually Pearce Wright separated from his wife and after his divorce he and Marshall moved in together. The relationship lasted until Wright died in 2005, after which Marshall moved into Pickering House, the Journalists' Charity retirement home in Dorking, Surrey.

Rita Marshall's pioneering stint as news editor at *The Times* was not to last. When Charles Douglas-Home became home editor he sacked Marshall from the job and in 1976 she went to Special Reports – advertising supplements – as assistant editor, becoming deputy editor of the section in 1981. She died in February 2008, aged 73.

Philippa Kennedy was the *Daily Express* first female news editor, and also the first woman to hold that position on a tabloid newspaper. She had previously worked in the newsroom at *The Sun*.

Her introduction to journalism was via the manager of her father's one-man medical practice in Hollywood, County Down. This young lady later married journalist Vincent Mulchrone, star columnist of the *Daily Mail*, and left her job with Dr Kennedy to accompany her husband to England.

Every year the Mulchrones would return to Crookhaven in Co Down, and the young Philippa would be enthralled by Vincent's tales of his journalistic adventures: 'how he had been on the last helicopter out of Saigon, or hobnobbing in the Bahamas with the Queen – and I would think: I want a life like that. And indeed, when the time came, Vincent sat with me at the kitchen table at their home in West Byfleet and helped me write my application to the *Mirror* training scheme in Plymouth.

'I remember how one of his sentences, 'I intend and mean to be a journalist' was picked up by my interviewer, Geoff Harris, who remarked how determined I sounded.'

In Crookhaven Philippa Kennedy would meet the leading journalists of their day, 'the friends who made their way to Vincent's 'little piece of paradise' – Colin Reid, Ken Donlan, John Winnington-Ingram, Terry O'Conner, Rod Tyler and a single guest appearance from Max Hastings.'

Her Fleet Street career began with a lucky – or unlucky – accident. 'At the Crookhaven regatta one year, a young lad's boat started taking in water, there were no safety boats, and there was panic. 'Get in there and save him' yelled Louie, and I had just time to take off my gold watch before diving off the quayside into the harbour in my new black velvet jeans.

'The poor lad was furious at being saved by a girl, but when I emerged dripping wet Ken Donlan, then news editor of new *Sun* newspaper, came up to me and said: 'If they don't take you on at the *Mirror*, come and see me.'

'And when I did exactly that, Vincent was waiting in El Vino with a chilled bottle of Veuve Cliquot to celebrate. I lived in awe and not a little fear of Ken, one of the most consummate operators of all time and I don't say that lightly. It turned into deep friendship and respect and years later, when Nick Lloyd offered me the news editor's job at the *Daily Express*, my first instinct was to turn it down, thinking I'd never live up to Ken.

'When I confessed over lunch that I'd turned down 'the best job in Fleet Street' he gave me the bollocking of my life, so I rang back and asked Nick to ask me again.'

Kennedy worked at *The Sun* for nine years before joining the *Daily Express* as news editor and later worked as a columnist. She joined the journalists' trade paper *Press Gazette* as editor in 1998, and stayed at the helm for four years. She was appointed an OBE in 2003 for services to journalism.

After freelancing for a few years, Philippa Kennedy went with her husband John to Dubai in September 2003 where she joined former *Daily Telegraph* editor Martin Newland's new English language paper, *The National*, based in Abu Dhabi.

Shan Lancaster was deputy news editor at the *Sunday Telegraph*, and has been a news editor at both the *Sunday* and *Daily Express*. She spent 12 years as a reporter at the Sun, and was then a royal reporter at the *Daily Star*. She left the *Telegraph* in 2001 to freelance.

In the early days, often venerated as the glory days, of newspapers, crime correspondents were definitely the stars of the show. And they were all... men. The *People's* Duncan Webb became a celebrity in his own right and a household name in the 1950s, as he fearlessly exposed villains in the manner of an old-style Hollywood film star. He would talk out of the corner of his mouth and adopt a variety of disguises to nail the villains of the day, then write up his successes with a seriously big showing in the paper.

But for all his flamboyant persona, Webb was a serious investigative journalist who assiduously courted the police and villains in equal measure. Webb's most famous campaign – and one that has reverberated down the decades to find an important place in newspaper legend – was his exposure of the Maltese Messina brothers for running a vice ring in London.

In those days, the *People* was famous for its hard-hitting, fearless investigations and had its own special investigations department, run by Laurie Manifold, his assistant Alan Ridout and secretary Barbara Spiegel. It was into this department that the young Shan Davies, aged just 23, found her way.

Davies, born in 1953 in East Sheen, South-West London, had left school at 16 and trained on local and regional newspapers. She started stringing and freelancing for the *Sunday People*, doing investigations under Manifold's expert, paternalistic eye. Her first assignment was to expose a farm in Wales that bred dogs for vivisection and this involved getting a job as a kennel maid there.

The story involved taking secret pictures and Davies just managed to nail the story before her cover was blown. She then made her excuses and fled, having already sent off rolls of film before her camera was smashed. This assignment, which resulted in the Welsh farm being closed down, was a wholly successful enterprise, and Davies seemed just the kind of young woman reporter Manifold had been looking for. She was taken onto the staff in 1976, first as a general reporter and then as Fleet Street's first female crime correspondent.

She says: 'I was the only woman covering crime in those days. I found the whole thing frightening and I didn't really know what I was doing. Everybody else seemed very experienced and knowledgeable, and what made it worse was that none of the photographers wanted to go out with me. They thought it was somehow beneath them to go out on a big story with a young woman.

'One of my very first stories was to interview the world's most tattooed woman and I went with Stan Jaanus, one of our leading photographers. After we had interviewed the woman, who was actually the daughter of comedian Jimmy Jewell, Stan said: shall we go for a drink? Stan was a Real Ale specialist and had his little book of real ale pubs with him all the time. We went past 10 pubs until we found a real ale one, and six pints later, went back to the office.

'He said: this girl can beat all of you wimps. She has just drunk six pints of real ale. That changed everything and I was in. People have often asked me how I could do such dangerous stories such as pretending to be a prostitute, having Charlie Kray as my minder and locking up a murderer in my bathroom but I would have done anything, anything, to get on the staff of a national newspaper and once I was in, felt I had to prove myself.

'I put myself in danger many times but I had to get the story; that was the main thing. The only thing, really. I was on my own a lot which, looking back, I should not have been. One on occasion I had to track down a bloke who had murdered someone but got off on a technicality. He was known as the vice king of Kings Cross and I went into a pub I was told he frequented. I had already made contact, and said I was from the *People*. He wasn't in that pub but the landlady told me he was in another just down the road. She actually took me there and in this huge pub a man tapped me on the shoulder and asked: are you the lady from the *People*?

'He had enormous cauliflower ears, a sideways nose and looked very frightening. I said I was here to get his story and there would be a few bob in it for him. We were sitting opposite each other in the pub when suddenly I found myself on the floor. I had been hit over the head and briefly knocked unconscious by this bloke's girlfriend who expected me to be a male reporter, and who thought he was cheating on her.

'The landlord threw the girlfriend out and then I got into a cab with the murderer, wondering whatever I was going to do with him. I took him back to my flat, stuck him in the spare bedroom and kept him there. My parents rang to say they were going to be in a nearby pub with some relatives and would I like to join them. I said to Mum, the only thing is, I've got a murderer with me. Mum was completely unfazed and said: bring him along. I got him to shave and then took him to meet my parents.

'I said to him, if you utter one swear word, you won't get a penny from the *People*. Mum and Dad were strict Welsh chapel and didn't like any kind of swearing. Anyway, he behaved himself and I got the story.'

Shan Davies soon earned herself a reputation for being tough and agreeing to undertake the kind of stories most female reporters simply turned down. When she was sent to walk in the footsteps of Peter Sutcliffe, the Yorkshire Ripper, somebody in the office asked about 'protection' and the response was: 'No, the Ripper can look after himself.'

On another occasion, where Davies had to pretend to be a prostitute, she made a check call to the office and the news editor, David Farr, asked: 'Are you in any danger, pet?' She said 'Yes, I am' to which his reply was: 'OK, jolly good.'

Davies reckons it's essential to be somewhat flamboyant, a bit of an actress, to carry off undercover work. 'You have to be able to turn into somebody else successfully and without alerting suspicions. I found I could pass as a kennel maid, a prostitute, or a cleaner in an old people's home. At my wedding to actor Hugh Lloyd, the former *People* editor Geoff Pinnington said: And Shan is quite a little actress herself.

'I think the ability to be somebody else has to be inbuilt into you. A lot of journalists couldn't, or wouldn't, do this work and it was much more difficult in those days as there were no mobile phones, no faxes, no computers and you had to make a check call every hour or so from a phone box – all without alerting anybody's suspicions as to what you were doing.'

Shan Davies left the *People* on her marriage to Hugh Lloyd, 30 years her senior, to freelance. She recalled: 'The job was very stressful but all tremendous fun. I can't remember ever having so much fun and the main thing was that I kept telling myself: I'm here! I'm not a freelance! I'm in Fleet Street! It was all a dream come true.'

There have never been many female Fleet Street crime correspondents but other names include Sylvia Jones of the *Daily Mirror* and Fiona Macdonald Hull who did undercover work for the *News of the World* and was later a showbiz columnist at the *Sun*. Rebekah Wade, later editor of *The Sun* also began her career hiding in cupboards to get stories, but in general, the nerve-racking and potentially dangerous world of undercover work has never attracted large numbers of women journalists.

Jane Reed became editor of *Woman's Own* magazine in 1970, having worked her way up on magazines from junior secretarial positions.

Just 29 years old, she was not only the youngest-ever editor of a mass-selling weekly, but also the magazine's first female editor. The weekly then sold 1.75 million copies a week. She remained at the helm for a decade through the 1970s, after which she became the publisher for a group of glossy IPC monthlies. In December 1983 she was appointed to the main board of IPC magazines and two years later left IPC to help launch the new newspaper *Today*, firstly as managing editor in charge of features and later as overall managing editor.

After four years at *Today*, she became director of corporate affairs at News International, at their Wapping headquarters, a job she held for 11 years. She partly retired in 2000 but has since acted as a consultant to the same company as well as being on many leading media councils and committees.

She says: '*Today* was not a typical Fleet Street paper of the time as the launch editor Brian MacArthur wanted to hire 50% women: he believed this would change the culture of newspapers and also encourage more women to buy the paper. He wanted women on every desk, from sport to city.

'For me, coming from a magazine environment where it was not unusual to have women in senior management, I found the very masculine newspaper culture very alien indeed. We knew that the men on the paper felt uncomfortable having so many women around, either telling them what to do or working alongside them as equals. Senior editors would lord it at features meetings and conferences and seemed to regard us, the women, as handmaidens rather than equals. We were not invited to discuss subjects, just accept the diktats.

'One senior editor, a man, re-angled a feature we were doing on Greenham Common women, wanting to imply that they were all 'single parent lesbian feminists' in spite of the fact that they weren't and in any case, our youngish readers saw them as freedom fighters, fighting for an important cause.

'I also remember all the female staff on *Today* sitting sedately in front of their brand-new computers while the men sat with their feet on the desk with their keyboards on their laps. The difference was that women worked to their keyboards, whereas the men made their keyboards work for them. The boxes in which the computers arrived had a woman sitting at the computer and a man leaning over her shoulder, helping the poor technically illiterate girl to cope with this nasty big machine.

'However, before long the male staff, all of whom had been used to completely male-dominated offices, got used to having so many women around and the atmosphere at the paper was very happy, productive and positive.

'When I first went into top management, I found we had to fall in with the prevailing masculine culture so as not to make the other – male – incumbents feel threatened. At IPC, senior women made a difference because for the first time women were making decisions about women and we were reacting as consumers as well as managers. We knew that most decisions in the home were made by women and eventually the men realised we could add to the bottom line with instincts and personal experiences as well as professionalism.'

In her long career in the upper echelons of magazine and newspaper publishing, Jane Reed has seen things improve greatly for women, but feels there is still a long way to go. 'There are still far too few qualified women making it to the very top. Some women, such as Sylvia Auton of IPC, Sylvia (Sly) Bailey of Trinity Mirror, Marjorie Scardino at Pearsons and Carolyn McCall at the Guardian Media Trust have reached the top, but they have all come from the commercial side of publishing rather than editorial.

'In some ways, though, not much has changed for women. Forty years ago, half of all mothers felt guilty if they went out to work and the other half felt guilty because they didn't. That is pretty much the same today. It is also depressing that there are still significant pay disparities, and that women with families still lose out in terms of career advancement.'

Jane Reed never married nor had children. Her sister was also a talented journalist and for 15 years wrote a humorous column in

Woman's Own under the name Polly Graham – the proviso being that Jane Reed herself had nothing to do with the contracts, fees or the column's content.

Women journalists have long been famous, or notorious, for their heroic drinking (Sandy Fawkes and Ann Pacey, to name but two), but until Jancis Robinson arrived on the scene, few if any women had ever actually written about drinking for a living.

There had been a number of famous male wine writers, such as Hugh Johnson and the legendary Cyril Ray, but the whole subject of wine – choosing it, drinking it, keeping a cellar, writing about it – was considered to be something so ritually masculine that few women even dared voice an opinion on it. Then Jancis Robinson became the first Master of Wine outside the trade in 1984 and instantly famous as one of the first women to write knowledgeably about wine in the popular prints. So here was another previously all-male bastion successfully stormed.

Robinson was born in 1950 and read maths and philosophy at Oxford. She has written a wine column in the *Financial Times* for many years and first started writing about wine in 1975, for the trade paper *Wine and Spirit*. She edited the *Oxford Companion to Wine* and also took part in a 10-part series on wine on BBC2.

Since she invaded this previously men's territory, there have been other women wine writers in newspapers, such as Jane McQuitty of *The Times* and Victoria Moore of *The Independent on Sunday*.

Although one of the most famous early photographers was a woman, Julia Margaret Cameron, the vast majority of newspaper photographers have been male, with – until recently – only a mere handful of women holding down major Fleet Street positions.

Possibly the first female newspaper photographer of note was Jane Bown, born in 1925, and at the time of writing still going. Her arresting and individualistic work first started appearing in *The Observer* from 1949, and she has been photographing – mainly portraits of interviewees – for them ever since. Other upmarket female photographers have been Sally Soames at *The Sunday Times* and Sue Adler on *The Observer*. Both were busy on their papers in the 1980s and early 1990s.

But the first woman photographer to work on a tabloid paper, and hold down the position for very many years on an otherwise men-only picture desk, was Doreen Spooner of the *Daily Mirror*.

Born in 1928, Spooner came from a long line of newspapermen. Her father, Len Spooner, was successively art editor of the *Daily Herald*, editor of *Illustrated*, a popular weekly magazine of the 1950s and also briefly, editor of *Picture Post*. Spooner's uncle was picture editor at both the *Daily Express* and the *Daily Mail*, so Doreen grew up in a household where newspaper photography was being talked about all the time.

She says she was always fascinated by pioneer female photographers such as Julia Margaret Cameron and Margaret Bourke-White, and determined to be a photographer herself. So, after leaving school at 16, she attended a photographic school run by the London County Council in Bolt Court, just off Fleet Street, to do a City and Guilds course.

She says: 'My Dad had bought me my first camera when I was eight, and so from an early age I was photographing children and family members. After Bolt Court a family friend suggested I went to Sweden where I worked in a studio. While In Sweden I went to Lapland and took pictures of reindeer being rounded up. They turned out marvellously and I managed to sell them to the famous Keystone Picture Agency.

'After coming back from Sweden I was offered a job with Keystone at five guineas a week. This was 1947 and I stayed there a year until the *Daily Mirror* opened its own picture agency and offered me more money. They soon realised, though, that they had overspent and shut the agency but offered three of the young photographers a job on the paper, including me.

'At the time,' says Doreen Spooner, 'I had never thought of working on a newspaper. This was 1948 and I was the only woman on the picture desk, among 10 or 12 staff photographers. I started going out on stories and thought: this is fantastic, there was so much adrenaline going. Then everything at the *Mirror* was unionized and my pay went up to £14 a week, which was fabulous money in those days.

'The *Mirror* was not then a closed shop as it later became, but it seemed a good idea to join the union. The picture editor there was Simon Clyne and he was very fair, didn't favour anybody. I absolutely loved it at the *Mirror* but after two years got a call from the founder of Keystone who wanted me to accompany him to America for six months as his official photographer.

'I decided to accept, thinking it would be a once in a lifetime opportunity, and handed in my notice at the *Mirror*. Simon Clyne said to me, young lady, you do realise that if you go you will never get a job here again. Even so, I went and took many pictures of the America of

134

the 1950s, which eventually became quite famous as they seemed to encapsulate an era.

'When I came back I didn't attempt to rejoin the *Mirror* but Audrey Whiting, then working in Paris, contacted me to say, why don't you come and work here?' Spooner went, met her husband, a French newspaper photographer, and secured lots of work as a freelance photographer. Three children followed and, says Spooner: 'My career was now on the back burner. We came back to the UK and financially fell on hard times so I rang the *Daily Mirror* and, as it happened, they were looking for somebody.

'They told me I could start on Monday. I thought I would perhaps be there two years but in the event, stayed for 25 years. This was 1962 and I was still the only female photographer on the staff. At first they put my byline as *Doreen Spooner Cameragirl*, but I objected and they soon stopped it.

'Actually,' says Spooner, 'I was nervous after a 10-year gap but discovered that nothing technically had changed. The cameras were still big and heavy and I think this was one reason for the lack of women photographers – simply carrying round the equipment you needed was daunting.'

One of her most famous photographs was of Christine Keeler and Mandy Rice-Davies sitting at an upturned barrel in a pub, chatting animatedly to each other. 'We got a call saying, if you want to know where these two tarts are, go the Long Bar in Holborn where you will find them sitting opposite each other, chatting. I went and saw them but how on earth would I get a picture without anybody seeing me?

'The bar was very dark and I didn't have a flash with me but I worked out the exposure and fired off three shots from the open door of the ladies' toilet. Keeler and Rice-Davies spotted me, started screaming and shouting and the bar owner yelled: who's taking these pictures? The reporter with me said, my colleague is only doing her job but we had to run quickly out of the bar before my camera was seized and smashed. This was a real scoop and it made the front page next day.'

Doreen Spooner made her name, however, with the fashion pictures she took when Felicity Green was fashion editor. The pictures, so unlike fashion shots of today, show the models leaping about, in all kinds of sinuous poses and, most particularly, smiling broadly as if they were enjoying the whole thing. In later years models look snooty, haughty and bored.

'The fashion pictures in those days were black and white so you had to think about line, background and simplicity to make the image strong and appealing. You can get away with more when using colour.

135

We had to remember our readership, that we weren't *Vogue*, and I always wanted to get plenty of movement into the shots. I was very much into shape and mood, and Felicity and I worked as a team and got on very well together.'

Anybody who imagines that size zero among top models is new needs to look at Spooner's pictures of the 1960s and early 70s. The models are rake-thin, easily as thin as the supermodels of today. Spooner also took glamour pictures, with the models successively becoming more glamorous or – as the years went by – shedding ever more clothes.

'When we first started doing glamour, showing a leg was daring,' she says. 'But then we graduated to topless. Many of the topless models felt more comfortable with me as a female photographer and again, I had to keep thinking of ways to make the poses interesting without being sleazy.

'I never liked swearing and if the other photographers started using bad language, Simon Clyne would say: do you mind, Doreen's here. The editor, Jack Nener, who became Audrey Whiting's husband, swore and used filthy language all the time.'

Doreen Spooner retired in 1988 and feels she blazed a big trail for female Fleet Street photographers. She survived the Maxwell era, accompanying him on stories. 'Maxwell always, always wanted his picture taking,' she says.

What qualities does she think are needed for success? 'Firstly, good health is essential. In the early days we had to have two cameras, one for black and white and one for colour, as the Irish edition used colour whereas the London paper only had black and white, so you needed a lot of stamina to lug all the equipment around. Then you have to be punctual, or early. A late photographer has probably missed the best shot.

'But in the early days as a woman I did not get equality of pay.' After retiring, Spooner sat on the board of the National Council for the Training of Journalists for photographers. 'I felt I owed something to the industry for giving me such a wonderful career all those years.'

The first woman to draw a front-page political pocket cartoon for a national newspaper was Margaret Belsky, in 1951. Belsky was born Margaret Owen in 1919 and attended Bournemouth School of Art where she won a *Punch* competition. She went on to study illustration and engraving at the Royal College of Art, which was where she began cartooning.

Her fiancé, the Czech sculptor Franta Belsky, showed her work to the editor of *Lilliput*, a popular weekly magazine of the time, and some of her drawings were accepted.

She became the *Daily Herald's* cartoonist but because she always signed herself 'Belsky' nobody knew she was a woman. She worked at the *Daily Herald* for 18 years, in that time drawing an estimated 6,000 pocket cartoons. In 1969 Rupert Murdoch bought the paper, by then renamed *The Sun*, but Belsky refused to work for him and from 1970 drew a regular pocket cartoon for the *Sunday People*. She also worked for the *New Statesman, Punch, The Guardian* and *Financial Weekly*.

Belsky thought of herself as the 'poor man's (or woman's) Osbert Lancaster' and although the first woman to draw political cartoons for newspapers, was so low-profile that most of the *Sunday People* staff had no idea of her identity. Nobody ever saw her although she did reportedly come into the office once a week to get ideas and discuss the week's pocket cartoon with the editor.

Sally Artz, born in 1935, also drew many cartoons for the *Sunday People*, and other newspapers and magazines. The daughter of painter Benjamin Artz, she studied graphic design at St Martin's School of Art and worked as a commercial artist before selling her first cartoon to the *Weekend Mail* in 1955. She later produced strips for the *Sunday People, Tit-Bits, Chat* and the *Daily Mirror*.

She says she was highly influenced by Disney and Nicholas Bentley, but her style, concentrating mainly on female foibles, is all her own.

Perhaps the best known female newspaper cartoonist is Posy Simmonds, born in 1945. She first came to national notice with her 'Bear' cartoons in *The Sun*, featuring a very lascivious bear and other naughty nursery characters. Simmonds was only 21 when she first sold the long-running Bear strips but since became famous for her wickedly witty social-comment strip cartoons in *The Guardian*, notably Mrs Weber's Diary and the more recent Tamara Drewe. Simmonds has never been a political cartoonist but concentrates on gently sending up aspects of contemporary society and, in particular, deflating the male ego.

One of the most successful female newspaper cartoonists was Kim Casali. Her 'Love Is' cartoons were syndicated all over the world and ran for a long time in the *Daily Mail* and *Mail on Sunday*. She was born Kim Grove in 1942, a New Zealander, and met her future husband, Roberto Casali, when living in California. She used to draw little cartoons illustrating her love for him, and he showed them one day to the *Los Angeles Times*. They immediately accepted them for publication, and started to syndicate them.

The drawings were of extremely innocent-looking, naked people, depicted as children but expressing rather twee adult emotions. Casali's beloved husband died in 1975, only four years after they were married. They already had two sons, and Kim made medical history when she had a child, Milo, two years later using her husband's frozen sperm.

Kim herself died in 1997, aged 55, but her oldest son Stefano has carried on the world-wide 'Love Is …' business, with the cartoons now being drawn by Bob Astley, while retaining the 'Kim' signature.

The astrology column has always been an important part of a popular newspaper and continues to be one of the best-read items, even by people who like to believe that astrology – determining your character and future luck by your star sign – is complete nonsense.

But a 'stars' column certainly makes sense to the newspaper proprietors as it is more or less a licence to print money. Most daily or weekly astrology columns have premium-line phone numbers which readers can ring for their own special forecast (at 75p a minute in 2008).

Certainly the astrologers themselves take their work seriously enough, however derided by scientists. In fact, the scorn and derision by which newspaper astrologers are held in so-called scientific circles has had the effect of making them ever more popular over the years.

Every time they are denounced by scientists and sceptics, more people turn to look at these columns, possibly because the anger and aggression which accompanies the scepticism has the effect of making ever more people intrigued.

Of course, nobody can say with absolute certainty whether there is 'anything in it' or not, which is why the debate is both endless and unresolvable.

At first, horoscopes appeared only in downmarket (or popular, big-circulation) newspapers, usually on or near the comic, puzzle and cartoon pages, but now most daily and Sunday newspapers, including the more upmarket papers, have an astrology column. The first broadsheet astrology column was introduced in the *Sunday Times* by editor Andrew Neil in 1992, and others rapidly followed suit.

The mainly male sub-editors on newspapers have certainly not always taken horoscopes seriously and there are stories that on some newspapers, space was so tight that the subs cut out the words 'not' 'don't' and 'no' from the columns. But senior staff have to take the horoscopes at least as seriously as the readers. When *Sun* readers complained that identical predictions were being made for, say, Scorpio on Tuesday and Libra on Thursday the editor at the time, Kelvin MacKenzie, instantly sacked the astrologer, telling him: 'Our readers aren't idiots, you know.'

So who are these mysterious astrologers? They are certainly not all female although women have always held their own here and this is one of the few areas in newspapers where there has never been any gender discrimination. Most newspaper astrologers are freelance although many are on exclusive contract with specific newspapers and the majority, it has to be said, have become extremely rich with their forecasts, phone lines and individual readings.

They are usually astute businesspeople, maximising their income with syndicated columns, online forecasts, personal horoscopes and books and television appearances. They are also usually quite willing to go head-to-head on television or public debates with out-and-out sceptics and disbelievers, thus elevating their public profiles all the time.

One of the longest-serving newspaper astrologers is June Penn, who lives in a splendid white house on the beach in Hove, East Sussex. Penn's grandfather built the row of houses in 1907 where many celebrities now have £3million-plus beach homes, attracted by the uninterrupted sea views and little area of private beach, the only such area in the country. In fact the Western Esplanade is popularly known in the area as celebrities' row.

June Penn began her psychic career on the *Brighton and Hove Herald* as 'Madame Crystal' later transferring to the *Brighton Argus*. She was discovered by Derek Jameson, then managing editor at the *Daily Mirror*, and for a time became the resident astrologer of both the *Daily* and *Sunday Mirror*. There may have been a psychic connection there as Jameson later bought a house right next to June Penn; the house was later bought by Heather Mills during her marriage to Sir Paul McCartney.

Penn transferred to *The People* after the death of the renowned astrologer 'The Great Lyndoe'. A story is told of Lyndoe which defies any rational or scientific explanation, and which makes even the most hardened newspaper hack shudder slightly.

Lyndoe, an eccentric character, insisted that his weekly column was fetched by hand every Tuesday. Because he was one of the most popular items in the paper, his every wish had to be indulged. Normally, his copy was ready on the dot but when, one Tuesday, the executive, Arthur Brown, turned up to collect the column as usual, Lyndoe said he hadn't written it because there would be no paper that Sunday.

Nothing could persuade Lyndoe to write the column and so Brown had no choice but to return to the office empty handed. The days went by but no column appeared, nor was there any sign of a dispute or strike at the paper. But at the last minute on the Saturday night, just as the presses should have rolled, the printers got into a serious dispute with management and refused to print the paper. The upshot was that – as Lyndoe had accurately predicted – no *Sunday People* came out that week. Now, was Lyndoe in league with the printers or could he see into the future?

Professional astrologers would say that there was no question of it, Lyndoe could see into the future, as indeed they all can.

June Penn certainly believes she has been blessed with psychic gifts, and was born a psychic. She says that although anybody can learn astrology, being psychic is as much of a gift as being an artist or musician. Her belief is that the future is fixed, that each individual's fate is predetermined, and that all this can be predicted with a detailed reading of their birth chart.

'You need to know the day, the date and the time, and that will tell you everything that is going to happen to the person, how many marriages they will have, whether they will make money, whether they will be blessed with good luck or have a difficult life. Even illnesses can be predicted. And nothing can alter this.'

Born in 1928, June Penn has been married twice, has one daughter, a former model and also a clairvoyant, and one grandson who is the Lord of the Manor of the Western Esplanade, according to an ancient tradition. Her grandson is also psychic she said, and the ability often runs in families.

The main point about newspaper horoscopes, says June Penn, is that they give hope. 'They are a guide to what should be happening, and what people in certain star signs will be going through at any given time. The thing to remember is that when certain planets move into your star sign there will be definite effects.'

How does she answer the sceptics? 'I say to them that if they were to take the time and energy to study astrology properly instead of just dismissing it, after one year their views would change. They would then realise that astrology can be extremely accurate.

'When casting newspaper horoscopes we use solar charts which take the sun's position and all the planetary positions. You do have to know a bit about astronomy as well. For example, I know where most of the planets are and how long they take to complete their cycle. Pluto, one of the newer planets, takes 248 years to complete its cycle whereas Jupiter takes 12 years, spending one year in each zodiac sign.

'Each planet has its own meaning. Mercury is the planet of communication, Venus is good for beautiful things, Saturn is a great teacher. I believe emphatically in astrology, as a great guide that can definitely help people.'

Marjorie Orr is one of the few media astrologers who had a solid journalistic background before branching out into the realms of the paranormal. She began her career as a reporter on the *Glasgow Herald* and then became a news and current affairs reporter on BBC TV. She helped to launch TV-am in 1983. She became interested in astrology and the paranormal after producing a television documentary on the subject, and has been the astrologer for the *News of the World, Daily Express, Woman* and many local newspapers.

She says that astrology was a revelation to her as she had been a complete non-believer when working for the BBC. She had her Damascene moment when her birth chart was read for the first time and says: 'Here was an information source that could not be discounted. From the time, date and place of birth, the astrologer told me in detail about my talents, temperament, strengths and challenges. As a philosophy graduate with a scientific bent, this shook my belief in a rational universe and made me decide to learn all I could about astrology.'

Orr decided to give up her television career to become a full-time astrologer and her particular interest is in political astrology which studies the horoscopes of world leaders and countries. Her fervent wish, she says, is to overcome the credibility gap and encourage even sceptics to see that astrology can be a useful tool which provides information on personality, behaviour and forthcoming events that is not available by any other means. The fact that science cannot explain astrology, Orr maintains, is not a good enough reason to discount it.

Debbie Frank, astrologer for the *Daily Mirror* and *Sunday Mirror*, plus several television shows, has a degree in American studies from Nottingham University and later studied at the Faculty of Astrological Studies. She became a professional astrologer in 1984 and has since written horoscopes for many media outlets including *The Sun, She* magazine, *Sunday Express* and *dailymail.co.uk*

Frank believes that astrology can be a powerful tool for self-understanding and says that in order to work it has to be interactive, with input coming from the subject as well as the astrologer. She says: 'We must play our part by making the right choices and knowing how to handle certain situations. Astrology can give us great insight into how to work with the patterns and forces that make up the cycles of both the planets and life. '

Debbie Frank shot to fame as Princess Diana's friend and astrologer during the last eight years of her life, and she also made headlines when she and her husband adopted a baby girl from China, who is a Scorpio, like her adoptive mother.

Mystic Meg, the *Sun*'s astrologer, is perhaps not as mystic as her name and byline picture suggest. Her real name is the more prosaic Margaret Anne Lake and like Marjorie Orr she has a journalistic background, having been a sub-editor on the *News of the World* and deputy editor of its magazine, *Sunday*. Born in Accrington, Lancashire in 1942, Lake learnt astrology from her gipsy grandmother, and read English at Leeds University before becoming a journalist. As Mystic Meg, she shot to national fame as the astrologer on the BBC's National Lottery programme but she never managed to predict the winning numbers in spite of exhortations to do so from Victor Lewis-Smith, for many years television critic at the *Evening Standard*. As well as her astrology columns, Mystic Meg owns racehorses under the company name Mystic Meg Ltd.

One of the most successful media astrologers of all time is Shelley von Struenckel, who became the *Sunday Times*' first astrologer in 1992. She was born in Hollywood and worked in fashion retailing in America before starting to write astrology columns in 1991, having studied at various American astrology institutes.

Her columns are now syndicated worldwide and she specialises in celebrity profiles. Her weekly column in the *Evening Standard ES* magazine always features a celebrity horoscope. Von Struenckel –her real (Austrian) name – is regarded, or regards herself, as the 'voice of reason' in horoscopes and it is noticeable that her predictions are much more negative than the sugary positivity of many of her rivals. Maybe this is considered more 'intelligent' as von Struenckel writes mainly for the more upmarket outlets.

Catherine Tennant, who writes a regular astrology column for the *Daily Telegraph*, comes from an aristocratic, horsey background which is perhaps unique in media astrologers. Sally Brompton, a former newspaper feature writer, has also made a great success of syndicated astrology columns.

Most newspaper astrologers have had another career before making use of, or developing, their psychic gifts and as June Penn has demonstrated, this is one aspect of a media career you need never retire from, and where your credibility as a 'wise old woman' may actually increase with age.

Although there are now many female sports presenters on television, there are still pitifully few in print journalism. One of the first was Julie Welch, who wrote on football for *The Observer*.

She was also the scriptwriter for the 1983 Goldcrest film *Those Glory Glory Days*, her autobiographical account of a football-obsessed girl who recounts her childhood experiences following Tottenham Hotspur in 1960-61 and then becomes the first female football correspondent on a national newspaper.

The film shows how Julia Herrick, a thinly-disguised Welch, struggles to make her parents and teachers understand her passion for football. Bewildered by her love of such a masculine sport, they send her to the school doctor who enrols her in Greek dancing lessons to try to interest her in more feminine physical pursuits. The passion continues unabated and Julia becomes determined to make a living from soccer in the only way she can in those days – by writing about it.

Little has changed. For although female reporters and photographers have now successfully penetrated most areas of print journalism, sports reporting remains almost a closed area. In spite of many women now having edited newspapers, there still has never been a woman sports editor of a national newspaper. The nearest has been Ginny Clark, who became the first female sports editor of *Scotland on Sunday* in 1998, although she stayed in the post for only one year before leaving. There remain very few women reporting on any sport, even sports played by women, such as tennis, and some sports psychologists feel this is a major reason why so few girls ever take up any kind of sport.

It just continues to be regarded as something for men.

The Sports Journalists Association has found that fewer than 10 per cent of British sports journalists are women, even 40 years after Julie Welch became a sports writer. One of the 10 per cent is Natasha Woods, chief sports writer for the *Sunday Herald* in Scotland. Woods started her career on the *Lynn News* in Norfolk as a general reporter and 'gradually drifted up the A1', joining first *The Journal*, Newcastle, and later the *Sunday Times* in Scotland.

Woods became a football reporter in 1994 with no previous experience of the job but maintains there were no issues either about her gender or the fact that she was English.

Other notable female sports writers are Sue Mott, of the *Daily Telegraph* and football writer Catherine Riley, formerly of *The Times*.

So why are so few women reporting on sport? Is there a lingering prejudice or sexism, or is it more the case that hardly any women coming into journalism actually want to be sports writers, as they are not remotely interested?

Possibly nowadays, the latter, as the days when women were seen as unwelcome intruders into male-only sports departments, are over. Yet the number of female by-lines on sports pages is vastly lower than on any other section of a modern national newspaper.

Judy Hobson's appointment made news in the journalists' trade paper, *Press Gazette,* in 1977 when the following item appeared:

> It is no use pulling on an old cardigan and going to the subs' table of *The Times* in search of the monastic life.
>
> Two more women will be seen subbing there during the summer, one permanently and one as holiday relief. The trail-blazer there has been Judy Walker (now Hobson) who last autumn [Sep 1976] became the first woman sub-editor on the paper's foreign table. Now she is to make it a double first by pioneering with the Home News subs.

Even as late at 1977, such an appointment could still make news. Here is Judy's story, in her own words:

'On leaving school with eight O Levels and 2 As in English and History, I knew I wanted a job writing and so I fired off letters to magazines in London and locally to the *Lincolnshire Standard* group of weeklies, who offered me a job at Louth as a junior reporter. There I covered everything from courts to the pop scene, and had my own column featuring local and visiting rock artists such as Manfred Mann, The Swinging Blue Jeans and Freddie and the Dreamers.

'During my apprenticeship I studied law, local government and shorthand. 'I then wrote to the editor of the *Evening Telegraph* series, was invited for an interview and subsequently offered a senior reporter's job on the *Scunthorpe Evening Telegraph* where I covered the education beat as well as borough and county council meetings.

'In those days, the early 1970s, the next step was to move onto a regional daily and so I joined the *Sheffield Morning Telegraph*, a leading regional daily, where I ran campaigns highlighting the pitiful state some of city's elderly were forced to live in and seeking improved access and employment rights for the disabled. I moved onto the news desk organising news coverage from the paper's regional offices and freelance agencies in addition to briefing and debriefing reporters in head office.

'I was keen to learn about all aspects of newspaper production, I asked my editor Michael Hides, a former chief sub of *The Guardian*, if I could join the subs' desk. He had no problem with the idea and readily agreed. There was already one other female on the news desk and another one on the features desk.

'I continued to write occasional features for the paper and felt subbing really helped hone my writing skills. I loved the immediacy of working on the stone and then hearing the presses roll.'

Fiona Millar, daughter of journalist Bob Millar a long-time executive at the *Daily Express*, was educated at Camden School for Girls and University College London. She trained as a journalist on the *Mirror* graduate training scheme at Plymouth where she met her life partner, Alastair Campbell.

Millar joined the *Daily Express* where she wrote about politics and left in 1988 to have a family. She continued with freelance journalism and in 1995 became a part-time adviser to Cherie Blair; this post turned into a full-time position when Tony Blair became Prime Minister. At the same time Alastair Campbell, a former political correspondent at the *Daily Mirror*, became Tony Blair's Director of Communications.

Since resigning as Cherie Blair's adviser, Fiona Millar has specialised in writing about state education, which she fiercely champions. She co-authored a book, *Remarkable Women*, in 1993 with Glenys Kinnock, wife of the then leader of the Labour party Neil Kinnock.

Cathy Couzens says: 'People often ask me what I miss most about not working on Fleet Street any more. Well free food! I cannot remember ever paying for my own dinner or lunch, either DX paid or the restaurant... Meeting the rich and famous... No, not really, it makes wonderful stories to tell but who the hell wants to hear them, just other hacks and hackettes.

'There are those who think I spent my whole time drinking and having fun.... Good god! I have been arrested, stuck down a nasty cave, stood outside people's houses for days door-stepping... Worked 20 hour days with no story to tell at the end (rarely!)... plus eight years in the provinces will give you enough council, court and pavement stomping to kill or cure.

'What do I miss? I miss the friendship and fun of Fleet Street, the gossip and the competition, the only way I can describe it is a brotherhood.

'Today there isn't as much friendship – they see it as a profession. We saw it as a craft and I can never ever remember anyone talking about money – I always got the feeling that all of us would have done it for free, it just came naturally.

'Every year when I see the names drop off the Christmas Card list I remember daft things that happened... typewriters flying across the room; Johnny Jones taking his clothes off in the newsroom (still don't know why)... Dougie Morrison trying to push my arse through the cave when I got stuck... Steve Wood scraping the whole of my side of the car off driving the wrong way down a one way street... Derek Jameson standing on a chair in a Manchester Hotel singing with his future wife Ellen Petrie trying to distract him by setting fire to his trouser leg.

'I know one thing – no one ever talked about self- esteem or sexual harassment in the workplace – we thought all that was part of the job! If you can't take the heat get out of the kitchen. So far as I was concerned, it just made it more fun!'

Traditionally, newspaper gossip columns were not only headed by men, they were called by men's names, whether real or made-up, or given some masculine-sounding name, such as Peterborough. William Hickey was one of the earliest, on the *Daily Express*, then there was Ephraim Hardcastle, Paul Tanfield, Henry Fielding, Nigel Dempster, Richard Kay or Garth Gibbs (some of the names being genuine by-lines). Even though female journalists had always worked on gossip columns, they did not normally run them – the single exception being Lady Olga Maitland at the *Sunday Express* – until Jessica Callan, daughter of *Daily Mirror* and *Daily Express* journalist Paul Callan, came along.

Callan, a graduate of the Trinity Mirror training scheme, was headhunted by the then *Daily Mirror* editor Piers Morgan to run a new type of column, staffed by young women and to be called *The 3am Girls*. The idea was that the 'girls' would be part of the story, partying along with celebrities and joining in their activities. The official launch, in 2000, read: *It's 3am. The music's pumping, the lights are low, the vodka Red Bulls are flowing. You're a superstar and you're misbehaving. Our new gossip columnists will be there too. All three of them.'*

Jessica Callan says: 'At the time, the showbusiness columns were run mainly by blokes in their 30s. I was the deputy editor of the *Daily Telegraph* Peterborough column when Richard Wallace, deputy editor at *The Mirror*, contacted me. I would be working alongside Polly Graham and Eva Simpson. I was to be the 'posh one'.

'Our brief at the column was to kick seven shades out of the showbusiness industry. We were to report on the disgraceful antics of
146

celebs and to name and shame publicists who acted like bigger prima donnas than the stars. The column became so successful that before long, the male-dominated gossip world was predominantly steered by women.

'*3am* was attacked for its banality and we were attacked for being victims of the Svengali-like Piers Morgan. But I didn't agree. I loved it and despite the hangovers, couldn't wait to get into work to cackle over the scandal we had witnessed the night before.'

Even so, Callan said that she heeded her father's wise advice not to spend more than five years in a gossip column and she left in September 2005 to go backpacking round the world. She says: 'My liver was intact but my love affair with the world of celebrity was over and I couldn't bear the thought of yet another champagne-fuelled celebrity party.'

Jessica Callan wrote a tell-all book, *Wicked Whispers,* about her years as a 3am girl,.

Journalism, in common with many other professions, can be extremely dynastic – some might say nepotistic.

Catherine Stott is the daughter of Mary Stott, pioneer woman's editor of *The Guardian*;

Penny Perrick is the daughter of the late *Sunday Express* journalist Eve Perrick;

Photographer Nikki English is the daughter of the late *Daily Mail* editor David English;

Emma Lee-Potter and Charlie Lee-Potter are the daughters of Lynda Lee-Potter;

Writers Claire Calman and Stephanie Calman are the daughters of the late newspaper cartoonist Mel Calman;

Jessica Callan is the daughter of *Daily Express* writer Paul Callan and American journalist Steffi Fields;

Bryony Gordon is the daughter of Jane Gordon;

Sisters Polly Graham and Jane Reed were journalists on *Woman's Own* at the same time;

Winifred Carr, formerly woman's editor at the *Daily Telegraph* and journalist Jean Carr are sisters;

Kate Molloy is the daughter of former *Daily Mirror* editor Mike Molloy;

Polly Hudson is the daughter of journalist and novelist Val Hudson;

Victoria Hopkirk is the daughter of journalist and novelist Joyce Hopkirk; Joyce Hopkirk and Heather Kirby are sisters, nee Nicholson;

Etiquette expert Drusilla Beyfus is the mother of *Vogue* editor Alexandra Shulman and writer Nicola Shulman; their father was *Evening Standard* TV critic Milton Shulman;

India Knight is the daughter of News International executive Andrew Knight;

Fiona Millar is the daughter of Bob Millar, former deputy editor of the *Daily Express*;

Petronella Wyatt is the daughter of Woodrow Wyatt, formerly 'the voice of reason' on the *News of the World*;

Journalist and TV presenter Claudia Winkleman is the daughter of Eve Pollard;

Bibi van der Zee is the daughter of former fashion editor Barbara Griggs;

Anna Tims is the daughter of Hilton Tims;

Vicki Woods and her daughter Octavia are joint agony aunts on the *Daily Telegraph*;

Anna Wintour is the daughter of former *Evening Standard* editor Patrick Wintour;

Amanda Shrimsley is the daughter of Bernard Shrimsley;

Katharine Hadley is the niece of the late *Sunday People* sports reporter Ralph Hadley;

Gillian Kemp is the daughter of former *Daily Mail* motoring correspondent Mike Kemp;

Agony aunt Caroline Buchanan is the daughter of former *Sun* writer Ann Buchanan;

Sophie Bower is the daughter of Veronica Wadley and Tom Bower;

Sophie Parkin is the daughter of journalist and artist Molly Parkin.

Does it help or make life easier to have a parent or relative already in the business? In some ways definitely yes. For one thing you know it's possible to get in, your journalist parents may well hold parties and events which other journalists attend, and there are often ready-made contacts to give at least a start.

But once in, you are not only on your own but likely to be judged even more harshly than somebody who does not have the same head start.

Nine

Brought to book

For some aspirants to the inky trade, journalism is a fabulous job in itself, but others secretly want to be 'real' writers; that is, to write novels, and in particular – with any luck – bestsellers.

After all, as journalists we become very used to having an audience of millions through our newspapers, and it is a potent dream to want to retain that audience with our own creative endeavours, rather than just reporting on the lives of others all the time.

In an ideal world, many writers would choose the hectic, exciting, minute-by-minute trade of newspaper journalism first, then mature into authors later, when the prospect of sitting alone at a computer all day long, with only invented characters for company, becomes more appealing than nailing villains or trying to obtain usable quotes from reluctant, monosyllabic celebrities.

When Mike Molloy – who himself later became a successful novelist – was editing the *Daily Mirror*, he used to say that half of his staff had written the first five chapters of their great novel while the other half had written the first chapter of five great novels.

Mostly, those five great chapters, or five great first chapters, would stay hidden in a drawer, but for a lucky – or phenomenally talented – few, the transition from jobbing journalist to highly-feted and high-profile novelist, actually happens. And although there are some male journalists who have become bestselling novelists, such as Molloy, Leslie Thomas, Colin Dunne, Frederick Forsyth and Ken Follett, spectacular successes have been achieved by women who plied the craft before hiving themselves off into a lone study. One thinks of names such as Shirley Conran, Penny Vincenzi, Celia Brayfield,

Barbara Taylor Bradford, Val McDermid and of course Jilly Cooper, all of whom achieved considerable success as newspaper journalists before going onto to becoming world famous authors.

Barbara Taylor Bradford, whose first published novel, *A Woman of Substance*, was an international success in print and as a television mini-series, started her career as a typist on the *Yorkshire Evening Post* at the age of 15. Six months later she became a cub reporter on the paper and, she says, woman's page editor at 18.

At 20 she determined to conquer Fleet Street and after a spell on *Woman's Own* as fashion editor, she worked for the London *Evening News*, seeing herself becoming a 'hard-bitten reporter in a dirty trenchcoat'. Instead she met and married American film producer Robert Bradford and went to live in New York.

Taylor Bradford believes that her early journalistic career gave her the thorough grounding that resulted in her later successful novels although it has to be said that little trace of her cub reporter days is evident in the blockbuster books. Her first big success, *A Woman of Substance*, is a traditional rags-to-riches story of a poor girl, Emma Harte, who gets a job as housemaid in the nearby manor house, is cruelly seduced by the caddish son, has a child out of wedlock and eventually becomes the owner of department store Harte's, a thinly-disguised Harrods.

This book, which was to make Taylor Bradford's name for ever, was adapted for television by novelist (and former journalist) Lee Langley and starred the young Jenny Seagrove, complete with Yorkshire accent.

Her other novels follow a similar blockbuster format, but she has become the total mistress of the genre and many of her books have become television mini-series, all produced and masterminded by her husband, Bob Bradford.

Shirley Conran, who also achieved success as a novelist, had a vastly bigger newspaper career than Barbara Taylor Bradford, including significant executive positions, before turning to fiction. Conran's first published novel, *Lace*, was also a genre novel which was made into a highly watchable, if excruciatingly clichéd, mini-series.

Conran has also had a much more interested and varied private life than many journalists turned novelists. Born in 1932 and one of the six children of the owner of a chain of launderettes, she was educated at St Paul's Girls' School, the alma mater of many leading career women, and then a finishing school in Switzerland.

She trained as a painter and sculptor at the Southern College of Art, Portsmouth and worked for several years as a textile designer and colour consultant. She became the first woman's editor of the then new

Observer Colour Magazine and later woman's editor of the *Daily Mail* where she was partly responsible for launching Femail in the 1960s. Her second husband was the furniture designer, restaurateur and general entrepreneur Terence Conran, with whom she had two sons, Sebastian and the fashion designer Jasper.

Conran first shot to international fame not with a novel but with a book that still lingers on many early feminists' and married home-makers' shelves: *Superwoman*. Published in 1975, it was a phenomenal success and responsible for introducing a lasting phase into the language: 'life's too short to stuff a mushroom.' The title of the book, which was really just packed full of cheating type of household hints, also ushered in the memorable phase 'superwoman' to describe a certain type of woman who wants to have it all; a phrase still very much in use. Much of *Superwoman* was actually written by Sheila Black, for which Black has never been given due credit.

A book on gardening for beginners, *The Magic Garden*, also became a bestseller before Conran's career as a novelist was launched with *Lace*, billed as 'the book every mother should hide from her daughter' and in 2008 available from Amazon for just 1p. This book also contains a memorable sentence: 'Which of you bitches is my mother?'

Several other novels followed, by now being written in the French castle Conran had managed to buy with proceeds from her books. A third marriage did not last and since her divorce from Terence, Shirley Conran has mainly lived alone.

Conran's abiding skill has been an uncanny ability to predict the female reading market accurately and lucratively, in much the same way as her husband Terence was able to do with his Habitat stores and later restaurants. *Superwoman* and its many spin offs arrived at exactly the right time, when women were wondering how to 'have it all' and juggle the multifarious roles of wife, mother, career girl, sexpot, fashionista, wonderful cook, brilliant gardener, which modern life seemed to be increasingly demanding.

Conran has also been a brilliant self-promoter and put every aspect of her life before the public, in particular her decades-long struggle with ME, myalgic encephalomyelitis, or chronic fatigue syndrome. She believes it was, paradoxically, the ME that led to her phenomenally successful writing career: 'It was 1970, I was aged 38, happily divorced and with a wonderful job as woman's editor of the *Daily Mail* when I was rushed to hospital with viral pneumonia. I saw three specialists, all of whom produced a different diagnosis, including one that I was workshy.

'Because I couldn't work I got ever deeper into debt and a friend fixed me up with a book contract. He thought I could write a book as I could take my time over it, and would not have to meet newspaper-type deadlines. I eventually produced a book about how to minimise housework, called it *Superwoman* and to my astonishment it became an international bestseller.

'Nowadays, when writing my books I have to be completely ruthless and never go out or answer the phone otherwise I would never get the book written as I have to pace myself very carefully. The symptoms have not improved in the last 35 years but I can manage them better.' And still the books come out, although Conran's later tomes have not matched the success of her 1980s novels.

There is, for many genre novels, a slot in time when the genre is popular, after which a new formula comes along. Thus, sex 'n' shopping was replaced by chick-lit, and hen-lit. Conran's early novels are full of brand names, which sounded exciting at the time but which now tend to come across as overly commercial, greedy, grasping and old-fashioned.

As well as writing her books, Shirley Conran has always campaigned hard for women to remain independent, particularly financially independent, and she has to a very large extent, lived the dream by becoming extremely rich and successful in her own right, even though once married to a very successful man. The Conran name doesn't hurt, as Shirley realised early on.

The journalist Angela Lambert, who died in 2007 aged 67, wrote seven widely-acclaimed novels as well as three non-fiction historical books. Of German extraction, Lambert (nee Helps) was educated at boarding schools and St Hilda's College, Oxford. She met her husband, Martin Lambert, at Oxford and they married in 1962. Five years later he left her to bring up her two children as a single parent. In 1971, she had an affair with novelist Stephen Vizinczey, author of *In Praise of Older Women*. This relationship produced a daughter, Marianne, but did not last and almost broke her heart.

Now with three children to support on her own, Lambert had to find a way of earning a living, and she first became secretary to Lord Longford and then one of the first female television reporters on ITN in 1972. In 1988 she joined the new *Independent* – she had been at Oxford with one of its founders, Andreas Whittam-Smith –and went on to work for the *Daily Mail* and *Daily Telegraph*. She then met television director Tony Price, who became her partner for the rest of her life.

Lambert's first novel, *Love Among the Single Classes*, was published in 1999, and draws on her experiences of being a single parent. Her other novels have recurring themes of sickness and ill-health and also draw heavily on Lambert's own life. Her 2002 novel *A Rather English Marriage*, was adapted for television by Andrew Davies and starred Tom Courtenay, Albert Finney and Joanna Lumley.

Like Shirley Conran, Lambert had recurring bouts of serious and often life-threatening illness and she died of the portal hypertension which had dogged her for two decades. Her final book, published in 2006, was *The Lost Life of Eva Braun*, Hitler's mistress.

Penny Vincenzi has also found success as a blockbuster novelist. The covers of her novels are very 'girly', and so is her website design, but this is deceptive; her books actually tackle tough contemporary themes, and ask readers to imagine what they would do if confronted with difficult or impossible scenarios such as losing all their money at Lloyds, coming into a sudden enormous windfall, or their husband asking them to perjure themselves in a serious court case. Vincenzi's novels always ask the question: what if, then proceed to answer the question through an imaginative, fast-paced story with plenty of twists and turns and realistic characters.

Vincenzi's first job after leaving school was working in Harrods' library aged 16. After this she went to secretarial college and joined the *Daily Mirror*, where she was originally Felicity Green's secretary. She later became a journalist, writing for women's pages of newspapers and women's magazines, and even had a go, with her husband, at starting up her own magazine, for Boots. This soon folded and after having her first two daughters she started writing novels. She says: 'I wrote the first chapters of my first novel at the kitchen table from 5 to 7 am while my children were still asleep. You can always squeeze time out of the day if you want to but you have to have a very strong idea for a novel.'

Vincenzi has made a lot of money from her novels, far more than if she was still scribbling for low-paying newspapers and magazines and says she would be totally terrified if she lost all her money along with her characters in the novel *An Absolute Scandal*. 'Money doesn't matter until you don't have it. I'd try to be very positive, start on a new book immediately, or finish the one I was writing and hope that one of the four daughters would take us in for a while until we got back on our feet.'

Vincenzi's daughter Sophie also became a novelist.

Her journalistic background comes in useful, she says, when it comes to research as she is used to talking to people. 'When researching *An*

Absolute Scandal, I found many people who'd been Lloyd's Names and who had suffered horribly. I talked to lawyers and to people who had worked in the City at the time. I even talked to someone who had worked at Lloyd's. You can't beat talking to real people when it comes to research. It's far better than just using the internet, which I try never to do as it wouldn't be original.'

So far as originality is concerned, for her 2005 novel, *Sheer Abandon*, Vincenzi reprised one of Shirley Conran's themes: which of three now-successful career women is the mother of Kate, the teenage heroine of the book. But there is no pornography in Vincenzi's books, soft or otherwise, just a fast-paced very realistic story with, thankfully, no attempts at 'fine writing'. Her journalistic background is evident in her novels from some of her themes. In *Sheer Abandon*, for example, she mentions columnists Amanda Platell, Lynda Lee-Potter and Carol Sarler by name and one of her characters is a reporter on a fictitious daily tabloid.

Celia Brayfield is another successful journalist turned novelist. Again educated at St Paul's Girls' School, the elder daughter of a dentist, she studied French at Grenoble University and then trained as a secretary. She moved into journalism via the typing pool at *The Times* and later became a television critic successively for the Evening Standard and *The Times* and *Sunday Telegraph*. Her first novel, *Pearls,* became a bestseller and she was to follow that with eight more novels and four works of non-fiction, including one about how to write a bestseller.

Like Penny Vincenzi, Brayfield likes to tackle tough, modern topics rather than historical or romantic themes, and believes it is her curiosity, the trait which first led her into journalism, which underlines the narrative drive of her novels. She has said that she likes to turn anything she finds curious and wanting to be explored, into fiction. Brayfield brought up her daughter, Chloe, as a single parent after her partner abandoned her when she was pregnant, and champions the cause of the One-Parent Families charity.

Former tabloid journalist Val McDermid has concentrated on crime fiction. She had a long career as a staff journalist at the *Sunday People* in Manchester before her writing career finally took off.

McDermid came from a working-class mining family in Kirkcaldy, Scotland, and was accepted to read English at St Hilda's College, Oxford. She believes she was possibly the first girl there to come from a Scottish state school.

Although she had always wanted to be a writer 'ever since I realised that real people produced all those books in the library' she was advised that it was impossible to make a living from writing books. So she trained as a journalist on the *Mirror*'s training scheme in Devon where she won the Trainee Journalist of the Year award. For the next 14 years McDermid worked on newspapers in Glasgow and Manchester, ending up, according to her website, as northern bureau chief for the *Sunday People* in Manchester, although McDermid does not mention the title of the actual paper.

One journalist who worked with her in the 1980s, Andy Leatham, has said that it was immediately obvious that here was a woman who could hold her own in any company and stand toe-to-toe with any man in the toughest of drinking schools:

> 'One Friday she confided in news editor Terry Lovell that her partner had been away all week and that she had booked a cosy dinner *à deux* at their favourite restaurant for a welcome home celebration that night. About six o'clock, just as thoughts were turning to after-work pints, Lovell despatched Val to Grimsby, on a so-called urgent job.
>
> 'So it was an apoplectic Val who gathered her belongings, muttering Gaelic oaths as she stormed off into the night. The news room door shuddered on its hinges as she slammed it behind her, followed by the sound of angry footsteps retreating along the corridor. Then there was a pause – and the sound of even angrier footsteps returning.
>
> 'The news room door flew open and Val's curly-topped head appeared around it. "See you, Lovell," she barked, "I hope your next shite's a hedgehog."
>
> 'An award-winning way with words, had our Val.'

McDermid also became the Father (or Mother) of the Chapel while working on the *People* in Manchester.

All the time she was working as a journalist, McDermid was attempting to become a 'real' writer. She wrote her first novel at 21, an effort that was summarily rejected by every publisher in the country, but later turned it into a play, *Like a Happy Ending*, which was performed by the Plymouth Theatre Company. She then tried to write a crime novel and her first attempt at this genre, *Report for Murder*, was published in 1984 by The Women's Press.

Financially, she was able to give up her job on *The People* in 1991 and has lived, very well, one assumes from her sales figures, by writing novels ever since. Now a leading crime writer, McDermid's books are heavily advertised on huge posters on station platforms and other public places and she has made a particular type of very sadistic crime novel her own. The novels are closely researched, pacily written, a clever, fast and entertaining read, often set in several countries and many locations, but they are very violent and definitely not for the squeamish.

She has won a Golden Dagger, the highest award for crime writers, for her extremely literate and well-written thrillers.

What prompted her to leave journalism for writing thrillers? In an interview to promote her book *A Place of Execution*, where some of the characters are journalists, she said: 'The book doesn't portray journalists in a very positive light.

'The world of national newspapers is particularly tough and cut throat. You get a certain level of cooperation among daily newspaper journalists, but when you're talking about looking for those exclusives, particularly for Sunday papers, the story is what counts. There wasn't a great deal of compassion in the trade of journalism as practised when I was doing it.'

She herself was as 'cutthroat' as the rest during her journalistic career, she said and added: 'I had to be. One reason why I left journalism was I realised there are two ways to go. You either become completely callous and shut off from the emotions of the people you're dealing with, or you invest in them, and either way is not a particularly emotionally healthy route to go down.

'I looked around in my early 30s at my colleagues on my paper and other papers and I thought: I don't want to be you when I'm 50. I have friends who are journalists, and there are decent, honourable journalists around, but even the decent, honourable ones will push the envelope when it's the difference between getting the story and not.'

Nicci French is also a popular crime writer, but this writer is actually the husband and wife writing team of journalists Nicci Gerrard and Sean French, son of film critic Philip French.

Jilly Cooper's forays into fiction have been internationally successful and as with her columns, she has tried very hard to please. Her caddish hero, Rupert Campbell-Black, appears in several of her novels, and her heroines are notable for loving lots of sex. Cooper has 'themes' for her novels and has tackled a television station (*Rivals*); showjumping (*Riders*); schools (*Wicked!*) and an orchestra (*Appassionata*). Many critics have said that the very explicit erotica in Cooper's novels verges on the pornographic; be that as it may, her novels are certainly a gripping read and much loved by teenagers.

Jilly Cooper has always made sure that the publication of each of her new novels is an 'event' and orchestrates massive publicity around each new launch. Apart from poster campaigns there are always loads of interviews in print and broadcast media. In fact, whenever an interview with Jilly appears, you can be sure it is always to herald a new novel. She is often extremely wily about pre-publicity as well, letting slip little diary items about a forthcoming blockbuster.

Many other, quieter, novelists envy the publicity Cooper is able to attract to herself whenever a new novel is on the horizon.

These are some of the most successful female journalists turned novelists, but very many journalists have had a go at writing fiction, although it has to be said, not always with the same degree of success as the bestselling writers profiled above.

Journalists Frankie McGowan, Hilary Bonner, Sarah Sands, Eve Pollard, Joyce Hopkirk, Val Hudson, Penny Perrick and Audrey Slaughter have all produced enjoyably readable – and published – works of fiction, but have not become as well known for their fiction as their work as journalists. Libby Purves has written about a dozen critically acclaimed and popular novels, and Jane Gordon, Diana Appleyard, Sally Brampton, Virginia Ironside and Sally Ann Voak are successfully combining fiction writing with daily journalism.

The late Unity Hall, women's editor of the *News of the World* for very many years, was also a prolific novelist, of light romantic fiction.

Molly Parkin, born Molly Thomas in Pontycymer, Wales, in 1932, is one of journalism's true exotics and eccentrics, noted for having many lovers, and she is a painter as well as a novelist and journalist.

Parkin actually started out as an artist, training at Goldsmiths College, London and Brighton College of Art. Her first husband, Michael Parkin, owned an art gallery, and Molly Parkin taught and painted throughout her first marriage, which ended in the early 1960s. She became unable to paint after her divorce and turned to fashion and fashion journalism.

Parkin's autobiography, *Moll*, published in 1993, details some interesting uses of wine bottles with an early lover, the bearded *Doctor in the House* actor James Robertson Justice. She also records having sex with an entire football team in one night, long before such exploits became part of footballer legend, or myth. Whether her account is strictly true or, given the amount of alcohol taken on that night, a slight exaggeration, is open to question but there is no doubt that Parkin has enjoyed a sex life many a famous royal mistress of the past would envy.

After her first marriage ended, Parkin worked in fashion with such 1960s luminaries as Biba and Mary Quant, then started writing on fashion for the innovative *Nova* magazine.

She later became fashion editor of *Harpers and Queen* and in 1969, joined *The Sunday Times*, which was where she made her name. It was while she was at the *Sunday Times* that she started writing novels with provocative titles such as *Love All*, *Up Tight* and *Breast Stroke*, starting a new genre known as comic-erotic.

Several of these novels are based on her experiences at the *Sunday Times* and they were notorious at the time for their explicit sex content. They were published in the mid-1970s to mid-1980s and managed to secure a lot of publicity for their author. The highly erotic cover of *Up Tight* was the work of Harri Peccinotti, a fashion photographer who made his name at *Nova* magazine.

Molly Parkin later married the artist Patrick Hughes but this marriage also ended in divorce. Their violent fights are chronicled in Parkin's autobiography.

During the 1980s, Molly Parkin and her two daughters Sarah and Sophie were famous for going to parties as a threesome, the three of them walking into the room with daring cleavages and exotic outfits, thus ensuring all eyes were upon them. Parkin appeared very jolly, the life and soul of the party, but in fact was by now in the grip of serious alcoholism, and this blighted her life, her finances and put paid to the entertaining comic-erotic novels.

After successfully drying out, Parkin resumed her original career as a painter but never toned down her appearance, and is still noted for her gaudy dress sense and particularly, her brightly-coloured matching headgear.

Of the younger generation of journalists and columnists, Zoe Heller, daughter of scriptwriter Lukas Heller (of *Whatever Happened to Baby Jane* fame) is becoming known as a writer of fine fiction and her debut novel, *Notes on a Scandal*, was turned into a popular film. Lynda Lee-Potter's daughter Emma has had several works of fiction published, including children's fiction. Other newspaper journalists who have published fiction include Caitlin Moran, Sabine Durrant, Kate Saunders and Julie Burchill.

Julie Burchill wrote two novels, *Ambition* and *No Exit*, which became bestsellers, and has also written teenage fiction. Jill Eckersley has specialised in teenage novels and short stories. Irma Kurtz, the long-standing agony aunt on *Cosmopolitan*, has also been writing successful novels for many years.

Claire Rayner's career as a novelist has run in tandem with her journalism and she has turned her hand to both contemporary and historical fiction; her series *The Performers* has been particularly popular. She submitted her first novel under the name Berenice Chetwynd, only to get a letter back from the publishers saying they liked the novel, but she would have to change her pseudonym as 'nobody could possibly have a name like that'. In fact, it is Claire Rayner's real name, the surname 'Chetwynd' being chosen by her father and registered by deed poll when he was trying to hide his identity escaping from debtors.

All three of Claire Rayner's children, Amanda, Adam and Jay, have published novels.

The acclaimed writer Jan Morris started life as a man, James Morris, a foreign correspondent on *The Times*, and was responsible for despatching the news of the conquest of Everest on the very day of the Coronation in June 1953. In the 1970s, Morris had a sex-change operation since when she has lived as a woman and produced many books including *The Haj*, a novel shortlisted for the Booker Prize.

As Jan, Morris has had a highly successful career as a book writer but as James, had an equally easy path into newspaper journalism because he was then a man, and Oxford-educated at that. So neither as Jan or James did Morris experience the prejudice or difficulties that would have accompanied her had she been a female trying to make her way as a foreign correspondent in the 1950s. In May 2008, Jan Morris entered into a civil partnership with her former wife, Elizabeth. They had to divorce when Jan Morris registered a change of sex, and later took advantage of the civil partnership legislation as they had never stopped living together.

Given that so many journalists aspire to be novelists, are the two writing skills very different, or just different aspects of the same kind of talent? With both, you are writing stories; it's just that one type – the journalistic – is supposed to be factual, whereas the other comes out of your head although it may be based on factual events, people or places.

The main difference is that with journalism you are supposed to stick to the facts whereas with novels, you are allowed – indeed compelled – to use your imagination. A journalist needs to have a certain level of writing ability, of course, but equally important are curiosity, a desire to get to the bottom of things, and a real feeling for what is topical.

A successful novelist must have these gifts too, but journalistic writing is always highly conscious, coming from the left side of the brain and although there may be moments of inspiration, the main skill required is the ability to put dry facts into palatable or entertaining form, to make them instantly readable and comprehensible to a readership that may just glance at the piece. There is also the important aspect that all pieces of journalism require a headline, so the subject must be able to be encapsulated into a few words.

The other thing about journalism is that it reads from the top-down, where the most important information is given right at the top of the story. Journalism is designed to be a quick read by people in a hurry and although a literary ability is a bonus, it is not an absolute requirement.

Writing fiction must eventually come out of the unconscious, often after much diligent and painstaking research has been done. But then it churns and churns in the mind until it comes out somehow of its own accord, as if the writer was taking it down from dictation. The children's writer Enid Blyton often remarked, after writing a chapter or two: 'I could never have written that' – and then reminded herself that, in fact, she just had written it. But she maintained she never knew where it came from.

Both types of writing require talent. They are different aspects of a writing and storytelling talent and sometimes, just sometimes they come together in the same person. The main talent for writing successful commercial fiction – which is what most journalists write – is the ability to keep the reader guessing and to have many twists and turns, to keep all the balls in the air until the final denouement.

The best novels by journalists are highly addictive reads, even if the characters tend to be stereotypes painted in broad strokes rather than complicated paradoxical individuals.

It is probably fair to say that many, if not most, female journalists have at least had a stab at writing a novel. Shirley Conran has said, along with Mike Molloy that most female journalists she knew had three chapters of a novel hidden away in a drawer – to explain why her sister scribblers tended to be so nasty about her own escape from the daily grind and into more timeless fiction.

In order to succeed, the fiction has to be going on in your head all the time. As Celia Brayfield said when asked where she gets her ideas from, the problem was not so much getting the ideas in the first place as stopping them from coming. They just arrive – then she has the challenge of trying to order these inchoate ideas into a readable, engaging novel.

A major reason why so many journalists aspire to novel writing is that, eventually, newspaper journalism, which is so exciting at first, can become all too ephemeral. After a week or so, the topicality of any newspaper story is lost and the article becomes a yesterday's forgotten item. Novels, by contrast, can last for ever – with any luck.

Another factor is that one can become tired of being bollocked by news and features editors, and want to be more in charge of one's own destiny. Yet another reason for moving into book writing is the desire not to have one's deathless prose 'improved' by soulless subs.

It is the case that around 80% of novels are read by women, even when not specifically aimed at the female market, so here again, female journalists probably have a head start on the men. And stories about love and betrayal, star-crossed lovers, adultery, forbidden sex, will always, always be popular. Rags to riches, riches to rags, reversals of fortune – all the eternal themes crop up all the time in both fiction and non-fiction, so the challenge is to capture them and give them a new twist, a relevance to the modern reader.

The final question for this chapter is: do journalists, or former journalists, make better novelists than others? To the extent that hacks have a low boredom threshold and have been thoroughly trained in readability, the answer is probably yes. But a lot of journalists' novels read a bit too much like non-fiction; again, a product of their training, where the imagination has to be reined in all the time.

There is also a tendency for some novels by former journalists to read like painting-by-numbers: here is some sex, here is some political content, here is a bit of travel, here is a description of an English village, here are the signs of success such as a Mercedes, a Docklands pad, first-class air travel. And I have never yet read a good description of sex by a journalist turned novelist – it's all a painfully embarrassing read and possibly the reason why *The Literary Review* magazine instituted its annual Bad Sex award.

But whether writing fiction or non-fiction, books or articles, it all comes down to whether you have something to say that the reading public want to hear. All journalists are scavengers, picking up stories, incidents, information, wherever they go, and the most talented have the ability to turn these scraps into satisfying works of art.

Because journalists have been writing all their lives, there is a good chance that their novels will be better than the usually dire attempts by politicians and former politicians, whose initial career has not been driven by the compulsion to write.

Most novels by former female journalists are basically beach or holiday reads, although not all. Although it is rare for a former journalist to write literary fiction, it is not unknown. Former Guardian woman's editor Clare Messud had a literary hit with her first published novel, *When the World was Steady*, and *Guardian* journalist Linda Grant has also written serious fiction.

Grant, born in Liverpool of Russian and Polish-Jewish immigrants, is a serious journalist as well as an award-winning novelist. Her novel *The Clothes on Their Backs* was short-listed for the Man Booker prize in 2008, and her novel *When I Lived in Modern Times*, won the Orange Prize in 2000.

As a journalist and a former *Guardian* columnist, she has written on subjects such as senile dementia, the drug ecstasy and on Serb nationalism and on Jewish and Israeli issues.

So – fiction and non-fiction can be successfully combined in the same career and in the same woman. Some critics have complained that journalists' fiction is all too often thinly-disguised autobiography. But if it's engaging, readable and a page-turner, does it matter?

Ten

The superstars

Some women journalists are such superstars from the word go and they are so far removed from the ordinary Joanna that that they often seem to be of an entirely different species.

Whereas writers like Jilly Cooper, Shirley Conran, Jean Rook and Katharine Whitehorn got to the top by a mixture of sheer hard work, slog and talent, the superstars seem to shine brightly right from the start, while humbler toilers in the vineyard can only gaze in wonder, awe and admiration.

Among the journalistic superstars are Anne Robinson, Janet Street-Porter, Tina Brown, Barbara Amiel and Anna Wintour, extraordinary women, very different from each other and all one-offs who somehow, attracted attention from their earliest years. For them, the media became the soil in which they flourished.

Of all the journalistic superstars, Anne Robinson has had the most solid and conventional Fleet Street career. In recent times known best for her dominatrix pose in the long-running television quiz show *The Weakest Link,* Robinson spilled the beans, or most of them, about herself in her candid autobiography, *Memoirs of an Unfit Mother*, where she told the harrowing story of how she lost custody of her only daughter, Emma, and of her struggles with alcoholism until she managed to give up drink completely. Robinson dedicates her book 'to all women who have struggled with a career and trying to do the right thing. Even if we achieve 20% improvement from one generation to another, we have done superbly.'

Robinson's book serves as a manual as to what it is possible to achieve if you are truly, madly, deeply – and ruthlessly – ambitious.

Anne Robinson was born in Liverpool in 1944. Her father, a university graduate, was a local schoolteacher and her mother ran a poultry business which became highly successful. Robinson always had, she says, an ambition to be famous, either as an actress or a writer, but never knuckled down at her expensive boarding school and left at 16 with only four O-levels. She went to a finishing school in France and then landed a job as a secretary to the editor of outside broadcasts on TV where she met her first lover, Frank Keating. They got engaged but the wedding was called off at the last minute, although Robinson confesses that she found sex 'fantastically delicious'.

More importantly for her subsequent career, she found the world of journalism delicious. The only problem was: how did she open the magic door and get in? What or who was her open-sesame? Although she had progressed from being a secretary to a researcher on a children's programme, she was at the time more attracted to print journalism than television, as: 'here was a career that with luck meant I could become someone but with the added bonus of being famous for being intelligent and able to write.' But – and there was a big but: 'I had no real qualifications or experience to enter print journalism...'

When Associated-Rediffusion did not renew her researcher contract, she replied to an ad for a reporter at the North London News Agency and was hired. She viewed this agency as the 'bargain basement' of journalism but at least it was a start and there she met a 19-year old lad, John Penrose, who would eventually become her second husband.

From the start a girl on the move, Robinson applied to the *Daily Mail* where Charlie Wilson was deputy news editor. She managed to get some shifts on the *Mail* and Charlie Wilson asked her out on a date to France. At 32, he seemed to Robinson like a real adult, and he was phenomenally ambitious. Wilson had begun his career as a teaboy on the *Sunday People* and he and Robinson soon began an affair. They were married in January 1968 but the marriage, Robinson confesses in her memoirs, was completely wrong from the start.

She does not reveal whether the sex in this marriage was 'fantastically delicious' but the relationship soon ran into trouble and was clearly never going to be a success. Unable to work on the same paper as her new husband – it was against the rules in those days – Robinson applied for an advertised job on *The Sunday Times*. There were 60 applicants for this post and Robinson was offered a week's trial.

She survived her trial period and was taken onto the staff, where she was sent to Northern Ireland to report on the troubles there, in 1968. Her marriage was by now in terminal decline and Robinson asked Harold Evans, the editor of the *Sunday Times,* for advice on what to do for the best. But Evans, although undoubtedly a talented journalist and editor, was hardly an expert marriage guidance counsellor, and Robinson reveals that he looked 'nonplussed' when his advice was sought on this intimate matter. In any case, Evans was soon to have serious marital problems of his own.

During her years at the *Sunday Times*, Robinson says she met wives of journalists who were clever and educated but doing nothing, just staying at home bringing up kids. She determined never to be remotely like them.

In those days, she says, women weren't estate agents, accountants, and even had to get a man's signature to rent a television set. Yet Robinson herself had been brought up by a career mother – her daughter calls her 'part monster, part magic' (a description she later applied to Robert Maxwell) – and from the start was determined to be a major earner like her mother. She certainly never remotely considered the life of a stay at home wife and mother for herself.

Her daughter, Emma, was born in 1970 and Robinson immediately went back to work after hiring a nanny. Charlie Wilson became deputy editor of the *Daily Mail* in Manchester and there soon followed a horrendous divorce and court battle for the custody, care and control of the infant Emma, which Wilson won. This is where the 'unfit mother' aspect comes in, as the judge in the case decided she was not suitable to bring up her own child. In those days it was usual to give the mother custody of the child or children, as it has been ever since, and the real drama of Robinson's book lies in her vivid retelling of this court case.

Charlie Wilson, who went on to become editor of *The Times*, among other jobs, has said that the main reason Anne lost custody of Emma was because she was alcoholic, something Anne Robinson herself has readily admitted.

She carried on working nonetheless and in spite of the growing alcoholism and loss of Emma, her career went ever upwards. She became the *Sunday Times'* correspondent n Rome, where John Penrose was also sent for the *Daily Mirror*. After the *Sunday Times*, Robinson went to the *Daily Mirror* which she found completely different: 'Here was not the unhurried scholastic atmosphere of an Oxford college, but something akin to the spirit today on a Stock Exchange trading floor dominated by brash young dealers. The *Mirror* executives were talented, dedicated, uncouth, their language foul, their skill at producing popular journalism of the highest standard unquestionable. Very few had formal qualifications of any sort.' This did not mean, however, that Holborn Circus was a house of philistines. 'It was just that the scholarship was heavily disguised.'

Again, Robinson was working with Penrose, who was assistant editor in charge of features on the *Daily Mirror* while she was a star columnist on the same paper.

Everything in newspapers, Robinson had noted, was totally male-dominated. The sports department, picture desk, advertising department, news room, were full of men with only the occasional token woman, apart from the fashion and women's pages. This was the case on every national newspaper at the time and the only aspect that distinguished the *Mirror* from other newspapers was the 'stupendous' level of entertaining and drinking that went on. The gender ratio on the *Daily Mirror* in those days was: men, 496, women, 22, including 123 journalists in Manchester, all of whom were male.

Male-dominated though it might have been, Robinson, at 37, was appointed assistant editor with token responsibility for editing the paper at times when the editor, Mike Molloy, was away. She had some idea she was making history as she went along and has admitted that she had no real idea about newspaper production or how a newspaper was put together. However, this did not prevent her from editing it and becoming the only women who was at least nominally editing a Fleet Street paper – in the days just before women were to storm into editorships on all kinds of newspapers.

She attracted the attention of Robert Maxwell when he bought the paper in 1984 and became one of the highest-paid staff there. Robinson-watchers say that she was always, always, angling for more money – and usually got it. After Maxwell fell overboard on his boat to his death in 1991, Robinson enthused: 'He enhanced all our lives' – a gushing tribute she had to retract when he was found to have embezzled the Mirror Group pension fund.

Her chance as a future television star came when she stood in for Barry Took on *Points of View,* and she soon established a loyal following with her trademark wink and catchphrase 'them upstairs' to describe the upper echelons of television management. It was soon clear that Robinson was a television natural and before long she was presenting the television consumer show *Watchdog*, where she replaced husband and wife team John Stapleton and Lynn Faulds-Wood. She was also a presenter on various radio shows, but her really big break came when she was asked to present a new kind of quiz show, *The Weakest Link*. This propelled her to international fame and the show for a while aired in America.

Her marriage to John Penrose hung on somehow for many years but also eventually ended in divorce. For many years, Penrose – as he was always known, at least by Annie – masterminded and managed Robinson's stellar career.

Charlie Wilson became editor of *The Times* during its first Wapping year, and later a high-ranking executive on the Mirror Group. After some years as a single father bringing up Emma, he married the magazine journalist Sally O'Sullivan, who became stepmother to Emma. This marriage, which produced two more children, also ended in divorce, and Wilson then married for a third time. All three marriages were to redheads.

Somehow, Anne Robinson has always had a gift for attracting publicity to herself, so that we all know about her losing custody of her daughter, her two marriages, her expensive facelift, and her struggles with alcoholism. Maybe, too, there is a gift for embroidering a plain unvarnished tale with journalistic licence, for dramatising an event in true tabloid style. For example, an account of her drinking bouts in her book concludes with the revelation that she woke up one day with her knickers round her neck, prompting many puzzled comments from readers as to just how knickers could somehow work their way up to the wearer's neck. Round the ankles, maybe, but up to the neck..?

But whatever embellishments Robinson has put on her story, there is no denying that hers is one of the great female journalistic success of the era. Print journalism gave Robinson her start, her high profile and then the much greater power of television allowed her to arrive at the pinnacle which, in her mid-sixties, she has retained. At the time of writing, Anne Robinson has been sober, and a teetotaller, for 35 years.

When Anne Robinson joined the *Sunday Times,* the editor was the great Harold Evans, an editor still remembered by hacks everywhere. At the time Robinson was there, Evans was a long-time married man with three children. His life was to change for ever when, at the age of 46 and the most glamorous editor of the most glamorous paper in the world, he met the 21-year old Tina Brown.

Cristina Brown, who had just left Oxford, was no ordinary 21-year old. While at Oxford, she had already networked like mad and thanks to making very close contact with well-known journalists such as Auberon Waugh, was already a published journalist in many national outlets. She had also enjoyed a well-publicised affair with the future novelist Martin Amis, son of Kingsley Amis.

Born in 1952, Tina Brown won the Catherine Pakenham Award at the *Daily Telegraph* in 1973, the same year in which the *Sunday Times* called her the most promising of all young female journalists.

She had also, by the time she met Evans, had two plays performed and she was to have possibly the fastest rise to international celebrity status ever known in the media. Although 25 years her senior, Evans fell instantly, totally, head over heels in love, and he and Tina set up home together while Evans went about dismantling his long marriage to Enid, the solid housewifely teacher he had met while both were studying at Durham University.

For her part, Brown thought that Evans was the sexy editor of all time, and together, they were to become an even more illustrious power couple than Eve Pollard and Nicholas Lloyd. Tina Brown had been writing for the *Sunday Times* but after setting up home with Evans decided this would not look good and so wrote for other papers, always making sure she was the star of her own articles. She managed to convey an almost manic enthusiasm for everything she wrote about, and her sheer energy and – one has to admit – clever writing ability soon attracted attention among media-watchers everywhere.

In particular, Brown attracted the attention of Gary Bogard, an Australian entrepreneur who had just bought the ailing *Tatler* magazine and in a stroke of pure genius, hired the now 25-year old Brown to edit it. As editor, Tina Brown put *Tatler* on the map and sought out expensive and talented writers. Brown was a talent-spotter as well as a gifted writer, and her *Tatler* became required reading among the literati and glitterati. Six years after meeting, Harold Evans and Tina Brown married, and Evans was made editor of *The Times* after Rupert Murdoch bought the loss-making paper from Lord Thomson.

The appointment was a disaster and Harold Evans' days at the Murdoch paper were numbered, for all that Tina Brown recorded her diary that she 'hugely' liked 'this vivid rascal' that was Murdoch. The couple went to America where Tina became editor of *Vanity Fair* and Evans went to work for the publishing company Random House, where he became president. Tina and Harry soon became the toast of the New York media superstars, and known as 'teenanarry'. They had two children along the way, George and Isabel. George was born when Evans was 57.

Tina Brown became successively editor of *The New Yorker* and a new magazine, *Talk*, but though she hired the best of the writing talent available, *Talk* soon folded. Many journalists and writers have their own tales of woe about working with Tina, who they regarded as 'talented but psychotic'.

Up and coming writers such as Toby Young and Tom Shone – who was headhunted by Brown for *Talk* when he was film critic of the *Sunday Times* – came to grief on Tina's magazines, mainly because nothing they wrote was ever published. Novelist Angela Huth was encouraged to send dozens of short stories, but all were rejected with an admonition to Huth from Tina to 'please, please, keep trying.' Tina Brown had had a fling with Huth's former husband, while at Oxford.

Since *Talk* folded, Tina Brown has tried writing a column for *The Times*, produced a book on Princess Diana, and tried to resuscitate a television career which stalled and stopped before it ever properly got going in the US.

At the time of writing Harold Evans – known in *Private Eye* as Dame Harold Evans – is 80 years old. He is the author of several books including classic works on newspaper style and design.

Janet Street-Porter had a similar rapid rise to fame to Tina Brown's, but came from a very different section of society. Tina Brown's father, George Brown, was a film producer and her glamorous mother, Bettina, was also a journalist. Janet Street-Porter, born plain (and very plain, according to her memoirs) Janet Bull, came from a working-class family living in Fulham, West London. The elder of two sisters, Street-Porter was tall and gangly, with protruding teeth and a horrendous accent which later became her trademark, or one of them. She studied architecture and married fellow architecture student Tim Street-Porter, who later became a successful photographer.

Both jacked in their architectural studies long before completion, and both from the start showed a kind of genius for networking. By the age of 22 Street-Porter was writing on young fashion for the *Evening Standard*, somehow already famous. In her own words: 'Over the next decade I would be at the centre of the art and music scene in London night after night, backstage with Pink Floyd or drinking with Janis Joplin. I'd model for Zandra Rhodes and put on a show at Joan Littlewood's theatre at Stratford East. I'd meet Barbara Hulanicki (Biba), Twiggy and Manolo Blahnik and Ossie Clark would design my wedding dress.'

Street-Porter refers to herself as a 'strange mixture of brash exterior and insecure interior. My hair changed colour about as often as I had sex. I tried owning pets, but they didn't last much longer than the husbands.'

Street-Porter landed a job at *Petticoat*, where so many future media stars. Jilly Cooper and Claire Rayner among them, were to make their name.

Petticoat was an untidy-looking, cheaply-produced weekly magazine, printed on poor quality paper and with blurred colour. It was aimed at young women, and its editor for most of its life was Audrey Slaughter, who started many big careers for women journalists. Everybody wanted to write for *Petticoat* in those days, and it was certainly a highly successful launching pad for Janet Street-Porter as Shirley Conran saw her work there and offered her a job as deputy fashion editor of the *Daily Mail*. This was 1969, when the actual fashion editor was Sandy Fawkes. Street-Porter calls Fawkes 'a red-haired, tempestuous journalist with a legendary temper and a huge appetite for booze and men. She was to be my mentor throughout my drunken two years at Associated Newspapers.'

Street-Porter was by this time having loads of affairs with famous men and her marriage to Tim was soon on the rocks. Her next husband was Tony Elliott, founder of *Time Out*, at the time a very new and radical departure from the staid, boring listings magazines of the time. This marriage lasted an even shorter time than the first one but her television career was now starting to take off and she eventually became the face of youth, or 'yoof' television.

She was one of the start-up team at the disastrous *Live* television company, along with Kelvin Mackenzie, and later became editor of the *Independent on Sunday*. She has also been in the jungle on *I'm a Celebrity – Get me Out of Here*, taken part in television documentaries, chat shows and she has also written two hectic volumes of autobiography and a book of beauty tips and hints.

One of the great media personalities of our time, Street-Porter is brash, loud, outspoken, not noticeably shy and a total, absolute survivor, having gone through many jobs in newspapers, magazines and television, many husbands and lovers, many homes – and somehow it has all brushed off so that she looks about 20 years younger than most women in their 60s.

As does the next superstar, the much more serious and ultimately rather tragic Barbara Amiel. Amiel first came to the attention of the media world big time when she was pictured with her fourth husband, newspaper proprietor Conrad Black, in fancy dress. Amiel was dressed as Marie Antoinette and Black as Cardinal Richelieu. It is a picture that has haunted the Blacks ever since as it has been reprinted dozens of times and is on the cover of Tom Bower's unauthorised biography. This picture is seen as somehow encapsulating everything one needs to know about the Blacks and is the consummate picture that is worth a thousand words.

But long before that picture was taken in 1999, Barbara Amiel had been trying her hardest to become a media star. She has attempted to achieve this by putting across an image of herself as both sexy and serious, as a seductive and alluring siren who is nevertheless extremely brainy. While writing quite serious and sometimes even explosive, stuff for serious newspapers, Amiel has also been at pains to present herself as one of the most glamorous and sexy women in the world; a hard double-act to pull off.

Barbara Amiel has been married four times, had countless affairs, but, in common with Janet Street-Porter, never any children to interrupt her ambition or rise to the top.

Amiel was born in London in 1940 of Jewish middle-class parents who divorced when she was eight. Her mother soon remarried and in 1952 the family, consisting of Barbara, her sister and a younger half-brother, emigrated to Hamilton, Ontario. Money was tight and Amiel had to take a series of menial jobs to survive. In 1959 she entered the University of Toronto to read Philosophy and English, after which she began making her way in journalism, firstly as an active member of the Communist party. This youthful idealism was a far cry from her later extravagance when married to Conrad Black, and the extreme right-wing views she began to espouse along with her marriage to him.

She started writing for Canadian magazines and newspapers and in 1983 became the first woman to edit a daily newspaper, the *Toronto Sun,* in Canada. In 1985 she came back to the UK and was a contributor to *The Times* and *Sunday Times* from 1986 to 1994. Other journalists remember Amiel sitting at her desk struggling with her copy; she was never a natural writer and her columns were as hard to read as they undoubtedly were to write. They never flowed in the same way as, say, Libby Purves' *Times* columns flow, and it was often hard to follow her train of thought.

She was always extremely flirtatious and definitely unhinged many of the men who encountered her. Her unofficial biographer Tom Bower, though, remained immune and unimpressed and his account of her shenanigans in his book *Conrad and Lady Black*, shows actual dislike.

After her marriage to Black in 1992, Amiel joined his paper, the *Daily Telegraph*, where she wrote a weekly column for a reported annual fee of £600,000. She was also editorial vice-president for a time of Hollinger, Conrad Black's company. One of the few journalists to champion the cause of Israel, she has been criticised for portraying Arabs in a racist fashion, and accused of making the *Telegraph* sound like a champion of Zionism.

She lost her column at the *Telegraph* in 2004 when her husband's financial activities on the paper started to be investigated, and – it has to be said – she loyally stood by him during his trial on criminal charges of fraud, at which he was found guilty and sentenced to six years' imprisonment. She then started writing again for the Canadian magazine *Macleans,* where she had begun her journalistic career.

Her various husbands have been: Gary Smith, George Jonas, David Graham and Conrad Black. The first three marriages were brief, the longest lasting just four years. It is said by onlookers that Conrad Black, who had also been married before, and Barbara Amiel, found true, if belated, love with each other.

Before their fall from grace, Amiel and Black were known for their parties and for living a ridiculously lavish lifestyle, provoking the comment from one journalist: 'Not many people can afford to live like Barbara Amiel, including Barbara Amiel.' The Blacks' lifestyle during their highest pomp became legendary and many commentators drew attention to the 'penny' test, whereby the sheets on their bed had to be so tightly drawn that a penny coin would bounce on it. They would rise at noon then work far into the night; Black composing his overblown biographies of figures such as Napoleon and Franklin Roosevelt while supposedly attending to the running of his newspaper empire.

During the good years, Amiel had a wardrobe stuffed with designer clothes and became famous, or notorious, for the comment: 'My extravagance knows no bounds.' Although by no means young when she married Black – she was 52 at the time and he was a few years younger – she was always elegant with a chiselled face and swish of jet-black hair. Tom Bower believes that much of her soignée appearance was due to cosmetic surgery but she managed to look stunning, however great the cost, in either cash or cosmetic enhancement, of achieving the effect.

It was always hard to take Amiel as seriously as she took herself. And when everything started to go into reverse for the Blacks, she confided to a friend: 'I never thought I would end up the laughing stock in three continents.' She was appalled, said former *Sunday Telegraph* editor Sarah Sands, by the way that London society turned against her when the Blacks' supposed riches were exposed as a Maxwell-style theft.

In his book Tom Bower (husband of *Evening Standard* editor Veronica Wadley) draws attention to Amiel's forty-year struggle to achieve fame and fortune and says that she has always tried to come across as an explosive and irresistible combination of brains and beauty, charm and attitude.

Privately, like many Hollywood stars and other adventuresses, Amiel has struggled with much ill-health, including a serious immunity deficiency disease, and she has also spent many years on anti-depressants.

The prevailing image of Barbara Amiel is of a rich bitch, dangerously demented and not only extravagant with her designer clothes, but also with the truth. In her autobiography, *Confessions*, she writes about being thrown into a Mozambique prison during a journalistic assignment for *Macleans* magazine and where, as a precautionary measure to protect herself and her colleagues, she ate her business cards. This 'confession' prompted the remark from one of her associates: but they were laminated!

However, along with a similar self-invented character, Jeffrey Archer, Barbara Amiel has provided entertainment and the opportunity for caustic comments from her journalistic colleagues, many of whom have revelled in her spectacular reversal of fortune. Gone are the two private jets waiting on the runway, the second jet there as a back-up in case the other failed for some reason, gone are the hundreds of designer outfits – well, they have probably not gone but have certainly not been added to recently – and gone are the retinues of servants and hangers-on.

Gone, too, one imagines, is the penny-tested bed on which clean Egyptian cotton sheets were put every day.

What does Barbara Amiel's story tell us about leading female journalists? Simply that with enough self-confidence, chutzpah and sheer brass neck, you can become rich, famous, feted – and have your own columns in leading newspapers for which you are paid am enormous salary. The lesser lights among us have the comfort of being able to ask: was the price for all this achievement and – for a time – envy, just too high?

Anna Wintour, born in November 1949, is the daughter of former *Evening Standard* editor Charles Wintour. She was educated at the North London Collegiate School – which Barbara Amiel also attended for a time – and she got her first job at the then new Biba boutique when she was 15. She dropped out of school a year later and went onto a training programme at Harrods.

Fashion was always in her genes and she became a journalist in 1970 on *Harpers and Queen*. In 1975 she went to New York to become a junior fashion editor on *Harper's Bazaar* and then held various editorial positions on American magazines until in 1986 she became editor of British *Vogue,* when the longstanding previous editor, Beatrix Miller, retired. In 1988, Wintour secured the much-coveted 'top job' , editor of American *Vogue*, for which she had been aiming all her professional life, and a job she has held ever since.

It has been said that Anna Wintour and Tina Brown, who had a similarly spectacular rise across the Atlantic, see each other as deadly rivals and even that they hate each other. Be that as it may, both British women have risen to the top in what is perhaps the toughest journalistic market in the entire world: that of big-time American magazines.

In her time, Wintour has dated many famous and prominent men including the writer Piers Paul Read, when she was just 15, the late gossip columnist Nigel Dempster, Richard Neville, founder of *Oz* magazine, and comedian Eric Idle. She also disappeared for a week with Bob Marley, but in the end married, in 1984, child psychiatrist Charles Shaffer, 13 years her senior, with whom she had two children. This marriage later ended in divorce, after which she had an affair with an American millionaire, Shelby Bryan.

Wintour's daily life and rigid discipline are well known. She gets up around 6am each day, plays tennis, has her hair and make up done and arrives in her *Vogue* office at 8 am. She is in bed by 10.15 each night and rarely stays at parties or functions for more than 20 minutes at a time. She is also famous for her never-changing hairstyle; a bouffant, fringed bob, for her dark glasses and for her rigidly-maintained size zero figure.

She became a figure of legend when she was fictionalised in the book *The Devil Wears Prada*, as the tyrannical editor Miranda Priestly. The lightly-fictionalised book, by former former *Vogue* intern Lauren Weisberger, became a bestseller, and the Miranda Priestly character became even more famous when the book was turned into a surprisingly successful, amusing and sympathetic film starring Meryl Streep.

Anna Wintour received an OBE for services to journalism in the June 2008 honours, even though she had worked in America for many years.

So do these journalistic superstars have anything in common, and do they have anything to teach journalistic aspirants of today? Three of them, Anna Wintour, Janet Street-Porter and Barbara Amiel, have concentrated hard on their appearance, so that they will be instantly recognised wherever they go. Janet Street-Porter is very tall and has perfected a kooky image; Anna Wintour is tiny, slim and always impeccably well-groomed in classic designer clothes; Barbara Amiel has gone for the alluring-siren look.

Anne Robinson's appearance is more ordinary and everyday but she has become instantly recognisable through her many television appearances. Tina Brown, although by no means a fashion plate, is much-photographed, often in evening dress and very often with her elderly husband Harold Evans. Brown has also been photographed in the presence of many famous people, and the 'teenanarry' pictures have been reprinted all over the world.

One way and another, all five women have become highly visible entirely by their own efforts. And what one can say is that they have absolutely no male equivalent. In the male-dominated world of the media, there are simply no men to touch these female superstars. Who was the editor of Vanity Fair after Tina Brown? Graydon Carter. Who? Few of us know remotely what Carter looks like or anything about him and the only reason most of us have even heard the name is through Toby Young's book and film, *How to Lose Friends and Alienate People.*

Who was the editor of the *Independent on Sunday* after Janet Street-Porter? Who edited *Tatler* after Tina Brown left? Who took over Amiel's column at the *Daily Telegraph*? Who presented *Watchdog* after Anne Robinson? Nobody knows, or can remember. Or even cares. And yet these singular women are firmly lodged in the collective unconscious of the media, at least for a generation.

They show us what can be achieved for the truly determined – and if you are prepared to accept the brickbats as well as the bouquets, to rise from the ashes of a previous failure or disaster and keep bouncing back, trying new things, never saying no, never giving up, never looking miserable but being able to put on an outward show of smiling, unshakeable self-confidence.

Plus, of course – always doing your very best to look glamorous, in charge and in control.

Eleven

Good old bad old days

The glory and glamour that was Fleet Street disappeared for ever in 1986. That was the year the old hot-metal technology was finally laid to rest and the once-mighty print unions lost their power for ever, after a bloody pitched battle with Rupert Murdoch's News International organisation at Wapping.

Once the printers conceded defeat, many centuries-old traditions came to a sudden end and one by one, newspaper offices began to move out of The Street.

This was a revolution as big in its way as the invention of the printing press itself in the 15th century. Along with the outdated print machines went the restrictive practices, the overmanning, the closed shops and the arcane rituals and traditions, some of which had been in place since Caxton's time.

Over the centuries the collective bargaining power of printers had become immense and was at its strongest in the newspaper industry.

The strictly men-only print unions had their various 'chapels', presided over by the Father who was elected yearly by ballot.

Printers, who had to serve a six or seven year apprenticeship, considered themselves superlative and very important craftsmen, a kind of priestly caste, and they continually fought against the introduction of new technology, including the linotype machine when it was developed in the late 19th century.

Owing to the bargaining power of the print chapels and the fact that no proprietor dare risk the loss of a day's print run by arguing, newspaper printers earned huge salaries for, often, very short working weeks. Not even the mightiest proprietor would lock horns with the

176

print unions, for fear of the Father of the Chapel bringing his men out on strike.

All printers knew that if their union card was taken away they would be unemployable, so all had to toe the union line. By the time of the Wapping dispute, there were two men for every job on some newspapers and intense bargaining over the years had meant that fractions of hours were charged as complete hours, and urgent news stories would always be paid extra.

Some post-Wapping journalists have wondered why nothing adverse about the print unions and their stranglehold ever appeared in the newspapers. The reason was simple: the printers would have refused to print it. In order to keep their newspapers on the streets, most proprietors had a policy of 'print at any price'. As long ago as the early 1970s, printers had refused to print an article by David Astor, then editor of *The Observer*, complaining about the overmanning and restrictive practices of the print unions.

In January 1984, the editor of *The Sun*, Kelvin McKenzie, wanted to run a readers' ballot saying: Tell us what you really think about the miners' strike. This strike was heavily supported by the print unions, which had raised £1 million in support of the miners. As soon as the Imperial Father of the composing room saw the anti-strike copy, he ordered his printers to stop work on it.

This led to McKenzie, never one of nature's calmest people, storming into the print room, only to be told that the proposed readers' ballot interfered with 'the democratic rights of the printing trade'.

These are just a couple of examples of the kind of incident that happened in the print rooms all the time. If a journalist tried to touch any of the type, this in itself could lead to the printers coming out on strike.

By the 1980s, not only were the print unions hanging on to a technology long out of date, but computer technology had actually been ready to use for many years already. The first woman sub on *The Times*, Judy Hobson, has told how an early computer stood unused and under wraps at *The Times* since 1978 – a full eight years before computer technology was actually used at that paper. In other countries with less strong or non-existent print unions, computers had long supplanted hot-metal type.

Yet the National Union of Journalists, to which most newspaper journalists belonged, played an almost equal part in prolonging the outdated, sexist, racist system operated by the printers. When the NUJ was founded in 1907 it slavishly copied the methods and tactics of the print unions, and this included the male, racist bias.

The NUJ was also composed of 'chapels' in newspaper offices, each presided over by the elected Father of the Chapel, and all members were known as 'brothers'. As newspapers grew in power, influence and wealth, so did the NUJ, eventually introducing a closed shop system in most newspapers, a training scheme in some, and insistence on pre-existing union membership for journalists working on national papers.

When newspaper circulations were at their height, the NUJ was a powerful organisation, and totally male-dominated. It set minimum hours, wages and conditions, and its bargaining power was also immense. In the 1980s the NUJ had attempted to modernise itself by setting up a (women-only) 'Equality Working Party' and also a 'Black Media Group'. Then, in 1984, when *The Times* journalists were locked in strife with the management, the NUJ decided to join forces with the main print union, the NGA (National Graphical Association).

The individual NGA chapels did not go for this idea which, as it turned out was a good thing as otherwise the journalists could have found their positions as untenable as those of the printers turned out to be.

This led to former chapel officers of the *Mirror*, which had been a closed shop, breaking away and forming their own union, the British Association of Journalists (BAJ). The outcome was that NUJ membership, formerly a compulsory requirement of employment at the Mirror Group, was no longer necessary and the NUJ soon lost all its bargaining power.

The whole complicated edifice for both the journalists and the printers came tumbling down with the demise of the print unions. After the Wapping battle was won by Murdoch, the closed shops opened up, union membership was no longer a requirement of employment, and anybody considered good enough could get an article, photograph or cartoon printed in a newspaper, even a paper that had formerly operated a closed shop.

It was at this time that Kelvin McKenzie made his famous speech to his staff at *The Sun*, telling them that 'what the NUJ has done for you, you could safely stick up a flea's arse.'

The NUJ limped on in spite of McKenzie's 'flea's arse' pronouncement, and in 2007 it celebrated its centenary. But now that ownership of a precious union card was no longer a mandatory condition of employment on a national newspaper, it became ever more difficult to rally the troops and on some papers, NUJ chapels disappeared altogether.

Former closed shops such as the *Daily* and *Sunday Mirror* now started employing non-union labour, which had not happened in living memory. It had previously been the case that every single employee of either paper, including temporary secretaries, had to be a member of an appropriate union. This went for freelance contributors as well.

Good news? Well, yes and no. On the good side, journalism was democratised, anybody could now get in, anybody could have a voice and in theory at least, every voice could be heard. Nobody could any more be silenced for having awkward views that might not please the printers, or for not belonging to an officially-approved trades union.

Because of the closed shop system, it had been difficult, if not impossible, for people to get into journalism in later life as, unless they were 'trained' and already in possession of an NUJ card – no other journalist's union would do – there was simply no way in. All that now came to an end and there was no longer any absolute necessity to train in the provinces before being thought worthy of a Fleet Street position.

Another benefit of the changed system was that the newspapers themselves started to become ever larger, and far from every journalist fighting for an inch or two of rare and precious space, it became a matter of trying to fill up acres of newsprint. As printers were no longer in a position to demand constantly higher rates of pay, newspapers could be produced much more cheaply than ever before.

In time, newspapers developed online versions and websites, and this opened up another significant and brand-new journalistic outlet.

Another important change was that the former uncrossable chasm between the so-called quality and the popular press began to close, and this created more opportunities again as it became possible to move freely between newspapers and not be pigeonholed as either a 'broadsheet' or a 'tabloid' journalist. The gap between newspapers and magazines also began to close as newspapers introduced magazine sections and glossy magazines of their own.

One positive effect of all this for women journalists was that opportunities now began to expand greatly. Journalism, always a many-headed monster, quickly began to grow more heads, particularly in female-friendly directions such as fashion, cookery, beauty, lifestyle, parenting and consumer issues. There was suddenly all the space in the world to write about domestic and family matters and to mouth off in endless columns.

Newspaper editors were now free to hire politicians, TV celebrities, sportspeople and specialists such as cooks, sex counsellors, sports coaches and fitness experts, to write for their pages, so the whole world of print opened up for everybody to have their say or provide their expert opinion.

Another advantage for women was that with the death of the old-fashioned print unions, the gender bias completely disappeared. The new technology was unisex and it seemed women could operate computers just as well as men – and without serving a seven-year apprenticeship, either.

Now that lengthy training periods and indentures were no longer a prerequisite to a job on a national newspaper, media studies courses began to proliferate at universities, and you could even take a degree in fashion journalism. Fashion journalist Catherine Wilson (now the Countess of St Germans) managed to secure a job on *The Guardian* straight after graduating from Central St Martin's.

All over the country, journalism courses began to be introduced at adult and evening classes and students who were good enough could get a piece published in *The Times* or *Guardian*, for example, after only a few weeks of being on the course.

Journalism, which had traditionally been seen as a man's occupation, became a profession eagerly considered by girls so that post-Wapping, around 75 per cent of students on journalism and media courses were female. This was a total change from the old days of the NCTJ training courses, where the ratio was around 10 men to every one woman.

Everything changed, and women began to flood into national newspapers at all levels. The old distinction between men and women in newspapers disappeared for ever and nobody was any longer shocked to discover they had a woman boss, a female photographer, a woman news editor. It no longer looked odd to have a newsroom composed 50-50 of males and females.

So far, so good. So what about the downsides of this revolution?

The immediate effect was that once the stranglehold of the unions was broken, wages were reduced and expense accounts disappeared. The print unions had been spectacularly successful in maintaining high wages for their staff so that by the mid-1980s linotype operators on wages of £45,000 a year were not uncommon.

Journalists' wages on national newspapers had also been kept high by the bargaining power of the NUJ, which kept demanding parity with the printers. Generous expenses were part of the package and many journalists considered their expenses as overtime. Overtime as such was not paid to journalists and as few worked strictly nine to five, the tax-free expenses were a useful way of increasing salaries as well as compensating staff for commitment beyond the call of duty.

When national newspaper journalists had to be fully paid-up members of the NUJ, it was relatively easy for the union to protect its members. But once journalism became a free for all with no requirement for

180

union membership, this protection ceased. Even long-serving members of staff were no longer protected and journalists could now be sacked on an editor's whim.

And when newspaper proprietors were freed from the shackles of having to employ union-only labour, they naturally set the wages at a vastly lower level and cut out all the expense accounts. One description of this situation at the time was that 40/40 – journalists in their 40s earning £40,000 a year, became replaced by 20/20 – journalists in their twenties earning £20,000 a year.

High profile writers and reporters could of course set their own levels but the collective bargaining power had disappeared and the capitalist system whereby a few high-flyers could command vast sums and the rest virtually nothing at all, prevailed.

At the same time, the chauffeur-driven cars went, the drinks cabinets and the boozy lunches went and, one has to say, the entire traditional Fleet Street lifestyle went with it. The *Private Eye* character Lunchtime O'Booze, intended to caricature a typical drunken journalist, disappeared; post-Wapping readers would not understand the reference.

Because there was no obvious place to meet, journalists no longer congregated in pubs to exchange gossip and stories, and the intense camaraderie that had characterised The Street in its halcyon days was no more, both inside the office and outside. Journalists working in offices were now marooned behind their computer screens and the once-noisy, bustling newsrooms became as quiet as cathedrals.

An article in the *Washington Post* in June 2008 lamenting the loss of the noisy newsroom reported:

'On deadline, the vast newsroom had always produced a cacophony. Typewriter keys pounded like an orchestra of percussionists until the volume swelled to fill the room... then one day modern times arrived. Computers. With their keys nearly silent to the touch, a forever quiet fell on the newsroom... Women and faces of all races became common in the newsroom. Ashtrays and liquor bottles disappeared.'

A more serious downside was that there was no job security any more. In the old days of the closed shop, no journalist could be sacked except for 'gross professional misconduct'. Writer Colin Dunne has said that when he was on the *Mirror*, it was 'strictly one-way employment'. New writers came in but old ones never went out.

But there was more bad news. For complicated reasons not necessarily directly connected with the loosening of union strangleholds, circulations began to plummet. The circulation of the *Sunday People*, for example, went from more than five million at its height down to just over 600,000 in 2008. Circulation of the *Daily Express* slid from over four million to around 800,000.

As circulations inexorably fell, so did profits and this brought in ever more savage cost-cutting measures. Here was another, previously unseen downside as, although the industry opened up to women in one way, it shut down in another as staffing levels were ruthlessly cut even as the size of newspapers kept increasing.

As an example, in the 1980s, the weekly magazine *Woman's Own,* with a circulation of around 1.5 million, was produced by a staff of 120; in 2008, the magazine *Take a Break,* with a similar circulation, was produced by a staff of just 35.

In the same way that the print unions had kept up high levels of manning (many called it overmanning) so the NUJ had demanded certain levels of staff. Now, wages and staffing levels could be cut to the bone and nobody would object. Newspapers that had formerly employed people of high talent and ability, now competed with each other to see just how cheaply they could fill the day's newsprint quota.

Young journalists were hired at cut-price rates or even for nothing at all if they were on work experience. It became impossible to earn a living on a local or regional newspaper and instead of journalists being sent out on genuine stories, they were set to rewriting press releases, a form of hackery the journalist Nick Davies has termed 'churnalism' in his book, *Flat Earth News.*

Perhaps the saddest aspect of this revolution was that news-gathering and dissemination which used to be considered the very purpose of newspapers, came to be seen as an expensive operation, too expensive to maintain, and more or less came to an end. News gathering had, of course, been one of the more exciting aspects of working on a newspaper and involved spending money entertaining and maintaining contacts, then going out of the office actually to get the stories.

By contrast, sitting in the office, having sandwiches at your desk for lunch and rewriting press releases and agency copy, costs nothing at all, except for the actual office costs. Post-Wapping, editorial pages became filled with comment instead of news that is, again, a cheap way of filling space. Comment – to adapt an old saying – may be free, but facts are expensive.

These changes were bad enough and meant that national newspaper journalism was no longer the exciting, fun-filled and stress-filled occupation it had been, but to many minds the worst aspect of the revolution, so necessary in many ways, was the end of Fleet Street itself as the nation's production centre. The Street, which housed most of the national newspapers, was handily near the Inns of Court, the

Houses of Parliament and the City and so was itself in the centre of things.

You could not walk down the old Fleet Street without bumping into a friend or colleague. But now that newspapers began to be housed in industrial depots all over London, everybody was isolated from each other. It was no longer necessary to be near main railway stations as the existence of motorways now meant that newspapers could be distributed overnight on lorries – and lorries could start out from anywhere.

As newspapers moved out of their Fleet Street locations to cheaper premises, the very heart of national newspapers was cut out. Could anybody imagine the Houses of Parliament decamping from Westminster and being split up all round London, with the Labour party in one building, the Tories in another and the LibDems and UKIP parties in Manchester or somewhere?

Could anybody imagine the Inns of Court, the Old Bailey, the High Court, being split up and cases being heard in Portakabins all round the periphery of the M25? Of course not. The geographical position of the main courts of justice and of parliament, right in the centre of the city, highlights their importance and status. Once newspapers moved out of central London, the whole importance of the media was called into question, and it began to be seen as something trivial and unimportant, dumbed-down, celebrity-driven.

The demise of the expense accounts also meant that something valuable was lost. Few journalists ever took a contact, or even a friend, to an expensive lunch without coming away with three or four stories the other newspapers didn't have. What kind of stories are you going to get eating sandwiches at your desk? On most papers nowadays, journalists have to get permission to take somebody to lunch and obtain prior approval not only of the restaurant but also of the contact.

Most journalists in the old days were ferociously ambitious and not trying to milk the system so much as nail the good stories.

There is no money for investigative journalism any more. When papers were flush with money, long-term investigations could be started which might or might not yield a fantastic story. Risks had to be taken; now, with ever more ruthlessly slashed budgets this cannot happen.

Yes, the old Fleet Street practices, the outdated technology, the stranglehold of the print unions and the male domination had to go. They had become a ridiculous anachronism, living in a bygone age and modernisation was long overdue. But it is sad that it has not seemed possible to retain the best of the old *and* of the new, to embrace the essential new technology at the same time as retaining the glamour, the high quality, the sense of doing something important and worthwhile for the readers, and also that wonderful, magical location between St Paul's and The Strand.

There is no point in mourning the demise of the old days, as there was much wrong with a system that discouraged articulate, opinionated and talented women from having an equal voice in the media. There was enormous sexism and racism in the old days, and women put up with sexual harassment and patronising attitudes, just seeing them as part and parcel of the job, the price paid for being allowed to join an exclusive men's club.

Those days are thankfully over but did all the glamour and fun, the sense of doing something both worthwhile and exciting, have to disappear as well?

When talking to women journalists in the course of researching this book, all drew attention to the extreme difficulty girls had in getting into newspapers in the past, but all agreed that with the demise of the old Fleet Street, the specialness of being there, went as well.

That potent feeling of walking down Fleet Street, experiencing with every step the almost unbelievable, thrilling sensation of being allowed entry to an exclusive enclave, has no equivalent in the days where all the newspaper offices are scattered around London and the drinking culture that was so much an integral part of the whole process, has completely vanished.

Every year in June, veteran Fleet Street journalist John Dale, editor of *Take A Break*, the biggest-selling women's weekly magazine in the UK, takes a group of his young journalists on a tour of Fleet Street. The reason? Dale said: 'As an editor employing mainly young or very young journalists, most of them women, it soon became clear that when I mentioned Fleet Street, they had not got a clue what I was talking about. We started these tours to remind people of how very important Fleet Street was, both as a place and a concept. To my young staff, it seems like life on another planet.

'When we walk down Fleet Street, we are taking a trip into bygone history. My staff has no idea of people sitting at typewriters, chain smoking, dealing with printers in the basement or congregating in pubs, nor have they any idea of the immense power of newspapers in the heyday of The Street.

'New technology has made everything much more efficient and means we can bring out better products with greatly lower staffing levels. And that of course has been a good thing. We have invented

184

new markets, brought exciting new products into being that would never have stood a chance with the old regime.

'But mainly, and so far as women are concerned, it's the culture that has changed beyond all recognition. Today's young journalists would simply not put up with the harassment and sheer rudeness that female journalists had no choice but to endure in the old days. When I was working at the *Daily Mail* in the 1970s, I was on a story about a serial rapist with Anthea Disney, a leading reporter.

'The detective we were interviewing said he could not talk in front of that young lady, meaning Anthea, and she would have to leave the room while he spoke to me only. She had to go, but no woman would put up with that kind of behaviour now.

'Sexual equality has happened but it's also important for young journalists of today to understand where journalism came from in the first place. Popular journalism originated and flourished in Fleet Street and in their heyday, newspapers had huge money, political power and influence. Newspapers were powerful in a way barely realised today, and this was why Fleet Street was so glamorous and awe-inspiring, to men as well as women.

'The Express newspapers made so much money they could afford, in 1931, to erect the famous plate-glass Art Deco building dubbed *The Black Lubyanka* by Private Eye. Now it is owned by Goldman Sachs; the money flowed out of newspapers and into the City, so it is no accident that banks have taken over these imposing old newspaper buildings.'

What do leading women journalists themselves think about the momentous changes since, for example, Doreen Spooner was the sole female photographer on the *Daily Mirror*, Felicity Green was the only woman on the board of a national newspaper and the only token women executives were the fashion editors?

Tina Weaver, editor of the *Sunday Mirror*, believes that gender is not an issue any more and says: 'Each reporter is judged on their own merit. Women get a good crack of the whip, whether it's covering wars, politics or the Asian tsunami. There are more women in newsrooms than ever before and Trinity Mirror has a female chief executive and a female national editor. This shows how far the industry has come.'

Eve Pollard believes it is still easier for men than women to get on in newspapers, but 'with every year, it gets less easy. We now have a constant three or four female newspaper editors, which is very different from when I was a number two.'

Sue Matthias, a founder member of the *Independent on Sunday*, says: 'When I joined, I was the only senior woman there. Even in 1990, it felt old-fashioned. We are moving towards a more balanced industry but we're not there yet. The old stereotype of women doing features and men doing hard news is changing and that kind of discrimination is being phased out but even so, you rarely see women in newspapers over the age of 50.'

Polly Toynbee was less impressed with the achievements of women like Eve Pollard and Rebekah Wade, saying 'they have been editors of pretty disgusting papers. They regard doing things just like the boys as a triumph. The *Daily Mail* is trashing women every day. Female journalists have a responsibility to look at the world through different eyes, not by mimicking men. They should think how to better reflect women instead of joining the lads' culture.'

Mary-Ann Sieghart reckons things have come so far that it's now an 'embarrassment' among male executives if there aren't enough women writers on their pages. 'When I first started,' she says, 'there wasn't a single female voice in the op-ed pages of *The Times*. Now there isn't a day without one.'

Well, that's the old guard talking. What do younger women journalists think of their trade these days? Elizabeth Day, a former young journalist of the year and reporter on the *Sunday Telegraph*, believes it is now actually easier to get a job on a newspaper if you are a woman.

She said after landing a job on the *Telegraph* diary at the age of 24: 'The kinds of things I was being asked to do – schmooze celebrities at book launches, film premieres or gallery openings, were somehow easier to get away with if you were a woman. A strange man who wandered up to you at a party and started asking all sorts of intrusive questions would be dismissed as lecherous or psychopathic whereas in a woman, the same traits were generally seen as out of the ordinary and charming.'

Elizabeth Day believes there are now more young women in journalism than men. When she won her Young Journalist of the Year title in 2004, five of the six nominees were female. As ever more women make their careers in journalism there will be more opportunities and 'we will no longer be a phenomenon but a normality.' Day adds: 'Journalism can be a rewarding, brilliant and challenging profession, and I truly cannot think of a better career.'

Journalism will always be tough, one way or another and the industry will always have its downsides. But all of the women featured in this book would, if they were to live their lives all over again, choose exactly the same profession. There are huge highs and terrible lows, but to be given an opportunity to write words that literally millions of people will want to read, is a very special privilege.

To its practitioners, journalism is simply the most exciting profession there is, and now that there is no gender discrimination, it is up to women, who now make up at least 50% of all journalists, to ensure it stays as exciting as ever.

Appendix 1

About the author

This book has described how a wide variety of ambitious, talented women fought, cajoled or inveigled their way into the male-dominated world of the old Fleet Street.

As for me, I was simply invited to join this elite and privileged group. I was contacted one day by Patricia Boxall, woman's editor of the *Sunday People*, to see whether I might be interested in a job on the paper.

So was this an instant rags-to-riches story? Well, not quite. Although my entry to Fleet Street may have appeared dramatic and sudden, it was actually the culmination of years of desperate effort and struggle to establish a writing career.

It all began in Newcastle upon Tyne, where I started married life at the age of 21. My young husband Neville Hodgkinson, also 21, had been accepted on the graduate trainee scheme of Thomson Newspapers in the north-east, where he had to sign up for three years' indentures. I, though, was not accepted onto the scheme and, unable to get any local jobs in journalism, went to work as a teacher in a girls' grammar school in Sunderland, after graduating from university with an upper second honours English degree.

There were few women on Neville's course, two at most, and about a dozen or 15 young men, all recent graduates. The young men were given low-paying jobs on the local newspaper the Newcastle *Evening Chronicle*, where they combined hands-on reporting of local events with block release courses in shorthand and newspaper law. After the three years were up, these young journalists were considered to be 'trained', and were then able to apply for jobs, either on other provincial newspapers, or on Fleet Street which was, of course, where most of them wanted to be anyway, although it was by no means automatic that they would get jobs there.

Although disappointed by not being accepted onto the training course, my dream of being a writer or journalist never went away and while teaching, I wrote and submitted countless articles to newspapers and magazines. All were rejected. Lowering my sights, I sent an article on the pros and cons of school uniform to my husband's newspaper, the *Evening Chronicle* and to my amazement they not only accepted it, but paid me £5 for it.

That one article led to a fortnightly column which led to a weekly column, all while I was still teaching. Neville and I had decided to start a family while we were young and when were just 24 our first son Tom was born. Will followed 18 months later, and although I gave up my teaching job when six months pregnant, I never stopped writing for the *Evening Chronicle*, even finishing an article from my hospital bed just hours after Tom was born.

Although by no means a professional artist, I was reasonably proficient at fashion sketches, the result of a misspent youth obsessively copying fashion pictures from my mother's magazines, and because I could do two jobs, as it were, I was eventually writing and drawing for four regional papers, the *Evening Chronicle, Newcastle Journal*, the *Northern Echo*, Darlington (where Harold Evans was once editor), and the Newcastle *Sunday Sun*.

I could not do news reporting or shorthand, but was eventually contributing enough articles to be allowed to join the NUJ, as journalism was now my full time job.

After his indentures were up, Neville became desperate to get to Fleet Street, and we both started applying to national newspapers. Eventually Neville was offered a job with the *Daily Telegraph*, but I could get nothing at all, not even any freelance work. Eventually, though, I had a breakthrough, of sorts. I replied to an ad for the position of deputy editor on *Modern Mother* magazine, and got the job. Here, my experience of being a young mother was actually a qualification. The magazine itself was a miserable, low-budget affair but it gave me some professional polish and I was soon asked to write a weekly column for the London *Evening News* as well, for £35 a time.

Pat Boxall had seen and liked these *Evening News* articles, but what clinched it for her was a big piece of mine in the *Sunday Mirror* on Hammer horror films, which included an exclusive interview with each of the main Hammer stars, Peter Cushing and Christopher Lee. I was paid £150 for this article, an almost unbelievable amount of money at

189

the time, and have Bob Edwards, the then editor, to thank for its inclusion in the paper, and the big showing it got.

So – thanks, Bob, for giving me this huge leg-up to my career.

I was also now writing for a new magazine, *Top Secretary*, and Pat had read these pieces as well. By the time of her phone call I had left *Modern Mother*, just before it folded, so was free to join any paper when and if the call came.

And so in August 1973 I joined the *Sunday People*. I can remember the thrilling sensation, when getting off the tube at Blackfriars, of finally having made it. For months I walked down Fleet Street, passing the black plate glass *Express* building, the *Telegraph* building and turning into New Fetter Lane, in a kind of dazed awe that I was now actually part of this glamorous and exciting newspaper world, that I was one of the Chosen.

There were, at the time I joined the paper, just four women in editorial out of a total editorial staff of about 150, including those at Manchester. They were: Pat Boxall, woman's editor; myself; Hilary Kingsley, TV and showbiz writer and finally, Sandy Brereton, 'special writer'. The newspaper would have been happier if it didn't have to employ women at all, but there were some jobs, such as the fashion, that couldn't be done by a man, or so it seemed in those days. Also, a few 'girls' were always needed for the kind of undercover work in which the paper specialised.

I stayed at the *People* for five years after which I felt it was time to move on, and my next job was at *The Sun*, where my old school friend and classmate Katharine Hadley was now women's editor. My place at *The People* was taken by Felicity Hawkins, from the *Mirror* graduate training scheme in Plymouth. She became, successively, editor of the *Mail on Sunday YOU* magazine, deputy editor of the *Sunday Mirror* and editor of *Classic FM* and *Pink Ribbon* magazines.

At the *Sun*, there was a fairly large women's department, known as Pacesetters. Although our office was tiny and crowded and we had to put up with Larry Lamb as editor, the women's page team was a talented and friendly group of women, and we all bonded.

Judy Wade, later a well-known royal correspondent, and the author Jean Ritchie, were then on the staff as was TV personality Nina Myskow, formerly editor of the teenage magazine *Jackie*, and Penny Perrick, later to make a name for herself as a serious literary critic and novelist. Philippa Kennedy worked on the newsdesk and Jean Dobson was fashion editor. Roslyn Grose, later to write the official history of *The Sun*, was a feature writer; Sally Ann Voak covered slimming and dieting and Claire Rayner was the agony aunt. We all had a fun, girly time there.

After *The Sun*, I worked for the Femail pages of the *Daily Mail*, edited by Gerald Rudge, known, naturally as Grudge. Again, I made some long-lasting friends, several of whom were to make big names for themselves in the media.

These included Lynn Faulds-Wood, later to become a television presenter with her husband John Stapleton; Frankie McGowan, later a magazine editor and later still a novelist; Carol Lee, author of many books on lifestyle issues, Yvonne Thomas, Jean Dobson (having moved from *The Sun*), Kathy Phillips and the young Deborah Moggach before she became a best-selling novelist. The columnist and biographer Rebecca Tyrrell was then a secretary there.

During my time at Femail Neville was medical correspondent on the *Daily Mail*, so finally we came together and were working on the same paper. By this time the old rule about husbands and wives not working on the same title had fallen into abeyance. My last office job was as woman's editor at *The Times* during its terrible Wapping year of 1986.

So what about my fellow females on local papers in the North-East? Anthea Hall went to the *Sunday Telegraph*, where she remained for the rest of her journalistic career; Jane McLoughlin went initially to the *Daily Telegraph*, became woman's editor of *The Guardian* and later wrote thrillers; Judith Hann had a big career as a presenter on *Tomorrow's World* and Liz Houghton, then Harris, who joined the training scheme in Sunderland, landed a job at the *Daily Express*. She later became a sub on *The Guardian*, job-sharing with her husband.

Anthea Linacre went to the Femail pages of the *Daily Mail* but was soon to leave journalism altogether. Jan Woodhead (later Fairfax) was the first female sub-editor on *The Journal*, Newcastle, and later joined IPC Magazines; later still becoming a freelance health writer. Leslie Geddes-Brown, woman's editor of the *Northern Echo*, later became a freelance writer on national newspapers.

Sue Hercombe became the last-ever Woman Journalist of the Year while still working in the provinces, and wrested the title away from bigger names such as Jean Rook and Lynda Lee-Potter. The judges had liked her fresh, new approach, and Sue said in her acceptance speech that although she was honoured to be awarded the title, she thought it was an anachronism to differentiate journalists by gender. As Sue Frost (reverting to her maiden name after her divorce) she became the agony aunt on *Woman* magazine.

As for me, since leaving office jobs in 1986 I have been combining freelance journalism with writing books.

Appendix 2

Further Reading

Books:

Bachrach, Judy: *Tina and Harry Come to America. Tina Brown, Harry Evans and the Uses of Power*. The Free Press, 2001

Bower, Tom: *Maxwell: The Final Verdict*. HarperCollins, 1995

Bower, Tom: *Conrad and Lady Black*. Harper Perennial, 2007

Callan, Jessica: *Wicked Whispers,* Penguin, 2007

Connolly, Ray, ed: *In the Sixties,* Pavilion, 1995

Conran, Shirley: *Superwoman,* 1975; *The Magic Garden*, 1983; *Lace,* 1985, all published by Penguin.

Dudley Edwards, Ruth: *Newspapermen Hugh Cudlipp, Cecil Harmsworth King and the Glory Days of Fleet Street*, Secker and Warburg, 2003

Dundy, Elaine: *Life Itself!* Virago, 2008

Edwards, Robert: *Goodbye Fleet Street*, Jonathan Cape, 1988

Glover, Stephen, ed: *The Penguin Book of Journalism: Secrets of the Press*, Penguin, 1999.

Greenslade, Roy: *Press Gang: How Newspapers Make Profits From Propaganda*, Pan Books, 2004

Grose, Roslyn: *The Sun-Sation.* Angus and Robertson, 1989

Hagerty, Bill: *Read All About It – 100 Sensational Years of the Daily Mirror*, First Stone Publishing, 2003

Hargreaves, Ian: *Journalism: Truth or Dare?* Oxford, 2003

Jameson, Derek: *Touched by Angels*, Ebury Press, 1988

Leslie, Ann: *Killing My Own Snakes*, Macmillan, 2008.

Melvern, Linda: *The End of the Street*, Methuen, 1986

Millar, Fiona and Kinnock, Glenys: *By Faith and Daring: Interviews with Remarkable Women*, Virago, 1993

Morgan, Piers: *The Insider*, Ebury Press, 2005

Parkin, Molly: *Moll: The Making of Molly Parkin,* Victor Gollancz, 1993

Patmore, Angela and Proops, Marjorie: *The Guilt and the Gingerbread,* Little, Brown and Company, 1993

Rayner, Claire: *How Did I get Here from There?* Virago, 2003

Robinson, Anne: *Memoirs of an Unfit Mother,* Little, Brown, 2001

Rook, Jean: *Rook's Eye View*, Express Newspapers, 1979; *The Cowardly Lioness*, Sidgwick and Jackson, 1989

Rozenburg, Joshua: *Privacy and the Press,* Oxford, 2004

Sebba, Anne, *Battling For News: The Rise of the Woman Reporter*, Hodder & Stoughton, 1994

Seymour, David and Seymour, Emily, ed: *Daily Mirror: A Century of News,* Contender Books, 2003

Scott-James, Anne: *In the Mink,* Michael Joseph, 1952

Skidmore, Ian: *Forgive Us Our Press Passes*, Revel Barker Publishing, 2008

Stott, Mary: *Forgetting's No Excuse,* Faber and Faber, 1975; *Before I Go,* Little Brown, 1985

Stott, Richard: *Dogs and Lampposts,* Metro, 2002

Street-Porter, Janet: *Fall Out,* Headline, 2006

Waterhouse, Keith: *Streets Ahead*, Hodder and Stoughton, 1995

Whitehorn, Katharine: *Selective Memory*, Virago, 2007

Wooding, Dan: *From Tabloid to Truth*, Theatron Books, 2004

Film:

Those Glory, Glory Days, Enigma Films, Goldcrest Films and Channel Four, 1983 (based on the life of football reporter Julie Welch)

Newspapers, and journals consulted include:

British Journalism Review, vol 12, no 1, 2001: *Brenda Maddox: Review of Class Act by Lynda Lee-Potter.*

British Journalism Review, vol 16, no 4, 2005: Deborah Orr: *Floundering in the Macho Media*

British Journalism Review, vol 14, no 2, 2003: Hilary Andersson: *The Wow Factor*

British Journalism Review, vol 14, no 3, 2003: Bernard Shrimsley: *Columns! The Good, The Bad, the Best.*

British Journalism Review, vol 17, no 4, 2006: Virginia Ironside: *The Last Great Agony Icon – Marje Proops.*

Evening Standard, Wednesday September 1, 2004: David Rowan, *Interview with Dawn Neesom, editor of the Daily Star.*

Evening Standard, Wednesday July 2, 2008: Chris Blackhurst: *Can Sly (Bailey) win her battle for survival?*

The Guardian, Tuesday, October 10, 1967: *Mary Quant talks to Alison Adburgham*

The Guardian, Thursday April 12, 2001: Jessica Hodgson: *Tina Weaves Her Way to the Top*

The Guardian, Wednesday November 21, 2001: Nancy Banks-Smith: *A Nice Little Job for a Woman at Home.*

The Guardian, Thursday June 6, 2005: Hadley Freeman: *Ladies of the Press*

The Guardian, Friday July 28, 2006: Stephen Brook: *Sarah Sands*

The Guardian, Wednesday, July 18, 2007: Jane McLoughlin, Woman's Editor 1984-5: *A Hiding to Nothing.*

The Guardian, Monday May 12, 2008: Peter Wilby: *Where are the female high flyers?*

The Independent, Friday 14 April, 2000: Virginia Ironside: *My Advice to Vanessa? Don't Give up the Day Job.*

The Independent, Tuesday July 6, 2004: Ian Burrell: *Dawn Neesom, The Cheekiest Editor in Town*

The Independent, 23 January 2006: Compton Miller: *Inside Story: The Big Stars of Astrology.*

The Independent,Monday 13 August, 2007: Sue Peart: *My Mentor: Sue Peart on Deirdre McSharry*

The Independent, Monday 7 April 2008: Sophie Morris*: Amanda Platell: My Life in Media*

Independent on Sunday, 24 October, 2004: Jane Thynne: *Where now for the angry old (and not so old) women of Fleet Street?*

Independent on Sunday, 6 November 2005: Jane Thynne: *Sarah Sands: Beauty, Fashion, Food, Health and Love: is that all women really want?*

New Statesman, 25 September 2000: *Lynda Lee Potter:* Profile by Michael Leapman

New Statesman, 11 December 2000: *The Future is not Rosie,* (profile of Rosie Boycott) by Bill Hagerty

New Statesman, 12 August, 2002: Lindsey Hilsum: *Who Wants to be a Mother?*

The Observer, Sunday January 10, 2003: Peter Preston: *Rebekah Wade: Redhead, Redtop, Red Alert.*

Press Gazette, the journalists' trade paper: various articles

The Spectator, 4 December 2004: Mary Kenny: *Why the Nuns Sacked Me*

Websites:

mirrorpensioners.co.uk (obituary of Ann Pacey*)*

womenofbrighton.co.uk (profile of Nancy Spain)

fuk.co.uk Sixties Fashion at the V&A (profile of Felicity Green)

vam.ac.uk (interview with Felicity Green)

tobyyoung.co.uk (interview with Lynn Barber)

gentlemenranters.com (various articles)

Index

Note: for simplicity, where there is just a brief mention, or list, of newspapers and journals, these are not referenced in the index.

Printed in the United Kingdom by
Lightning Source UK Ltd., Milton Keynes
138749UK00001B/98/P